IMAGES
of America

The Lost Communities of Lake Oroville

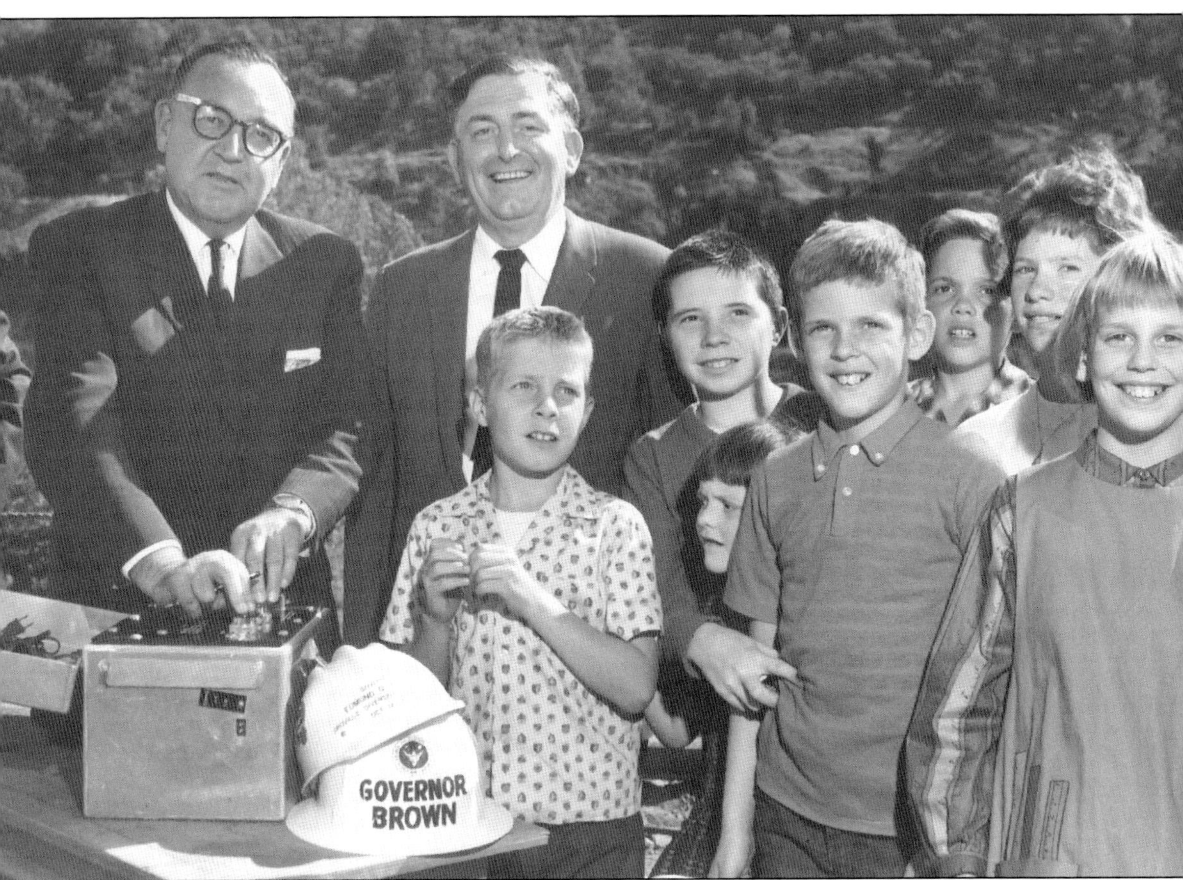

Gov. Edmund G. "Pat" Brown presses the button to set off the first dynamite blast for the construction of Oroville Dam on October 21, 1961. He is joined by William S. Warne, the director of the California Department of Water Resources. The children in the photograph are, from left to right, Kenny Wallace, Cody Wallace, Ellen Mackay, Billy Mackay, David Mackay, Robyn Foster, and Jeanibeth Torkelson. They were invited to the event because their community of Las Plumas and their one-room schoolhouse were slated to be inundated by Lake Oroville. Robyn (Foster) Payne wrote, "I remember that event all too well. It was the beginning of the end of a way of life for me." By the end of 1968, Las Plumas had been burned down, and the area was several hundred feet under the lake. (Courtesy of California Department of Water Resources.)

On the Cover: Sunbathers enjoy the beach and the cool water of the Middle Fork of the Feather River at the Curry-Bidwell Bar State Park on August 18, 1962. Other visitors look down from the Bidwell Bar Suspension Bridge that was built at that location in 1856. (Courtesy of California Department of Water Resources.)

IMAGES
of America

THE LOST COMMUNITIES OF LAKE OROVILLE

Larry R. Matthews and Scott C. Roberts

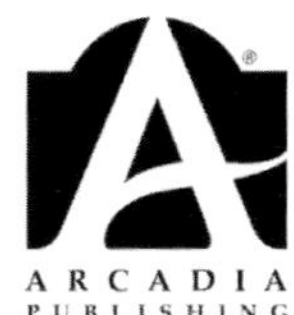
ARCADIA
PUBLISHING

ISBN 978-1-4671-2399-0

Published by Arcadia Publishing
Charleston, South Carolina

Printed in the United States of America

Library of Congress Control Number: 2016947830

For all general information, please contact Arcadia Publishing:
Telephone 843-853-2070
Fax 843-853-0044
E-mail sales@arcadiapublishing.com

Visit us on the Internet at www.arcadiapublishing.com

This book is dedicated to all of the former residents of the Lost Communities.
It is especially dedicated to those residents who contributed to this book.

Contents

Acknowledgments 6

Introduction 7

1. The North Fork and West Branch 9
2. The Middle Fork 43
3. The South Fork 65
4. Mooretown and Feather Falls Village 79
5. Saving Historic Icons 103
6. Relics 115

Acknowledgments

The various agencies and individuals listed here have authorized the use of their photographs for this book.

These agencies and organizations provided multiple photographs. Our thanks go to Bill Kelley, Paul Hames, and Veronica Case of the California Department of Water Resources Graphic Services (CDWR); Nancy Brower and Sally McCoy of the Butte County Historical Society (BCHS); Elizabeth Bell and Rosemarie Mossinger of the Yuba-Feather Museum (YFM); Raymond Cooper and the Butte County Public Works Department (BCPW); Meriam Library of California State University, Chico (MLCSUC); and the *Chico Enterprise-Record* (ER).

Oroville residents who contributed multiple photographs include Audrey (Coombes) Aiston (AA), James Lenhoff (JL), Wheeler family collection (WFC), Norm MacKenzie (NM), Lois (Spencer) Edwards (LSE), Herman Presentati (HP), Esther Wilson (EW), Wayne Wilson (WW), Allen Stolz (AS), Glenda "Sue" (Soderberg) Sinkey (SS), and Marlene Wright (MW). Thanks also go to Robyn (Foster) Payne (RP) of Carmichael, California; Marcella (Rodgers) Hansford (MH) of Rosedale, Indiana; and Ron Turner (RT) of Juneau, Alaska.

Single photograph contributors from Oroville are Gary E. Johns, Bob Jackson, John Hastie, Phil Ravert, the South Feather Water and Power Agency, and Gonzalo Peewee Curiel. Also contributing single photographs are Bonnie Baron of Paradise, California; Steve Hayes of Soulsbyville, California; Mollie Fitzsimmons of Redding, California; Diane Lloyd of Spokane, Washington; the Pacific Gas and Electric Company; the California Department of Transportation; and the Vickie Brown Miller/Rookie Davis family.

Image sources in this book are identified either by name or by the abbreviations included here.

Special thanks go to Audrey (Coombes) Aiston, Norm MacKenzie, Robyn (Foster) Payne, Ron Wheeler, Lois (Spencer) Edwards, and Sue (Soderberg) Sinkey, who agreed to be interviewed by the authors. In agreeing to share their personal histories, they greatly helped us in our attempt to preserve the history of these areas.

Thanks also to Ron Wheeler, John Hastie, John Sheldon, and Darryl McElmurry, who gave us several hiking and/or boat tours of the Big Bend/Las Plumas/Enterprise areas in 2014 and 2015. The authors also wish to thank our family and friends for their enthusiastic support during the 16 months that it took to complete this book.

Introduction

It has now been almost half a century since Oroville Dam was completed and the canyons of the West Branch and the North, Middle, and South Forks of the Feather River were flooded by Lake Oroville. At 3,537,577 acre-feet, Lake Oroville is the second-largest man-made lake in California, after Lake Shasta.

Time seems to fade the memories of older residents, and recent generations of Northern Sacramento Valley residents do not remember a time before Oroville Dam existed. Many current residents have no memory, nor have they ever heard, of the communities that were inundated by Lake Oroville. They may only see the roads that seem to end, and go nowhere, at the shoreline of the lake.

But there are still residents who remember just how much fun it was to swim in the Middle Fork of the Feather River at Curry-Bidwell Bar State Park. At the time of inundation, that area's 1856 Bidwell Bar Suspension Bridge, Tollhouse, and Mother Orange Tree were historic icons that dated back more than a century.

Many remember the winding road that took them into the canyon to Enterprise and the old one-lane bridge that crossed the South Fork of the Feather River. Some remember that the same road, Lumpkin, also took them up the hill to Feather Falls Village and the beautiful Feather Falls.

In the North Fork, there was the Big Bend Powerhouse that was an early-20th-century pioneer in generating power in Northern California. Right across the river from it was the small community of Las Plumas, which was populated by the families of those who worked at the Big Bend Powerhouse.

For centuries, various Maidu Native American tribes had made their home in the canyons. Beginning in 1849, gold-seekers had made their way into the area.

William Swain is a good example of those who arrived early to mine for gold in the area. In November 1849, following a seven-month overland journey from Independence, Missouri, Swain and three of his fellow miners built a cabin on the north shore of the South Fork of the Feather River. It was located several miles west of where Enterprise later would be established. Over the next 11 months, Swain searched for gold in the South Fork, Bidwell Bar, and North Fork areas. He arrived back at his home in New York in February 1851 with little gold to show for all of his efforts.

Many descendants of the Native Americans and gold miners continued to reside in the canyons until they were required to leave in the 1960s.

Preliminary work had begun on the Oroville Dam in 1957. Formal construction began in 1961, and the dam was completed in 1968. Between those dates, most buildings were either removed or burned down, cemeteries were relocated to higher ground, roads and railroads were realigned, vegetation was removed, and all residents were relocated.

Bridges were a big part of the area. After all, there was a multitude of rivers and creeks to cross. They are well represented in this book. Most of those bridges were removed and scrapped prior to the area being flooded.

Most chapters of this book are broken down into geographical areas: the North Fork and West Branch, the Middle Fork, the South Fork, and the Feather Falls area.

Those chapters feature the communities of Las Plumas and the Big Bend Powerhouse, the area of the Berry Creek Station, Enterprise, Bidwell Bar, and Hansell's Bridge. All these areas, with the exception of Hansell's Bridge, were inundated by Lake Oroville. Hansell's Bridge was blown up and removed as the dam's embankment encroached upon its northern support.

Also included is the village of Feather Falls, which was not covered by the lake but has its own story to tell. The road to Feather Falls was rerouted due to the creation of the lake, and the village was still accessible. However, it fell victim to changing circumstances and is now just a wide spot in the road.

There is also a chapter of rare photographs regarding how the iconic Bidwell Bar Suspension Bridge, Mother Orange Tree, and Tollhouse were prepared for removal from the bottom of Bidwell Canyon and relocated to higher ground.

Finally, there is a chapter called "Relics." There are reminders of these communities that can be viewed today. Some were exposed by the recent drought that lowered the level of Lake Oroville.

How did this book come about? In 2014 and 2015, the authors were involved in book signings and presentations regarding *The Building of the Oroville Dam* book. At several of these events, people made comments about how their families had been uprooted by the State of California and just how much they missed living in those areas covered by Lake Oroville. Some had bitter memories about being forced out. However, one thing they all had in common was a deep love and nostalgia for the areas in which they had lived for so many years. They were also afraid that the history of those communities would cease to exist.

A turning point came when we received an e-mail from Robyn (Foster) Payne. She had seen her photograph with Gov. Pat Brown in the Oroville Dam book. He was pushing the button to set off the first dynamite blast for the construction of the dam in 1961. Robyn said, "I remember that event all too well. It was the beginning of the end of a way of life for me." She and her schoolmates in the image are from the Las Plumas School that would be covered by Lake Oroville in 1968. Another photograph version of that event appears in this book.

All those comments impressed us, and this book is the result. We felt that a book that would preserve the history of these communities was a valuable project.

We were so fortunate to find past residents of the area who were willing to be interviewed and who shared rare photographs. They were all very happy to share stories of their lives and their families. Some of their experiences encompassed several generations.

This book does not claim to give a complete history of each of the lost communities. What it does claim to do is to provide a window for the reader to view just a little bit of the rich history that each community has to share.

Within this book, we have collected some of the memories of residents and their photographs for all to see and share. We also included just a few comments of what some of the residents did in their lives after they moved from that area.

The lost communities of Lake Oroville still exist. They are there in the memories of those who resided in the area. The physical foundations are also still there—hundreds of feet below the surface of Lake Oroville and at a wide spot on Lumpkin Road.

One

The North Fork and West Branch

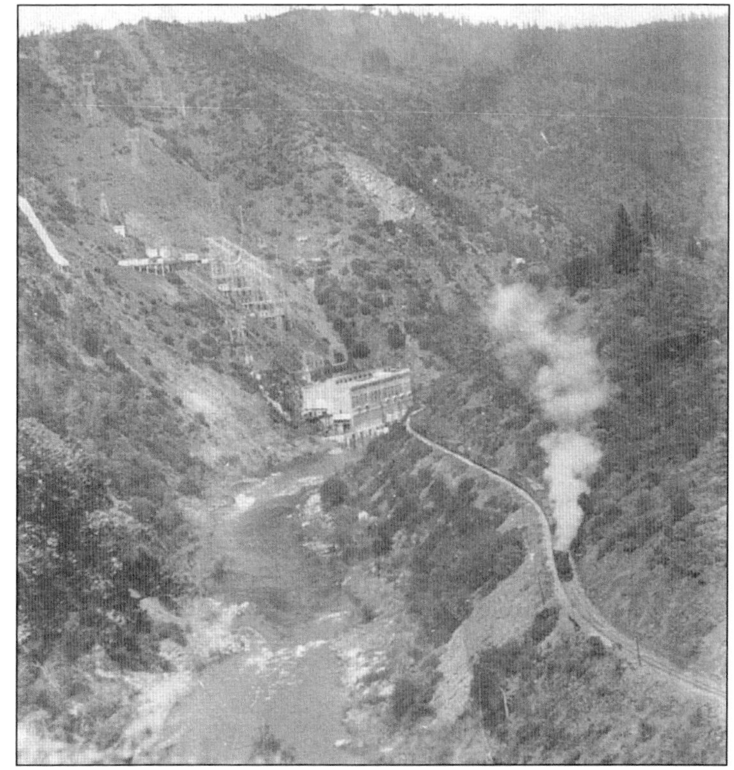

This chapter includes the communities of Las Plumas and the Big Bend Powerhouse, the rail junction of Berry Creek Station, and several sites around the West Branch. The area lies about 16 miles northeast of Oroville. When Lake Oroville is at its maximum height of 900 feet, this area is submerged under about 400 feet of water. This photograph depicts the Big Bend Powerhouse in the 1920s. A Western Pacific Railroad train has just left the community of Las Plumas on its way south toward the Sacramento Valley. (Courtesy of RP.)

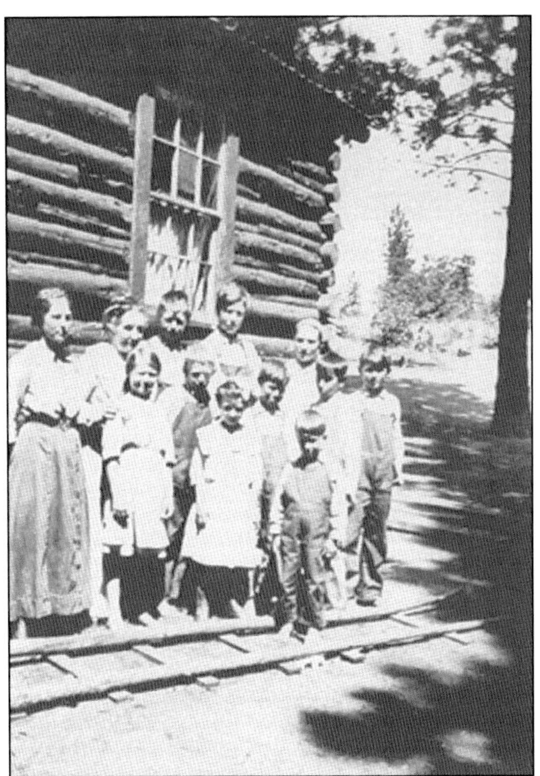

One of the earliest photographs from the Big Bend area is this c. 1883 view of the very first Big Bend School. The teacher is Miss Pettys. The one-room, log-cabin-style school served the children of gold miners, ranchers, and farmers for about 25 years. Big Bend was named after the 13-mile, horseshoe-shaped bend in the North Fork of the Feather River. (Courtesy of MLCSUC.)

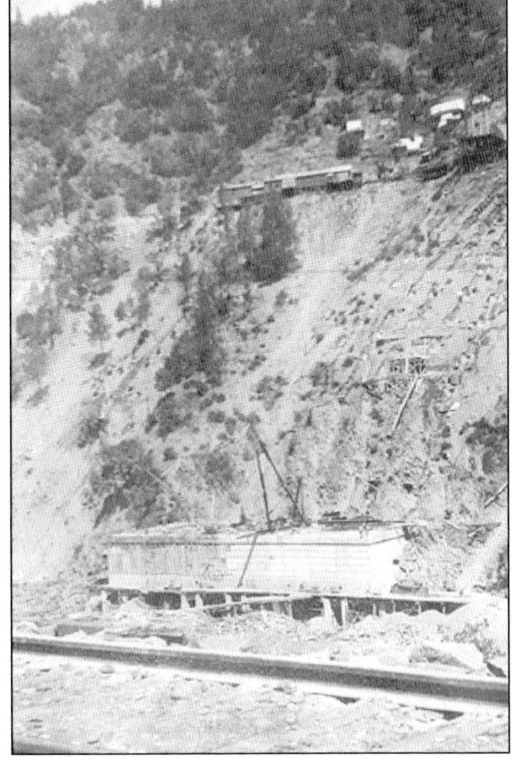

Construction of the Big Bend Powerhouse began in the late summer of 1906. Located on the north side of the Feather River, the powerhouse was built of concrete and steel and had a foundation of concrete pillars that were sunk 35 feet into the hillside and riverbed. The railroad transported the sand and gravel for the project, and the material was brought all the way from the Yuba River near Marysville. (Courtesy of MLCSUC.)

This is the still incomplete Big Bend Powerhouse around 1908. At the beginning of work on the project, material was brought in by horse and wagon from the rail station in Oroville. By early 1908, the Western Pacific Railroad had progressed into the area, making the transportation of heavy supplies and machinery much easier. About 1,100 men worked day and night to complete the powerhouse. (Courtesy of BCHS.)

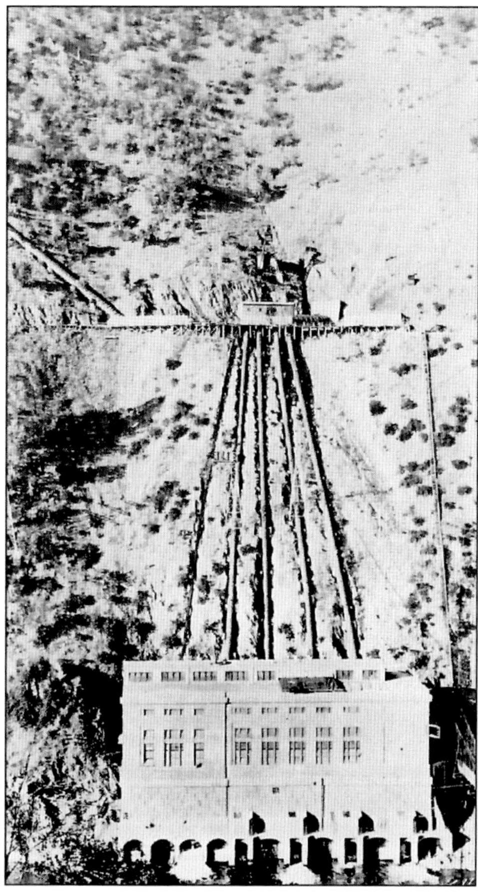

The Big Bend Powerhouse is seen in operation during a high-water event in 1910. The cost of construction was $7.6 million, but the investment really paid off. Shortly after construction, the powerhouse was providing service to the San Francisco Bay Area—a distance of about 164 miles. That was the longest circuit of its type on earth. (Courtesy of RP.)

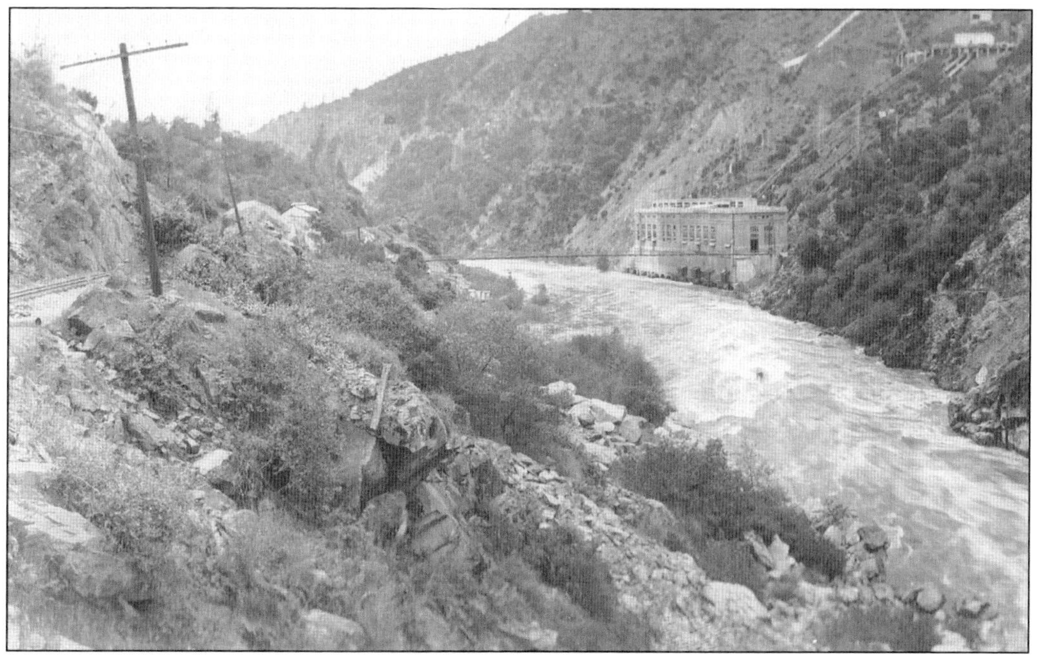

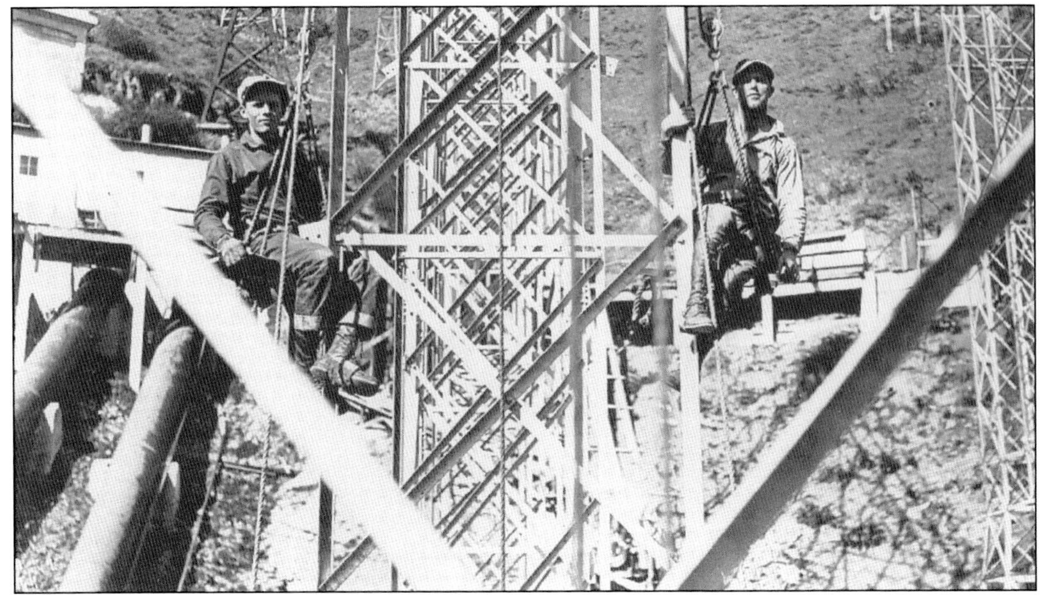

These are two photographs of construction workers as they work on the power transmission towers located in the upper right section of the powerhouse in 1923. This was an upgrade to the powerhouse. The West Coast Construction Company had built the powerhouse, designed by the firm of Viele, Blackwell & Buck. Power from this location was transmitted to the Brighton Substation in Sacramento and then on to Oakland. The Great Western Power Company was very reliable and paid its workers in cash on a regular basis. Nevertheless, due to a worker shortage, other firms attempted to recruit workers from Great Western. More than a few times, the representatives from these other firms were run off at the point of a rifle. (Both, courtesy of RP.)

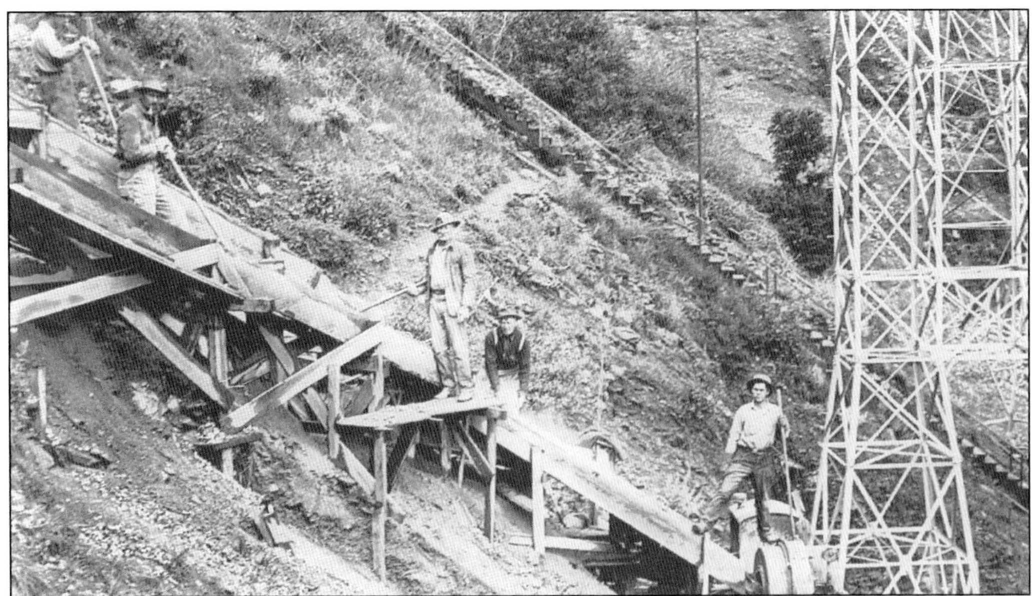

Here are two photographs of the inside of the Big Bend Powerhouse. The first four 10,000-kilowatt General Electric generating units were placed in service on December 23, 1908. At a later date, two larger units were installed, increasing its generating capacity to 70,000 kilowatts. Transmission voltage was increased from 60,000 to 100,000 volts in November 1909. The power was sold to the new Pacific Gas and Electric Company in the San Francisco Bay Area. The first customers served by the powerhouse were the Cowell Cement Works in Contra Costa County and residences in Berkeley Heights. At the time, Big Bend was the largest hydroelectric operation west of the Mississippi River. (Both, courtesy of AA.)

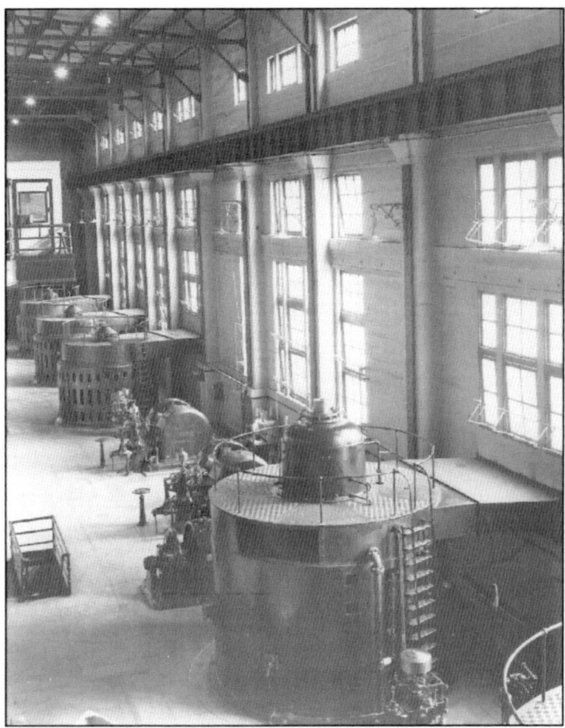

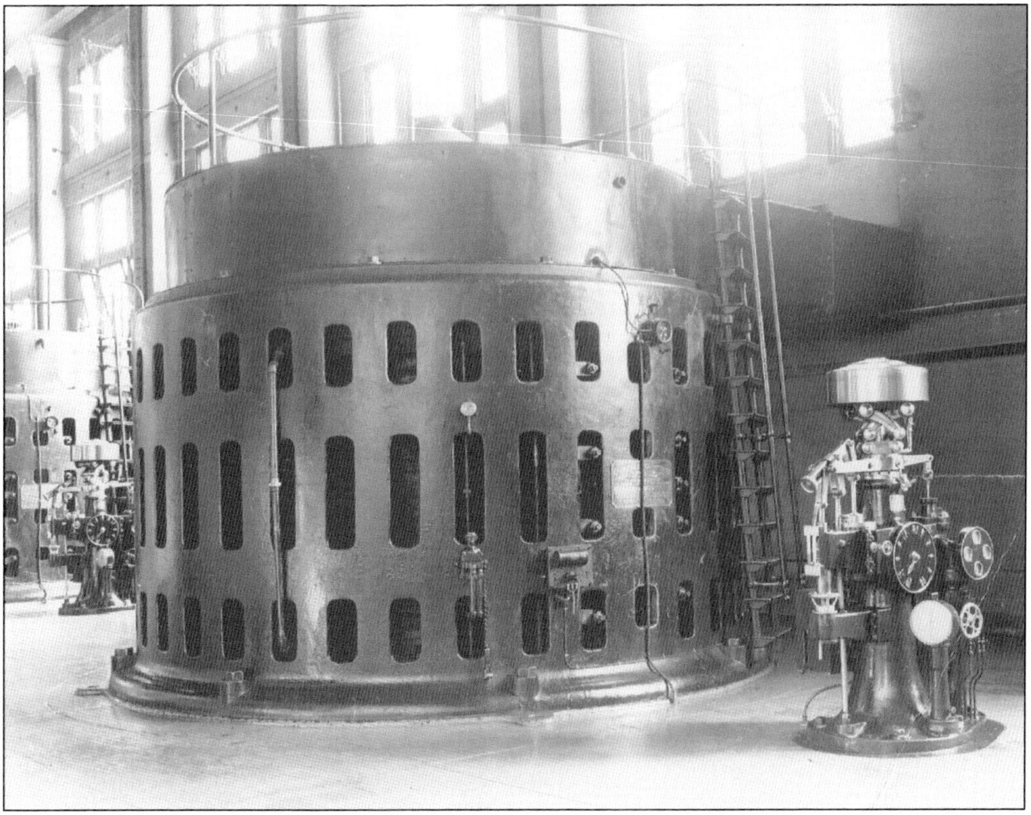

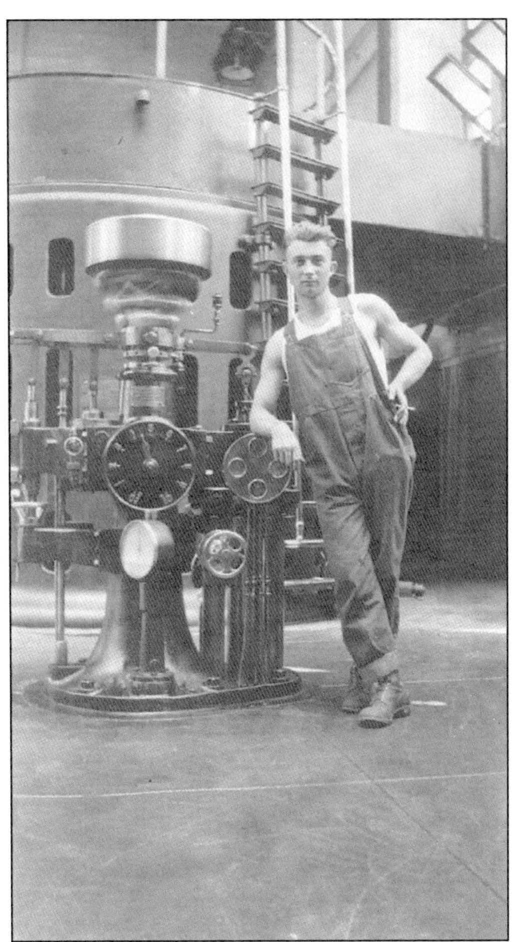

This is a set of photographs showing employee Bill Vanderburgh in the early days of the powerhouse. Here, he can be seen standing by the governor control and operating the power switches. The governor was used to monitor and control the speed of the turbines. During the early years, a crew of five operated the plant: a plant foreman, first and second operator, and two oilers. In addition, a support staff of laborers, painters, plumbers, machinists, and technicians was needed for a well-run powerhouse. The plant ran for 24 hours a day, and the employees worked in three shifts. (Both, courtesy of RP.)

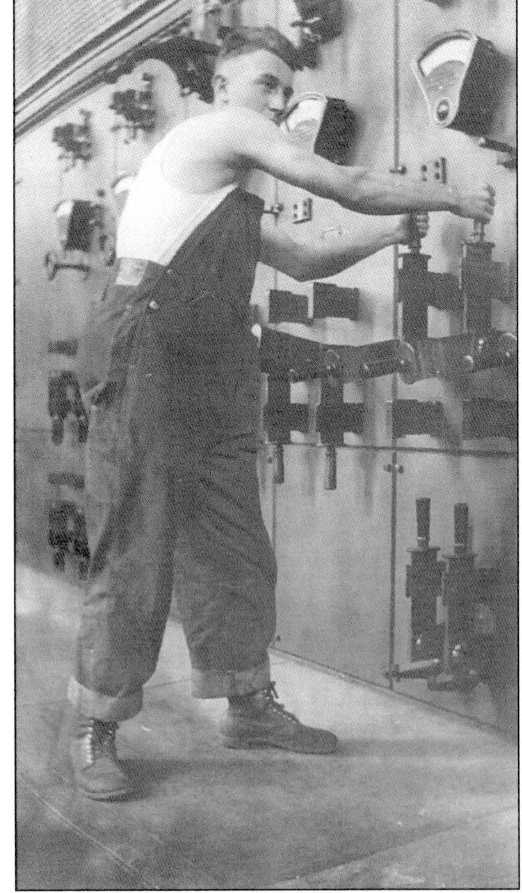

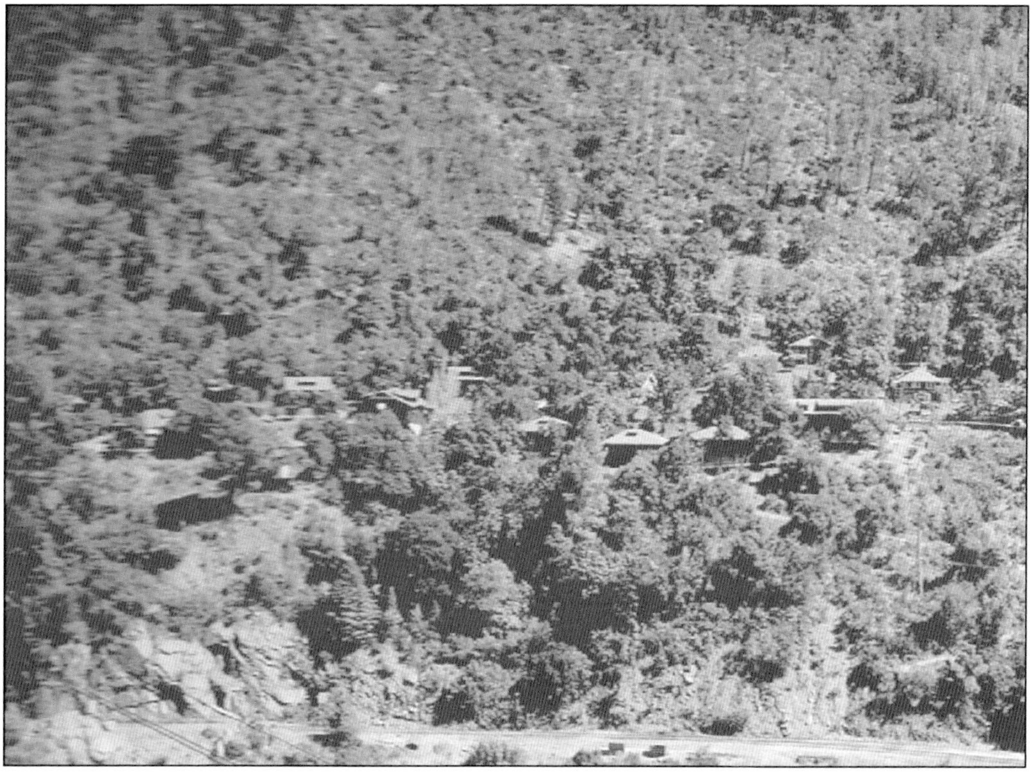

This is an early view of the Las Plumas community taken from near the top of the powerhouse. The living quarters for the construction employees were located on the north bank of the Feather River at Island Bar, just a short distance east of the powerhouse. Once construction was completed and the powerhouse became operational, this community was built for regular employees and their families on the south shore of the river, right across from the powerhouse itself. This photograph shows the theater, clubhouse, three shift houses, and the dormitory. All were located on the east side of the community. (Courtesy of NM.)

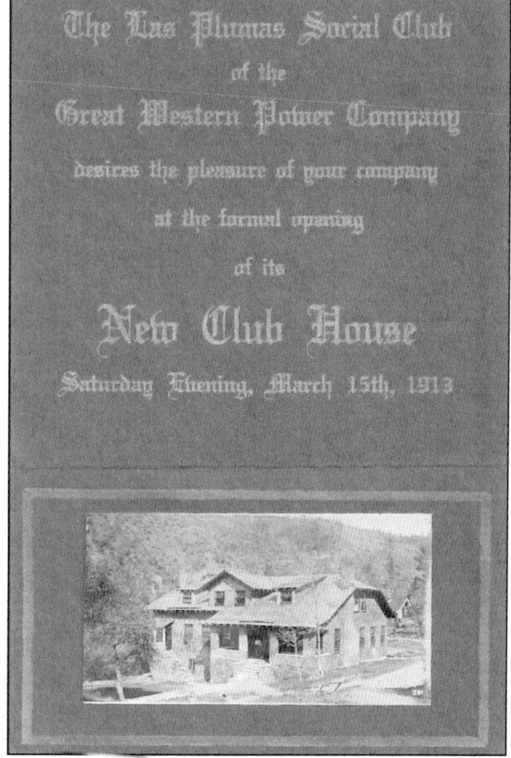
The Las Plumas Social Club
of the
Great Western Power Company
desires the pleasure of your company
at the formal opening
of its
New Club House
Saturday Evening, March 15th, 1913

One of the main centers for social functions was the Las Plumas Social Club. This is the invitation for the grand opening of the new clubhouse on March 15, 1913. The highly anticipated dances were held once a month and were attended not only by local residents but also by visitors from the valley and other mountain areas. (Courtesy of BCHS.)

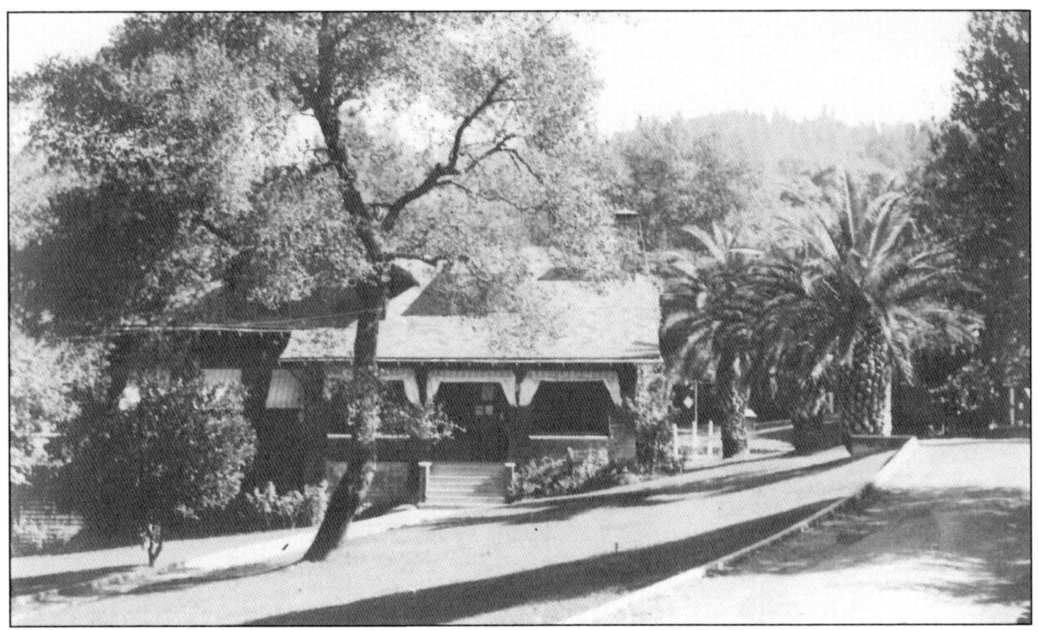

This is the Las Plumas Social Club a few years later. It may be noted that several good-size palm trees have quickly and mysteriously grown next to the club. In actuality, many of the trees, plants, and shrubs in the community were brought in from outside the area. Some were imported from the 1915 Panama-Pacific International Exposition in San Francisco. (Courtesy of BCHS.)

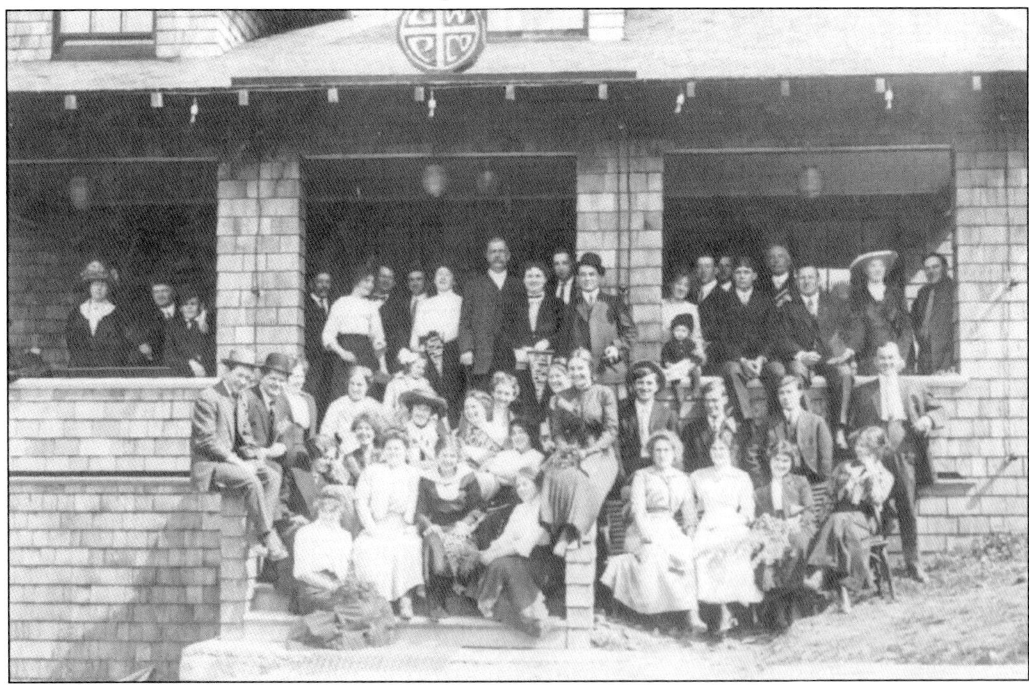

Employees, their families, and guests gather on the porch of the Las Plumas Social Club at Las Plumas in 1928. This might have been just prior to one of the much-anticipated monthly dances that were held at the club. The Great Western Power Company logo appears above them. (Courtesy of Phil Ravert.)

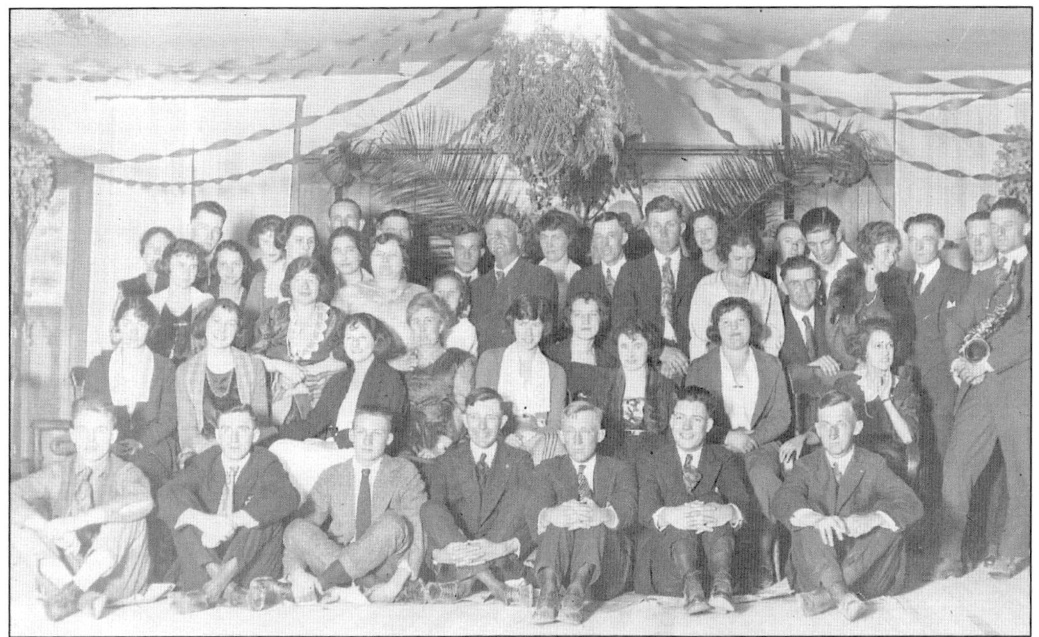

In the early days of Las Plumas, a special train could be chartered to bring guests and musicians in from valley towns for the Saturday-night dance. Here is a scene from one of the social occasions at the Las Plumas Social Club. This photograph includes employees, spouses, and a rather tired-looking saxophone player. Some of the dances went on way past 2:00 a.m. (Courtesy of RP.)

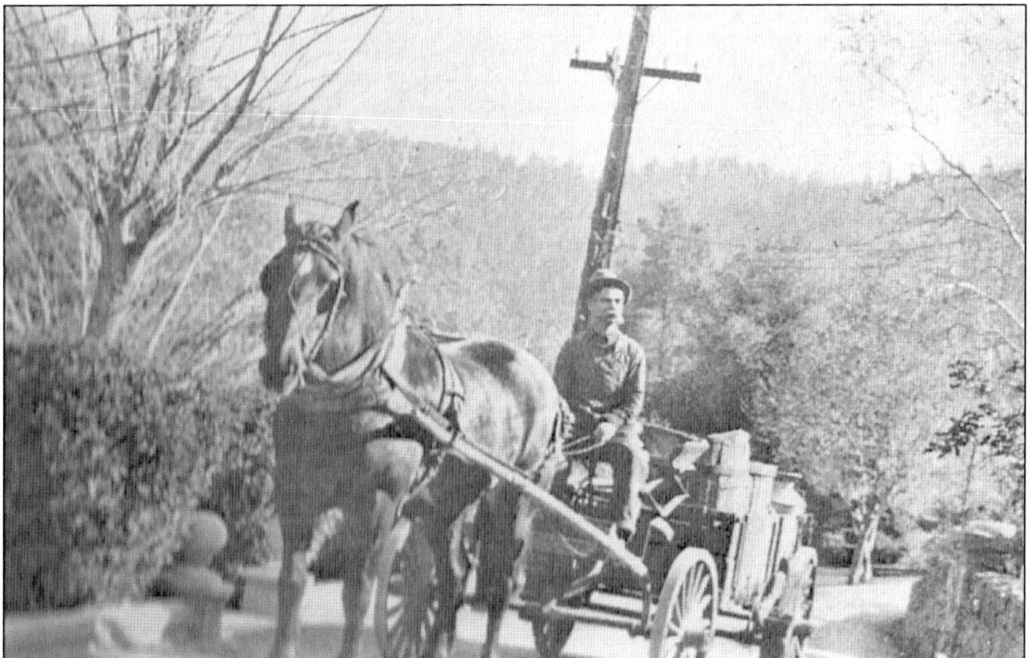

In every community, there is always someone who has to do the dirty jobs. Here is Bill Cox with his horse and wagon. Two of his duties were collecting garbage and delivering ice. These duties became especially important during the summer when temperatures would normally reach well above the century mark. (Courtesy of RP.)

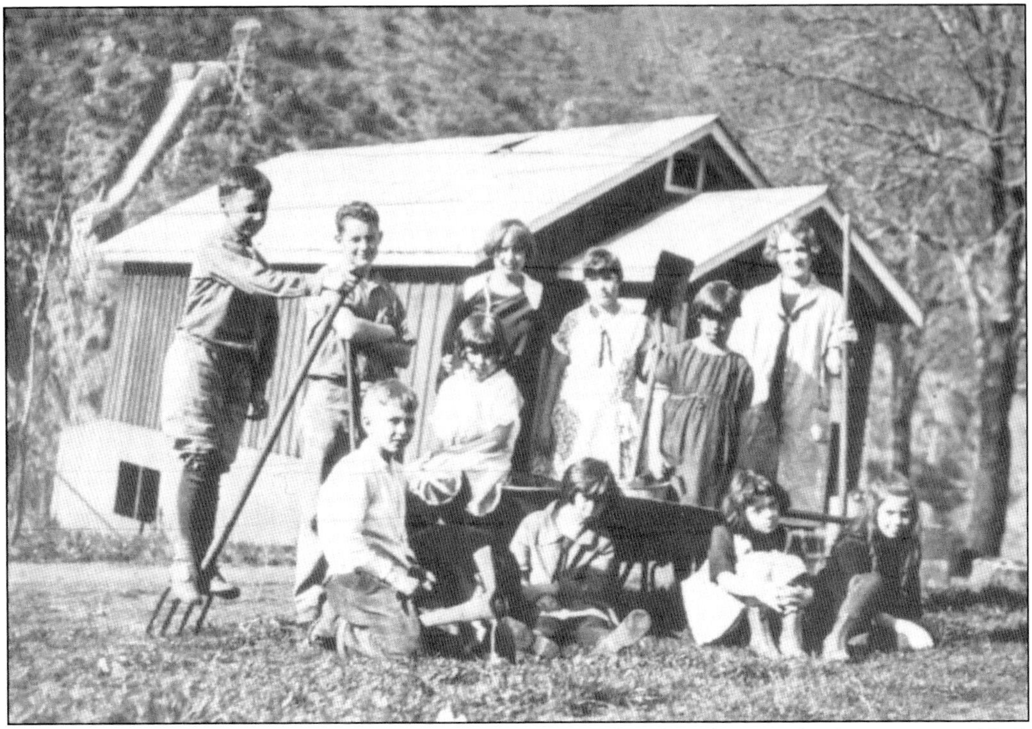

When families began to reside in Las Plumas, it was decided that the time had come to establish a new school on the south side of the Feather River. Both photographs show the second Big Bend School. Above, teacher Minnie Hefner is pictured with the class of 1928. Below, a class from about 1940 is seen with their teacher Mary Ann Spooner. The building was an improvement over the original Big Bend School, but it was not fancy. It was a one-room structure that was left over from the powerhouse construction days. The school served children from kindergarten through eighth grade. (Above, courtesy of BCHS; below, courtesy of RP.)

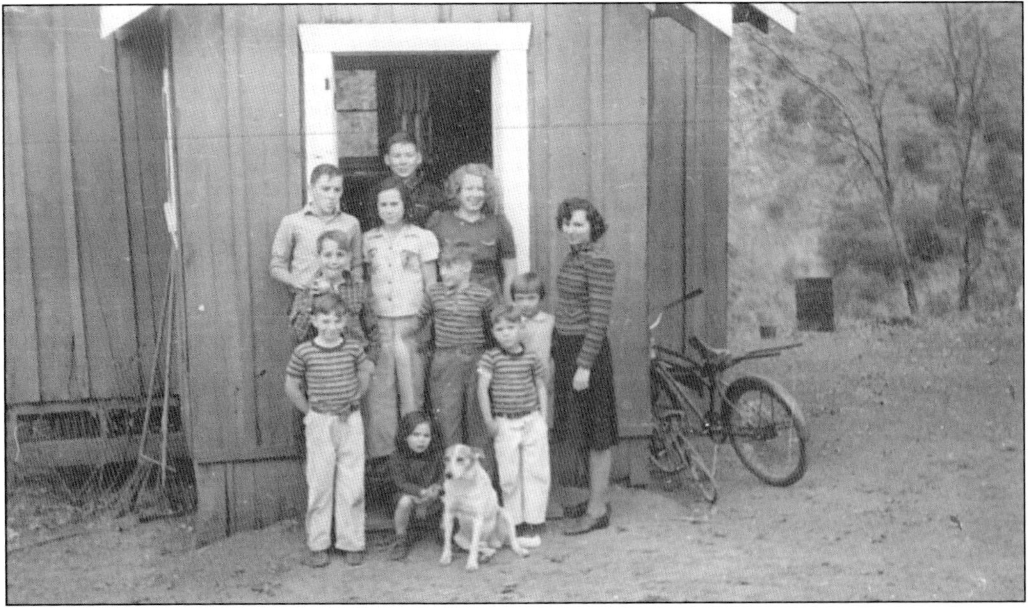

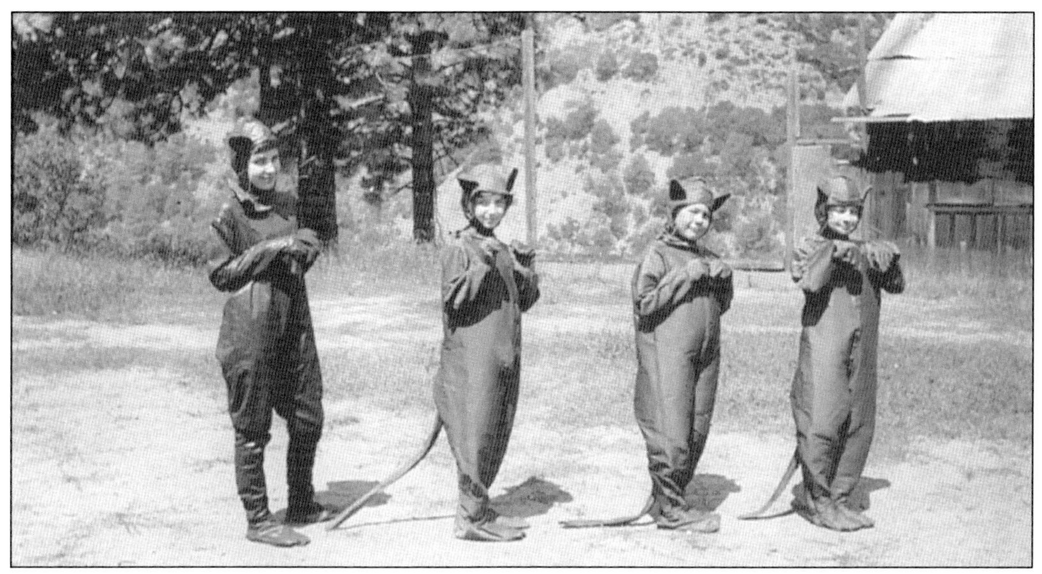

Being in such a remote location, people had to keep themselves entertained. Some of these activities were card parties, community dinners, picnics, softball games, miniature golf, and beach or pool parties. The Big Bend teachers also came up with school projects and events. In these photographs from 1933, the girls' teacher had suggested that they make costumes and dress up in them. In both cases, the children's mothers made the outfits, and the girls modeled them. The girls in these photographs are, from left to right, Edna Johnson, Audrey Coombes, Dorothy Campbell, and Lorie Roulette. (Both, courtesy of AA.)

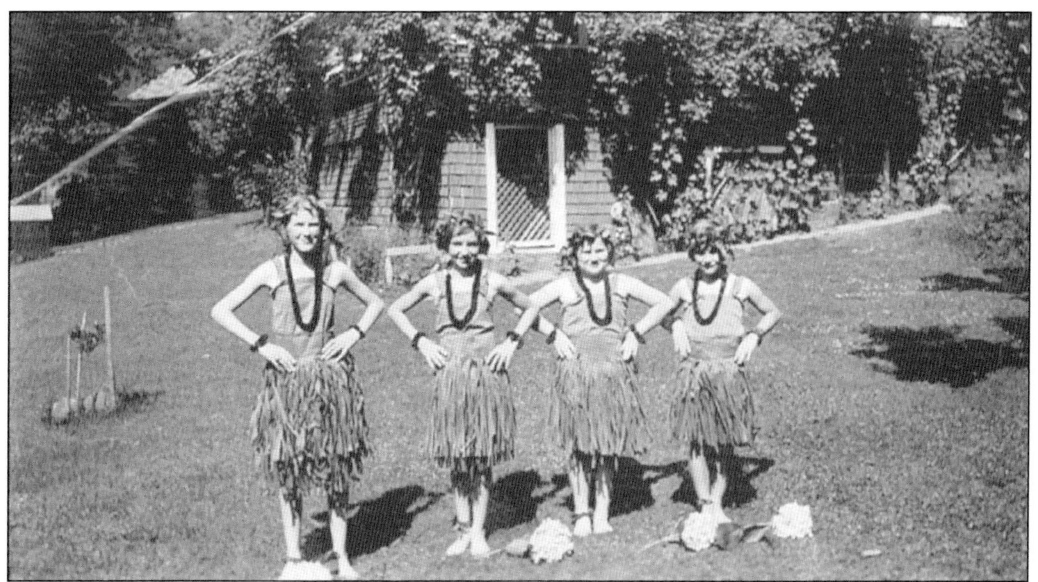

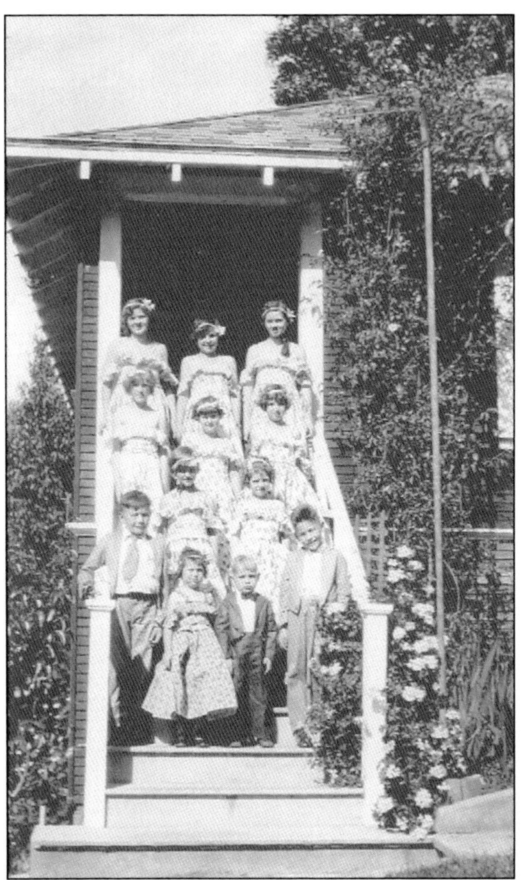

In June 1932, the Ogle family sponsored a party for all Big Bend School students who were interested in music studies. From left to right are (first row) George Roberts, Charlotte Campbell, Wallace Odneal, and Lewis Roberts; (second row) Loris Roulette and Beverly MacKenzie; (third row) Edna Johnson, Dorothy Campbell, and Audrey Coombes; (fourth row) Florence Toland, Nellie Jean Ogle, and Francis Toland. (Courtesy of RP.)

In the mid-1920s, the Las Plumas employees established a very unique theater. It was determined to be the smallest theater in California at the time. At only 20 feet wide by 52 feet long, it could seat about 75 attendees. By 1929, the venue had achieved another milestone in being the only electrically heated theater in the world. (Courtesy of BCHS.)

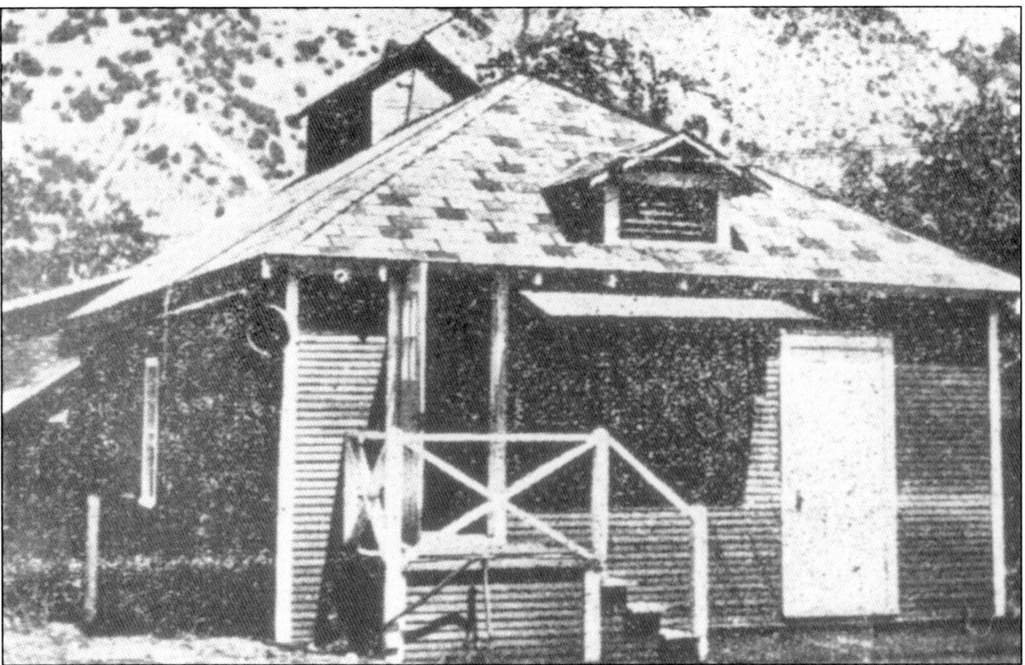

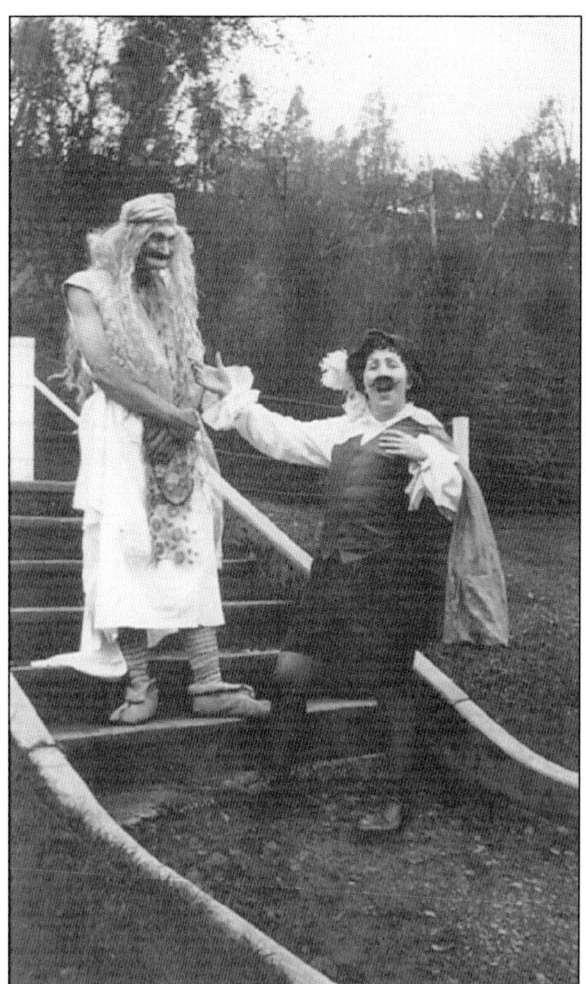

Here are two examples of Las Plumas Theater live productions. At right, Ty Lockerman and Myra Odneal appear in a production of Shakespeare's *Romeo and Juliet* in 1928. Note that Ty plays Juliet and Myra plays Romeo. Below is a Camp Fire Girls program from 1934. Additionally, movies of the era were shown on a regular basis. The seats were wood-slat settees. As a matter of routine, if patrons did not have money to pay for their tickets, they could get credit until payday. (Both, courtesy of AA.)

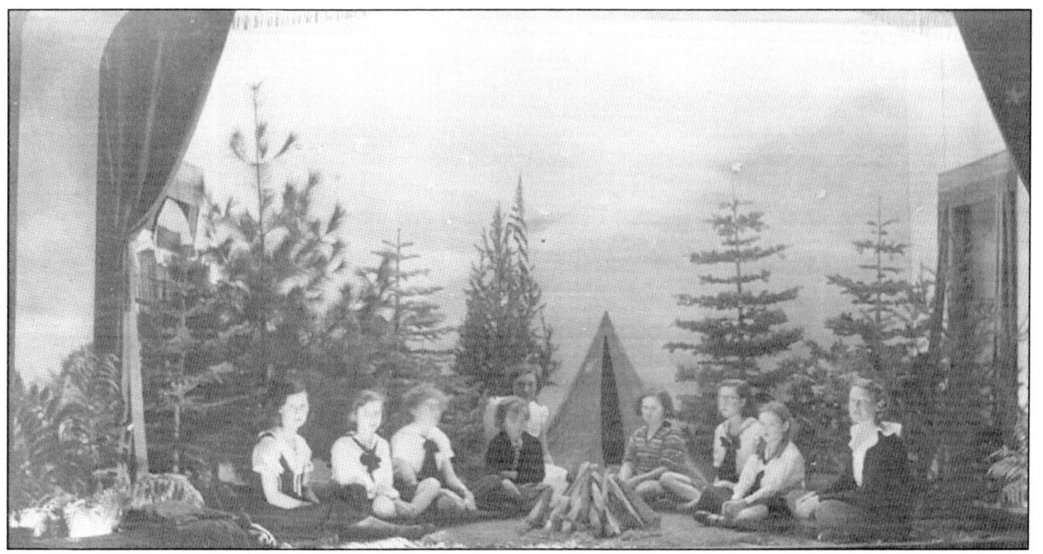

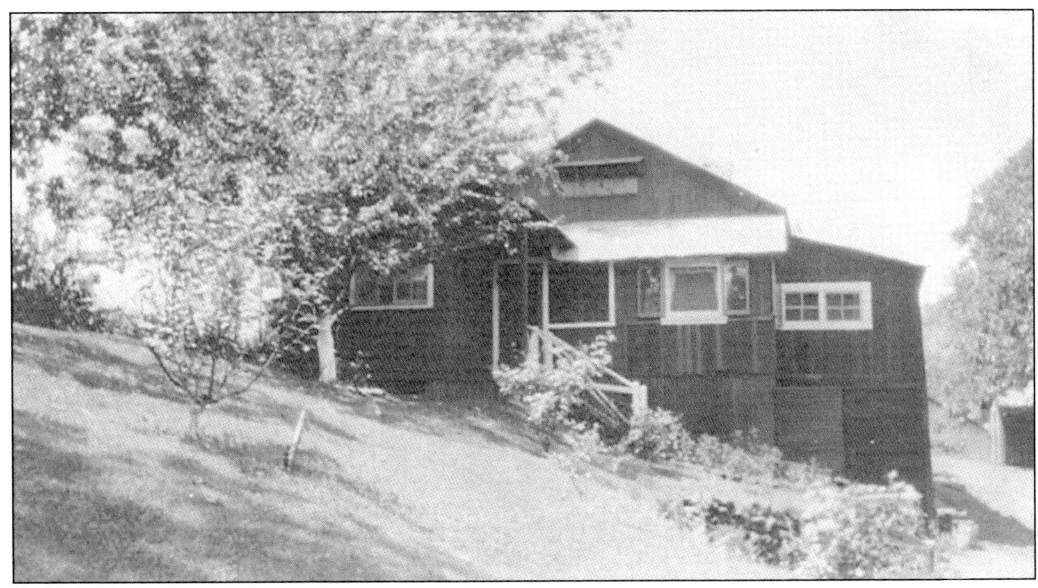

These two photographs feature examples of the residences at Las Plumas. This community originally consisted of a small number of temporary houses, a one-room schoolhouse, an office, a planing mill, a hospital, and a doctor's residence, as well as a combination mess hall and dormitory. Once construction ceased and families began to move into the area, new buildings were erected, including a dormitory, a school, a social clubhouse, modern homes, three shift houses, a guesthouse, a theater, an office, a post office, a train depot, and a warehouse. The new, permanent community was built just northeast of the old camp. (Both, courtesy of AA.)

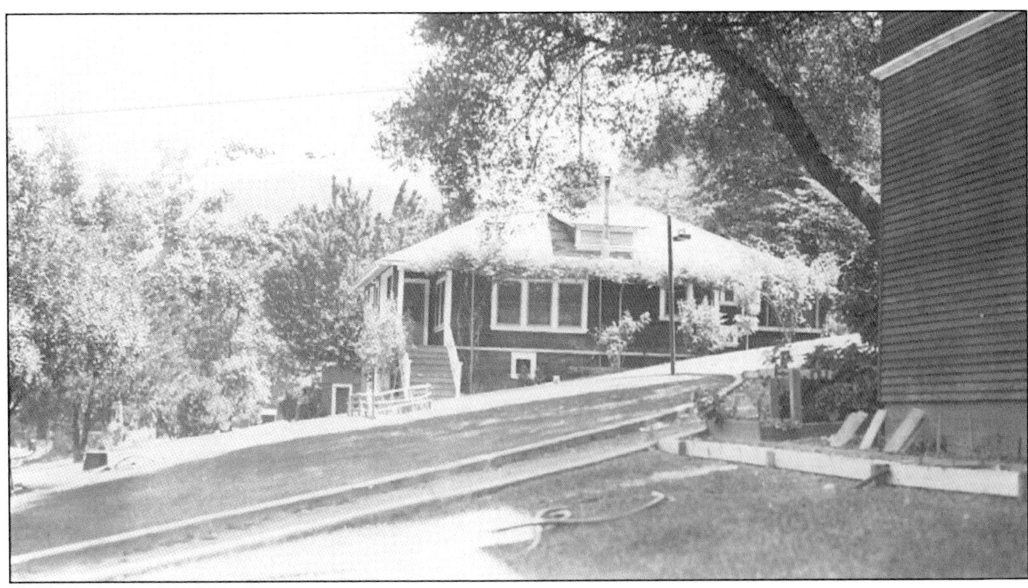

These are two views of residents cooling off in the river during the hot summer days of 1933. The swimming area on the North Fork was extremely popular, especially when the temperature hit 100 degrees. In the photograph at right are Howard Coombes and his daughter Audrey. The Coombes family, including Howard's wife, Hazel, resided in Las Plumas from 1926 to 1936. He was a power plant operator. The photograph below shows the main swimming beach, which was located just east of the suspension bridge that allowed access across the river. The beach could be accessed by a trail that began just north of the railroad. (Both, courtesy of AA.)

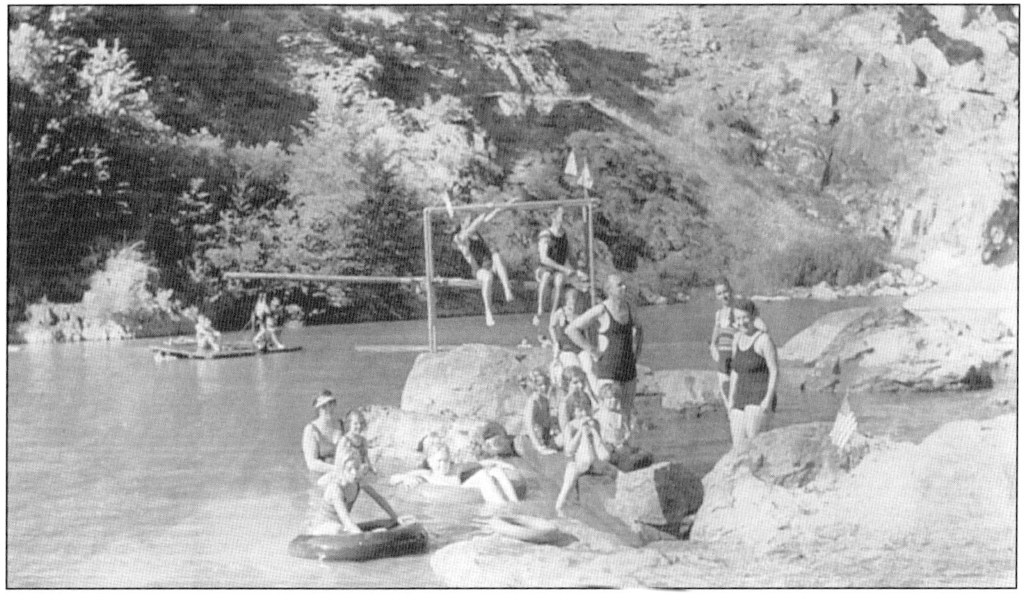

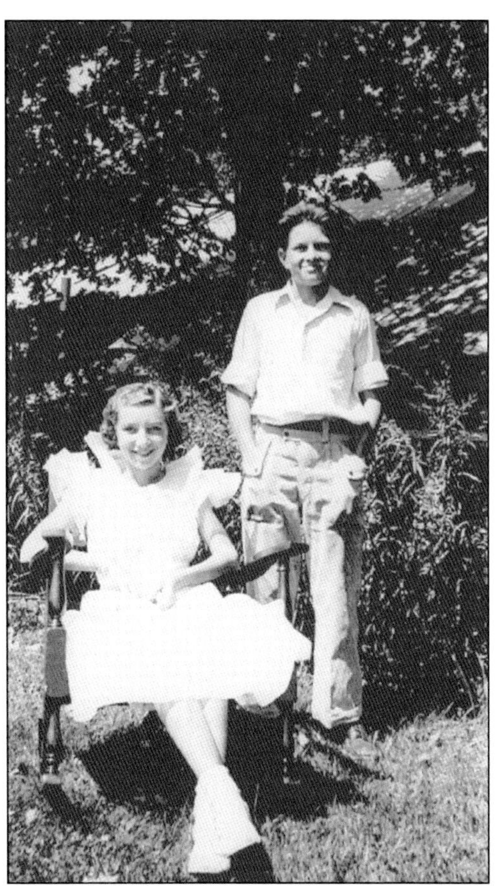

Audrey Coombes, age 11, and Bill Aiston, age 13, are shown at Las Plumas in 1934. They married in 1944, raised two daughters, and owned and managed Aiston's Men's Wear in Oroville from 1958 to 1987. At various times, Bill worked for Oroville's KDAN radio station and for the local newspaper. After retirement, he wrote a regular newspaper column called Looking Back at Oroville. (Courtesy of AA.)

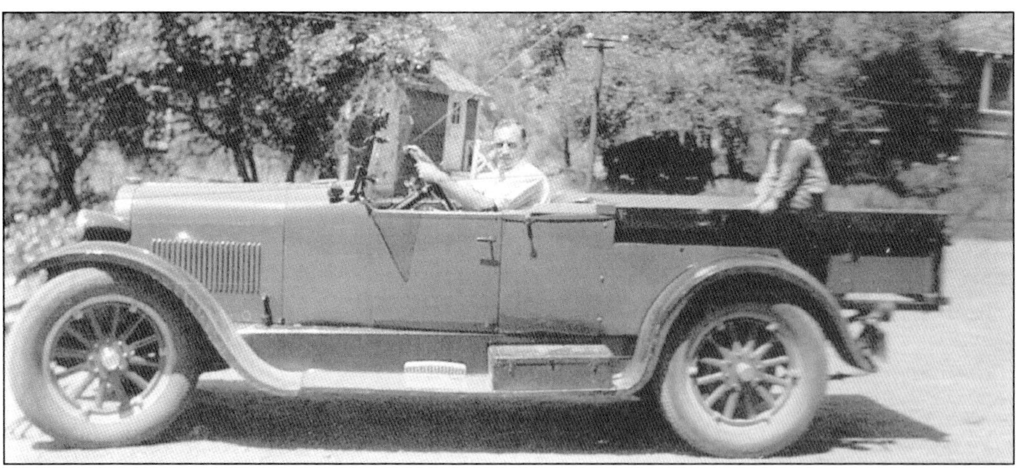

Kenneth McKenzie and his son, Norm, are shown riding around Las Plumas in 1935. Kenneth was a power plant operator. Also in the family were his wife, Mayme, and daughter, Beverly. Getting an automobile in and out of Las Plumas was a chore. There were four different roads, two on each side of the river, to access the location. However, they were unpaved, narrow, extremely crooked, and sometimes dangerous. To drive any of those roads was nerve-racking and exhausting. The opening of the Feather River Highway in August 1937 made access from the north much easier. (Courtesy of NM.)

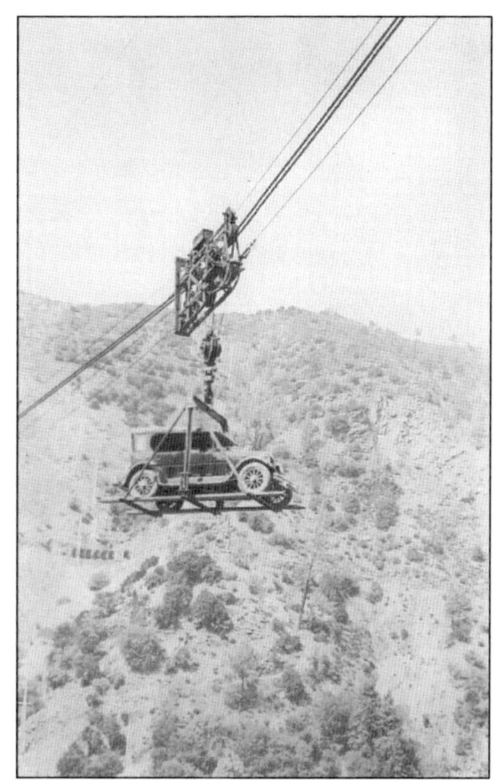

During construction, materials needed to be transported from the railroad depot on the south bank of the Feather River to the powerhouse site on the other side. To solve this problem, two cable tramways were suspended across the 1,200-foot span. A steel-frame skip was built, and material was moved across the chasm via what was called the "Molly Hogan" ferry. Over the years, the high lines transferred everything from vehicles and big-tonnage items to passengers. Apparently, the ride was quite a thrill. Both photographs illustrate the technique. The Molly Hogan served from the beginning of construction right up to the time the powerhouse ceased operation in 1967. The term "Molly Hogan" refers to a type of cable splice. (Right, courtesy of NM; below, courtesy of RP.)

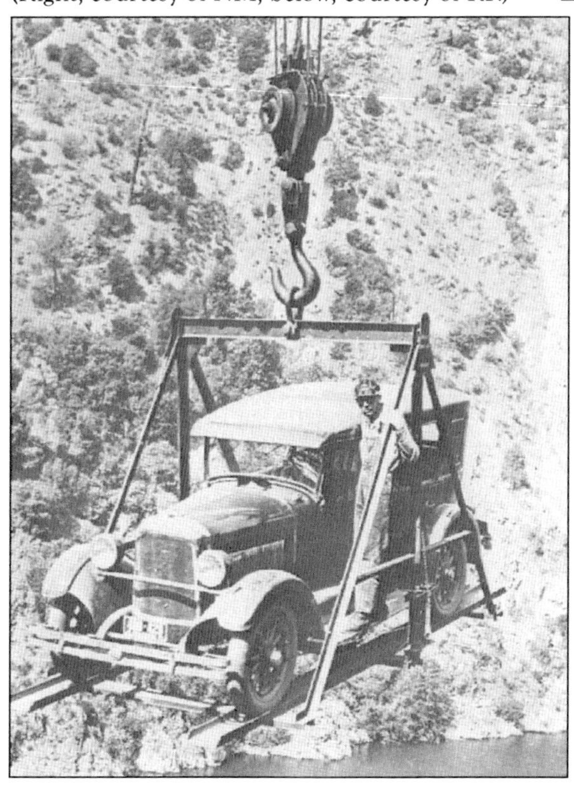

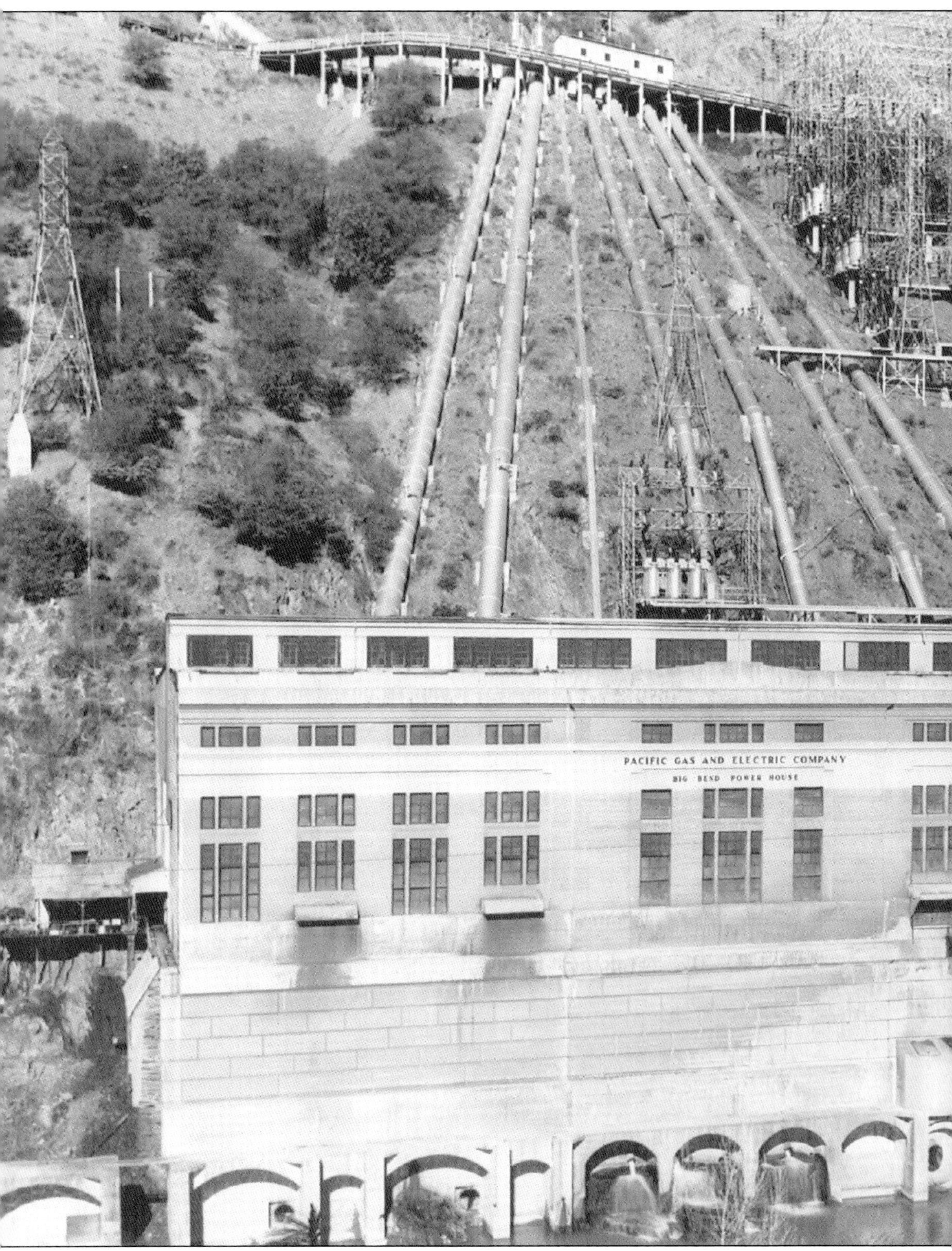
PACIFIC GAS AND ELECTRIC COMPANY
BIG BEND POWER HOUSE

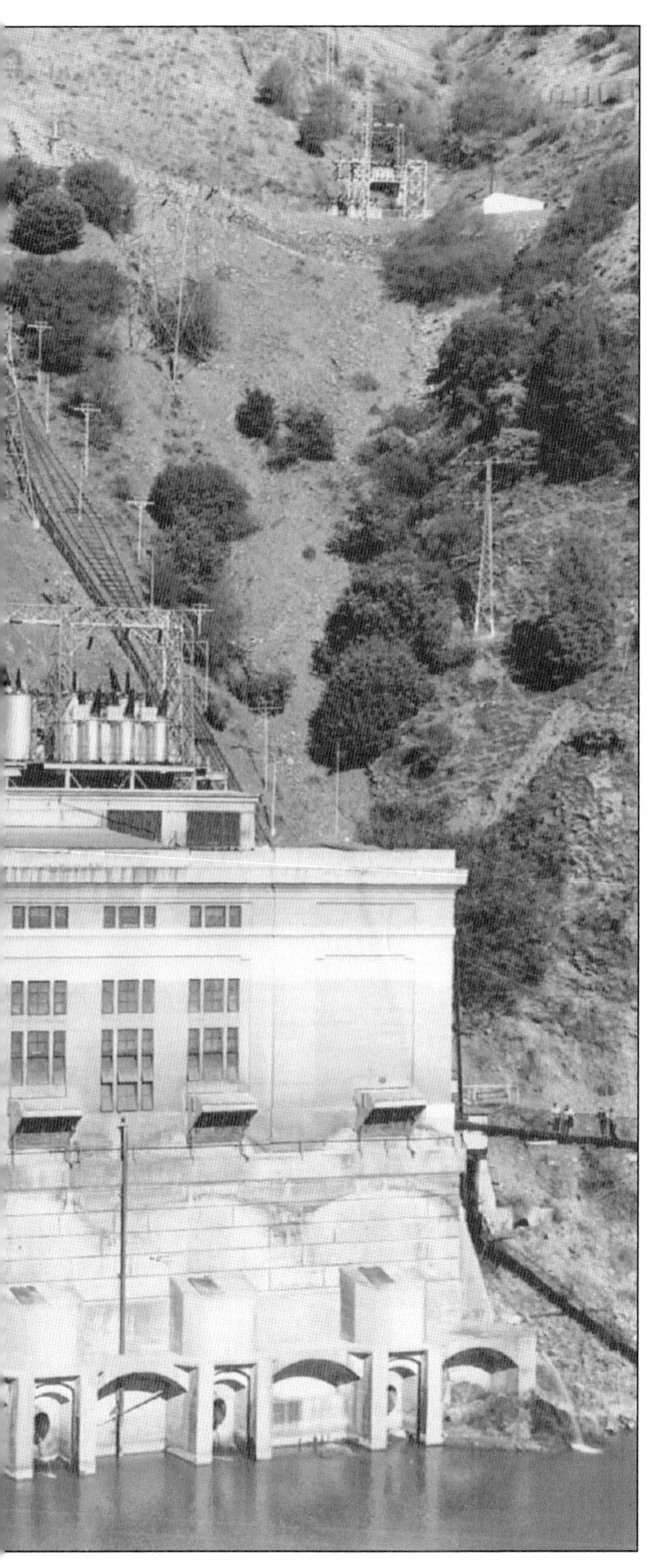

In 1930, the Great Western Power Company merged with the Pacific Gas and Electric Company. At that time, the names "Pacific Gas and Electric Company" and "Big Bend Powerhouse" were added to the front of the powerhouse. The water for the powerhouse was provided by a three-mile tunnel that diverted water from the north end of Big Bend directly to the powerhouse at the southern end of the bend. The tunnel diverted water that normally would have gone around all 13 miles to the south end of the bend. A 12,007-foot tunnel had been built in 1882 as part of a failed mining project. In 1906, a new 3,400-foot tunnel was built to connect the new powerhouse with the southern end of the old mine tunnel. The water was directed to separate sections of penstock pipe, each of which was 450 feet long from the mouth of the tunnel to the powerhouse. The water was then directed to the turbines. At the time, the generators turned by those turbines were the largest of their kind ever constructed. (Courtesy of RP.)

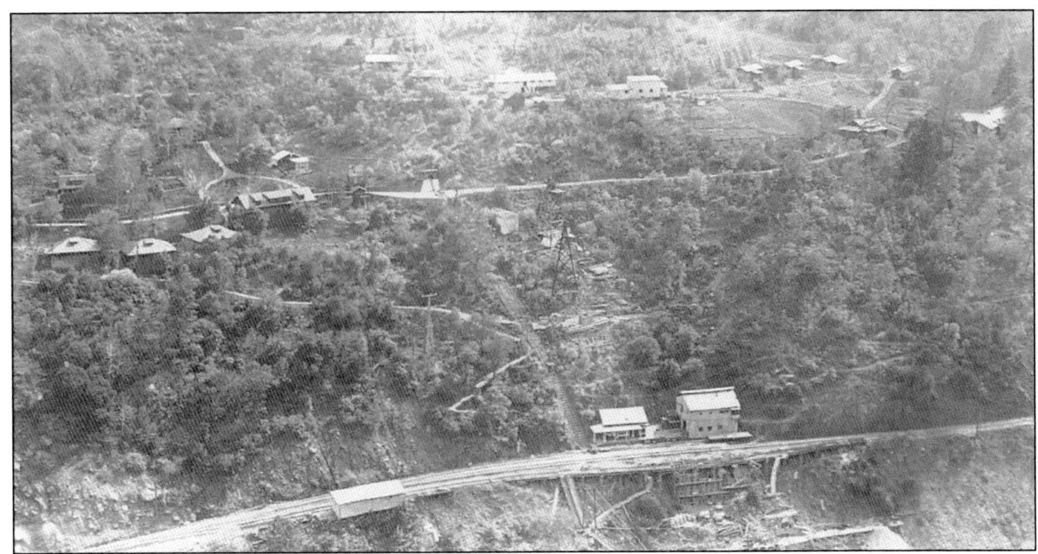

The above photograph of Las Plumas has a view looking south and covering the middle and western part of the community. Running across the bottom of this view is the Western Pacific Railroad. The two buildings along the railroad are the depot and the storehouse, also seen below in a close-up view from 1935. The tramway travels up through the center of the photograph, where the large hospital building is located. The hoist house for the tram is seen where the tramway intersects with the road. The building to the left with the circular paths is the dormitory for single workers, and the superintendent's house is situated just above it. Following that road to the right of the photograph is a private dwelling and the school. They are the last two buildings on the right. (Both, courtesy of NM.)

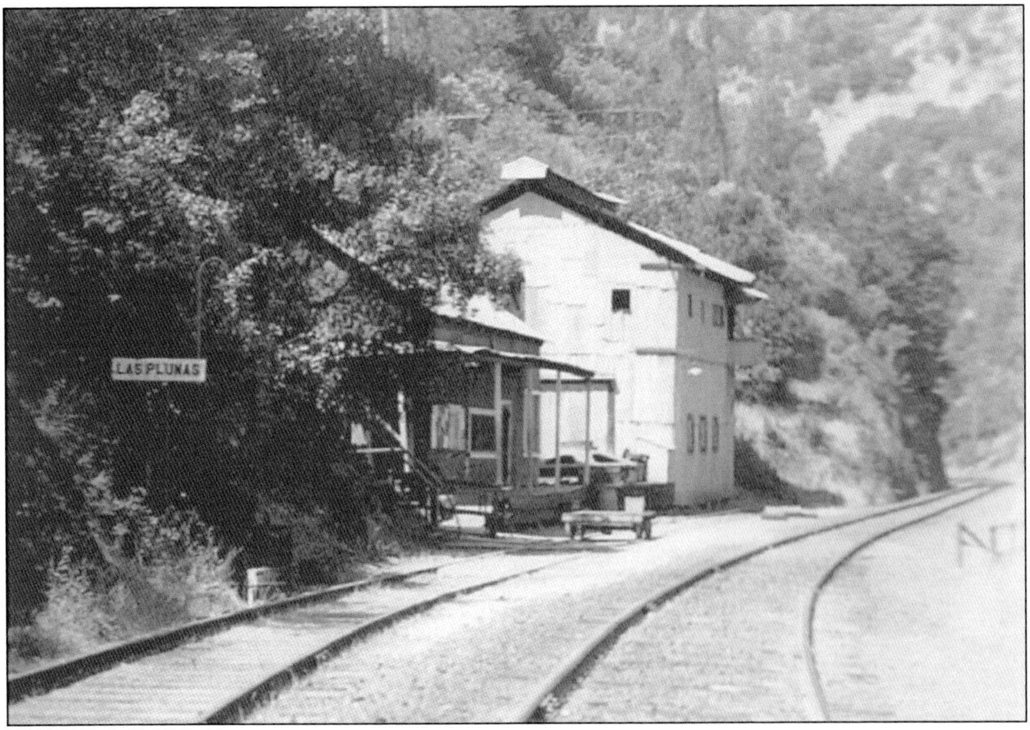

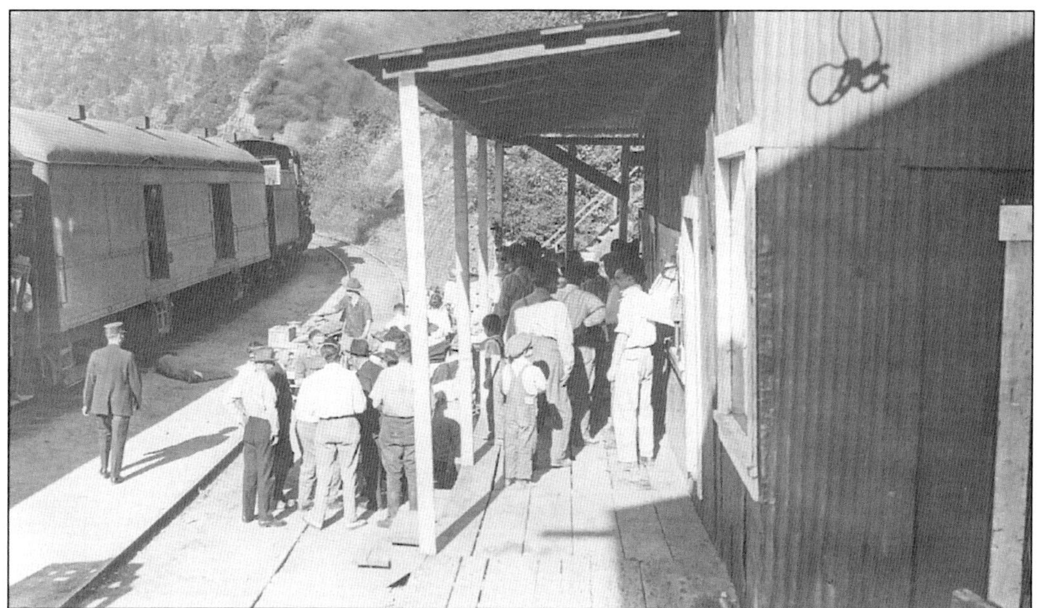

A group of residents is shown meeting the afternoon train at the Las Plumas depot in 1923. Other than traveling uncomfortable dirt roads by car, the only means of traveling to Las Plumas was via the Western Pacific Railroad. The trains carried mail and passengers on a daily basis between the Bay Area and Portola. (Courtesy of RP.)

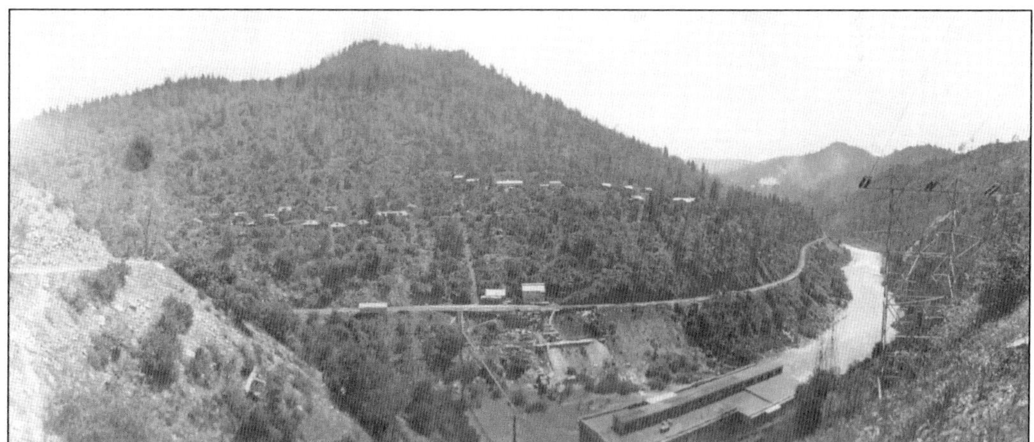

This is a rare photograph from about 1925 showing the top of the Big Bend Powerhouse. The rectangular piece of roof on the right would slide back to allow large pieces of machinery, such as generators and turbines, to be moved in or out of the building. This image also provides a nice view of the river and the railway as it leads off toward the south. (Courtesy of RP.)

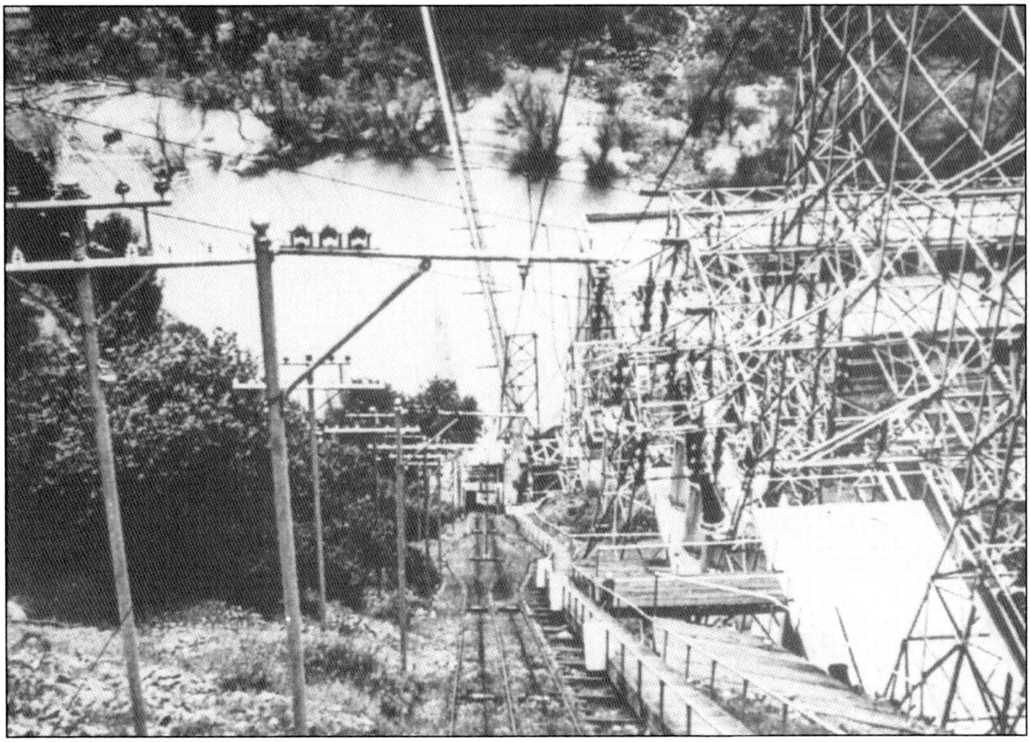

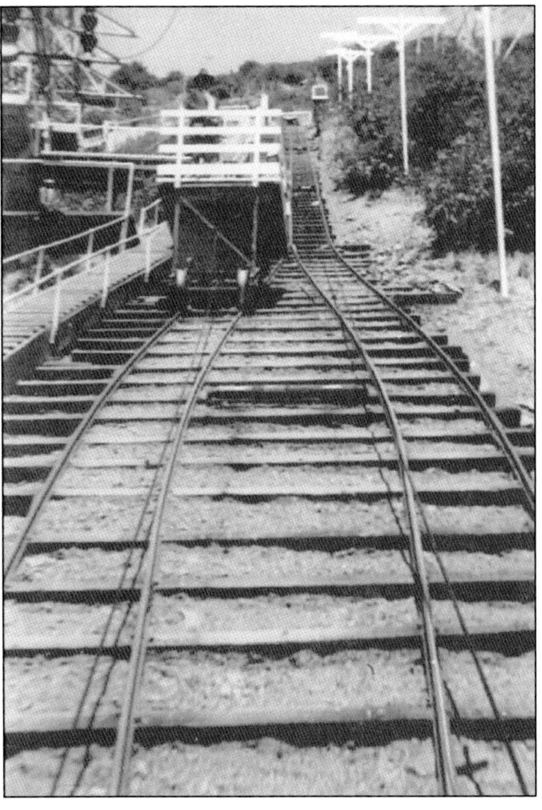

There were two tramways at Las Plumas. One ran up the hill from the Western Pacific Railway depot to the camp on the south side of the river. On the north side, the tramway ran up the hill from the powerhouse to the south portal of the tunnel. In the early days, one could always get a ride on the north side by ringing a bell that would alert the tram operator to start the tram. However, on the south side, sometimes the tram operator was not available, and one would have to walk up the steep trail to the camp. This problem was solved in the 1930s when both tramways were converted to an automatic system. Both of these images show the north side of the river. The above photograph has a view looking down the hill, and the view in the photograph at left is looking up the hill. (Above, courtesy of BCHS; left, courtesy of NM.)

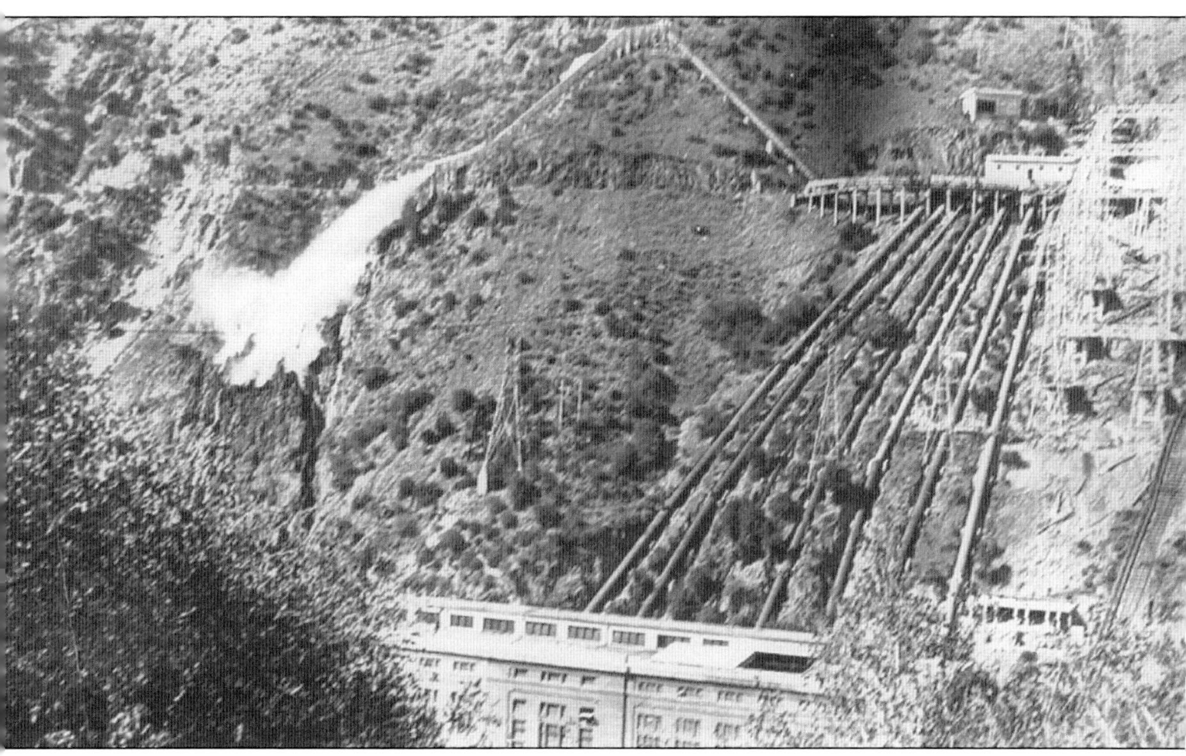

This photograph shows the spillway overflow in operation, which occurred when water from the tunnel was not being pulled into the turbines and was vented out to the river. In 1914, Great Western vice president Guy C. Earl addressed the possibility of the lack of water in dryer years. He had a dam constructed at Big Meadows, about 40 miles north of the powerhouse. The dam flooded a historic Yamani Maidu village site and caused part of the town of Prattville to be moved to higher ground. In 1926, a larger dam was built that increased the lake area to 1,308,000 acre-feet. Earl named the lake after his three daughters—Alice, Martha, and Eleanor. That is why Lake Almanor was created and how it got its name. (Courtesy of NM.)

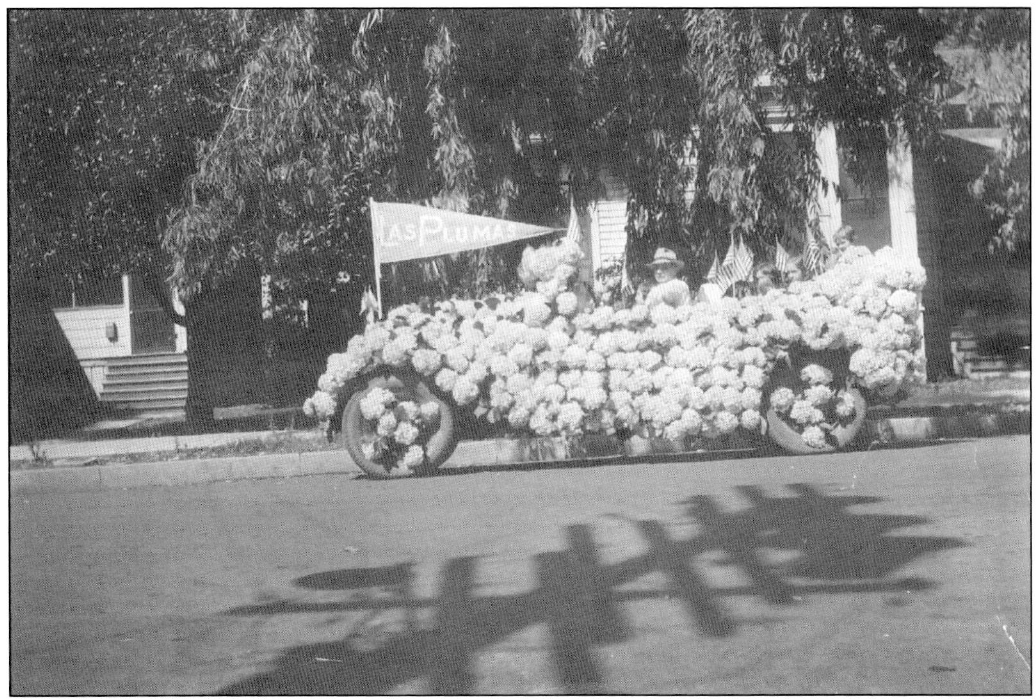

Oroville was the closest good-size city to Las Plumas and the other communities located in or near the Feather River Canyon. Most of their high school students went to school in Oroville. This is Las Plumas's award-winning entry in the annual Oroville parade in 1930. (Courtesy of RP.)

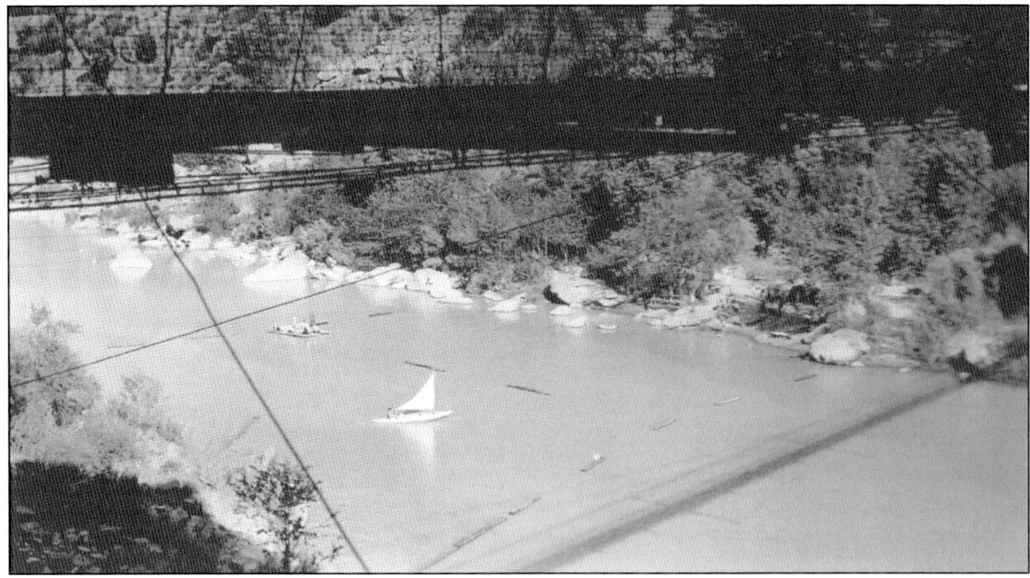

The silhouette of the suspension footbridge is shown above an idyllic scene from a summer day on the river. During the heat of the summer, residents used rafts and sailboats to navigate the waters of the Feather River. The swimming beach can be seen to the right. It was located on the south bank of the river. (Courtesy of NM.)

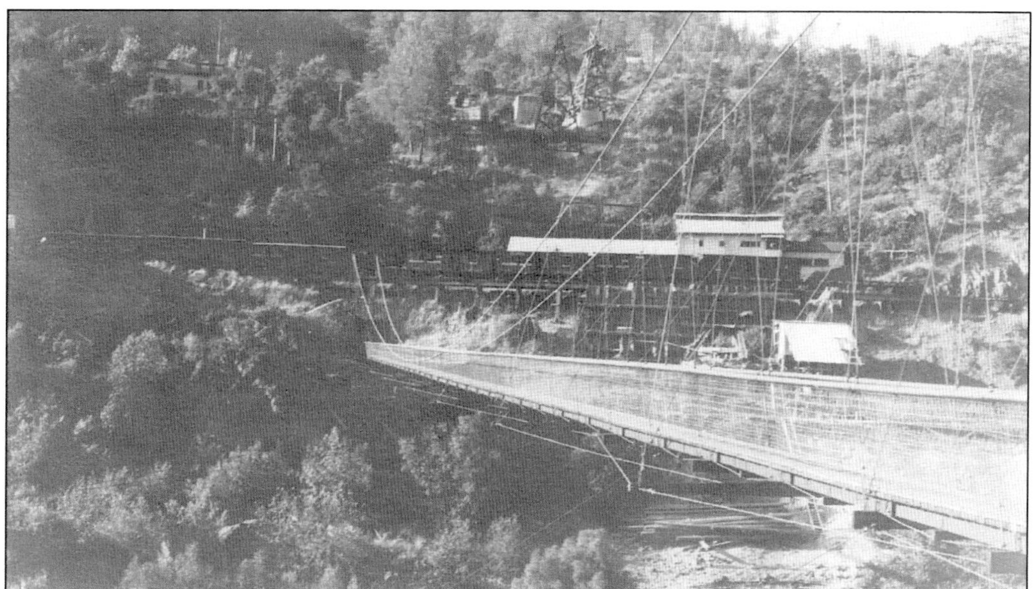

These photographs from 1923 show the suspension footbridge that spanned the 1,200-foot gap between the camp and the powerhouse. Both views look toward the south, or the camp side of the river. Above, a train can be seen stopped in front of the depot. In addition to the daily train, a local freight and passenger train also ran three times per week each way, from Las Plumas to Oroville. At right is a close-up view of the footbridge. It should be noted that rails were laid to facilitate a pushcart that made it easier to transport supplies across the footbridge. (Both, courtesy of RP.)

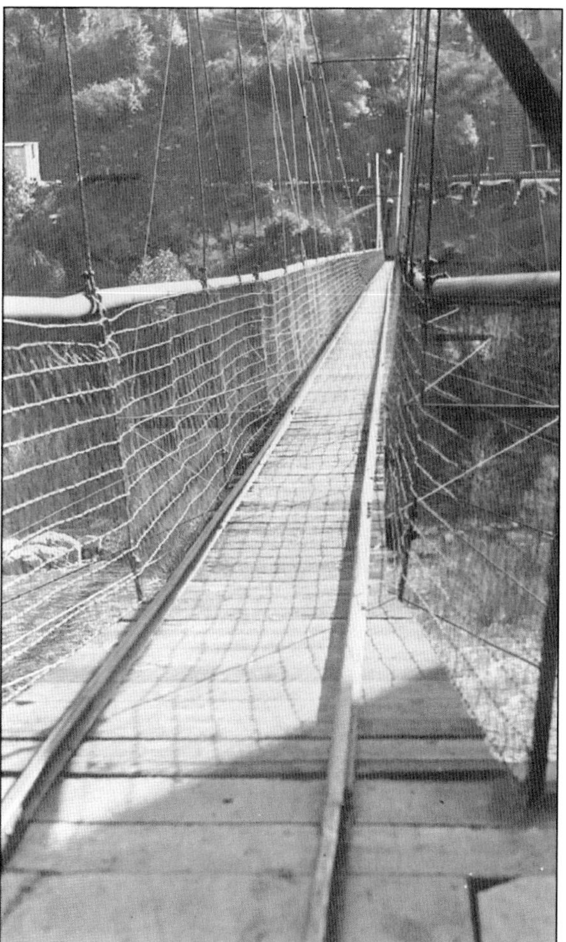

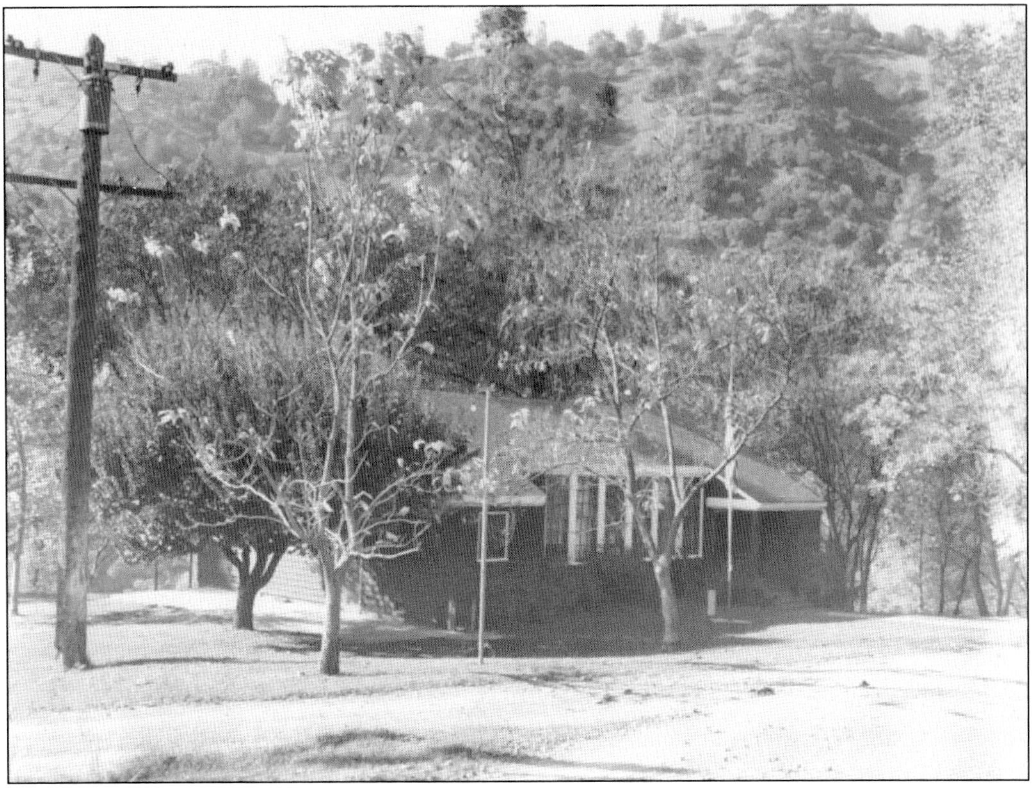

This is the third, and last, Big Bend School. Due to the deterioration of the existing school, bids went out in 1940 to build a new one. Architect Charles F. Dean designed the one-room, one-story frame structure that was built in 1941. On November 19, 1945, the school was renamed the Las Plumas School, and the district was renamed the Las Plumas School District. The new school served for more than 25 years. (Courtesy of MLCSUC.)

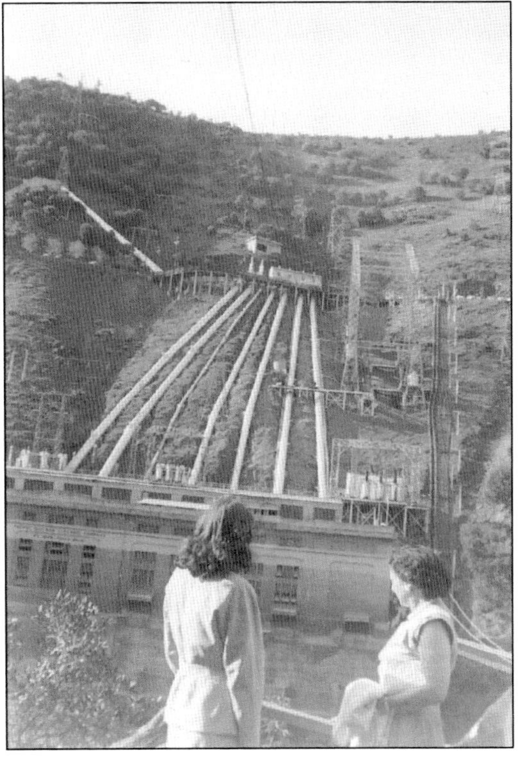

An unidentified woman and Marilynn Foster (right) are pictured observing the Big Bend Powerhouse in the 1950s. The tramway is shown on the right side of the powerhouse. Sometimes the trams were down for maintenance. During those occasions, a decision had to be made whether to wait or hike the 383 steps to the top. To many children in Las Plumas, climbing those steps was a rite of passage. (Courtesy of RP.)

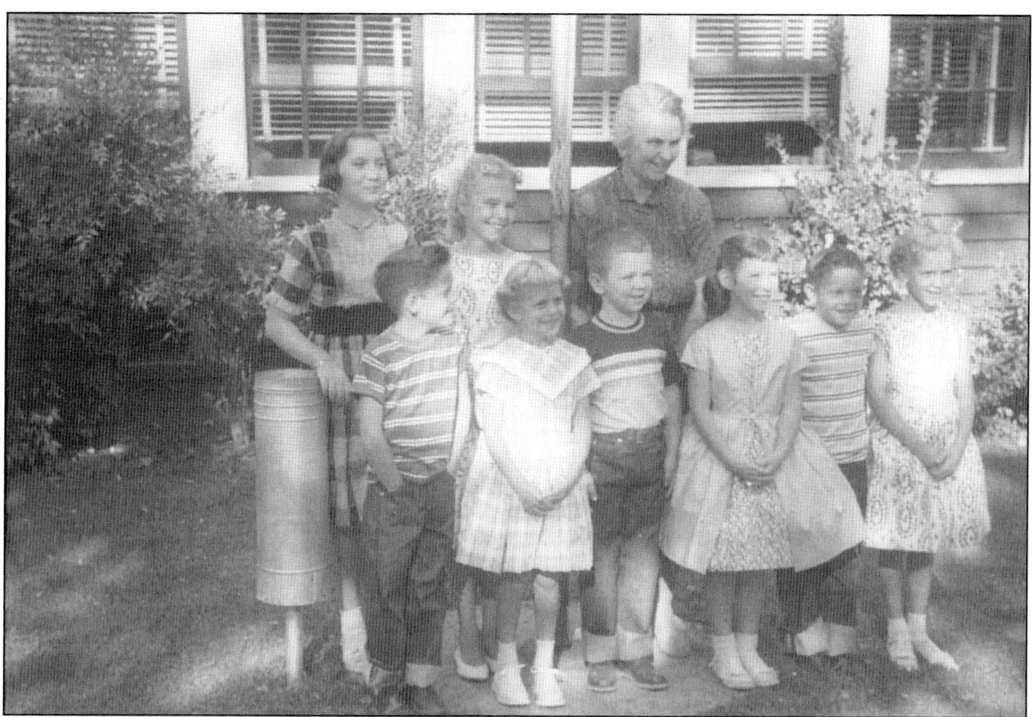

A class of the Las Plumas School is pictured in May 1958. From left to right are (first row) Billy Mackay, Jeanibeth Torkelson, Craig LeMaster, Robyn Foster, David Mackay and Debbie Howe; (second row) Shirley Moak, Cindy Howe and the teacher Lola Self, who also taught at the Mountain Springs School at Enterprise and at Feather Falls School. Torkelson was the last graduate of the Las Plumas School. (Courtesy of RP.)

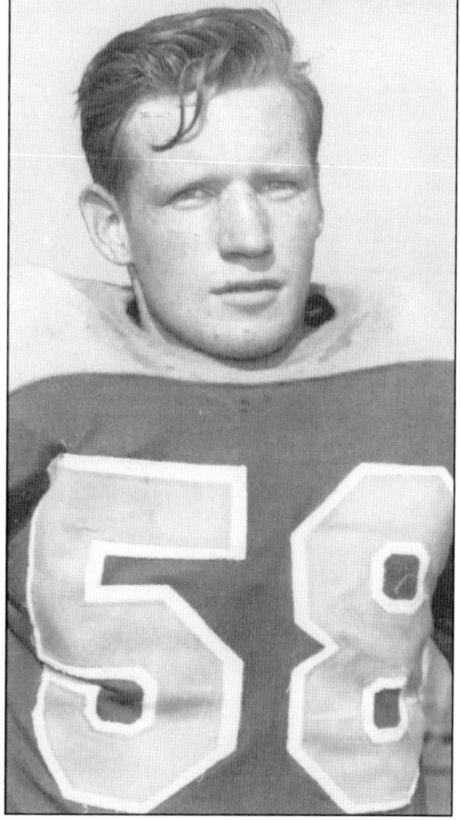

The Las Plumas School only served students through eighth grade. Due to the distance involved, the Oroville Union High School District offered to pay the parents of high school students living in Las Plumas 50¢ per day to live in Oroville. One such student was Norm MacKenzie, pictured here in his Oroville Tigers football jersey in 1947. He lived in Oroville for the last three years of high school and graduated in 1948. MacKenzie taught physical education at Oroville High School from 1956 to 1961, and he served as athletic director and head coach at Las Plumas High School from 1961 to 1996. (Courtesy of RP.)

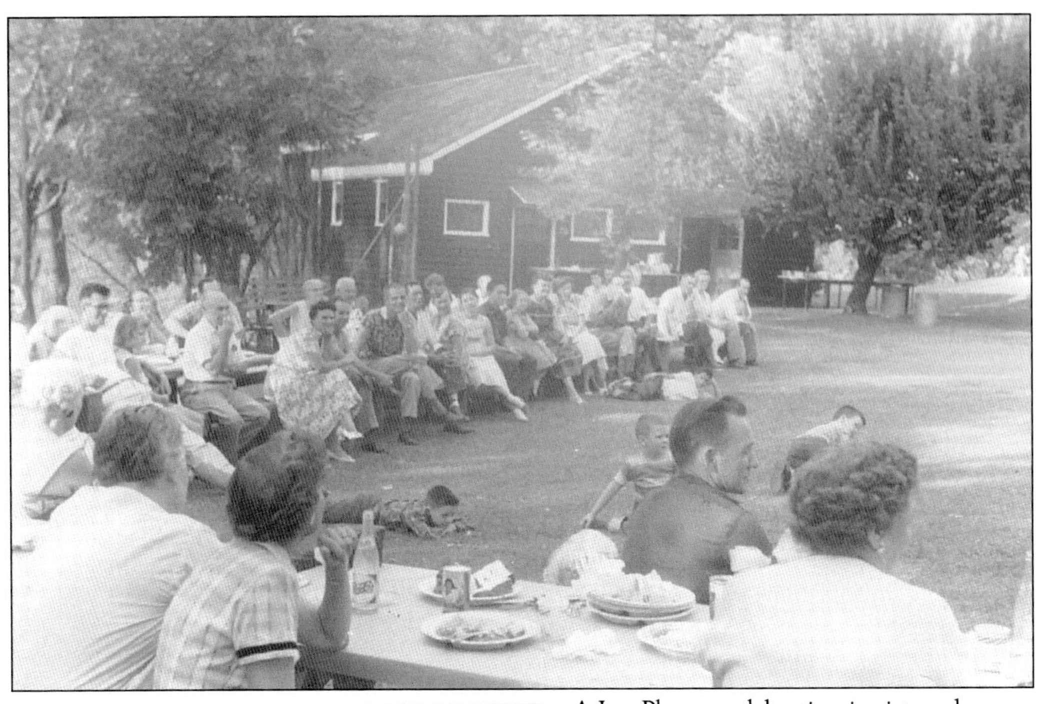

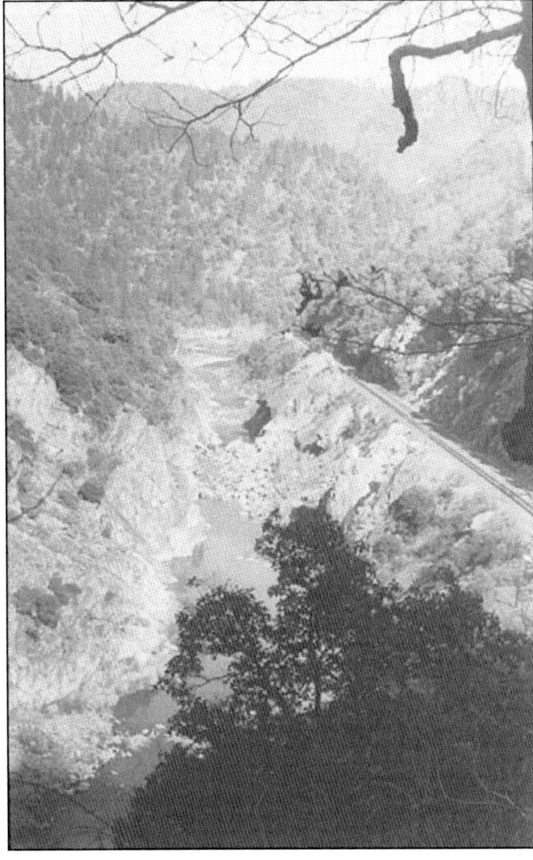

A Las Plumas celebration is pictured in 1958. This might be a retirement party. The Las Plumas School is seen in the background. Even as early as the mid-1950s, the residents recognized the fact that Lake Oroville would someday flood their community. On June 1, 1957, Gov. Goodwin Knight arrived in Oroville to celebrate the area's selection for the location of the Oroville Dam. (Courtesy of AA.)

This is a 1955 view of the Western Pacific Railroad between Las Plumas and Berry Creek station. The railroad ran east-west on the south side of the Feather River for a distance of four miles. One of the two rough roads that one could travel to access Las Plumas ran on the south side of the railroad all the way to Berry Creek station. From there, the road headed due south for about two miles to where it connected to Oroville-Quincy Highway. (Courtesy of MLCSUC.)

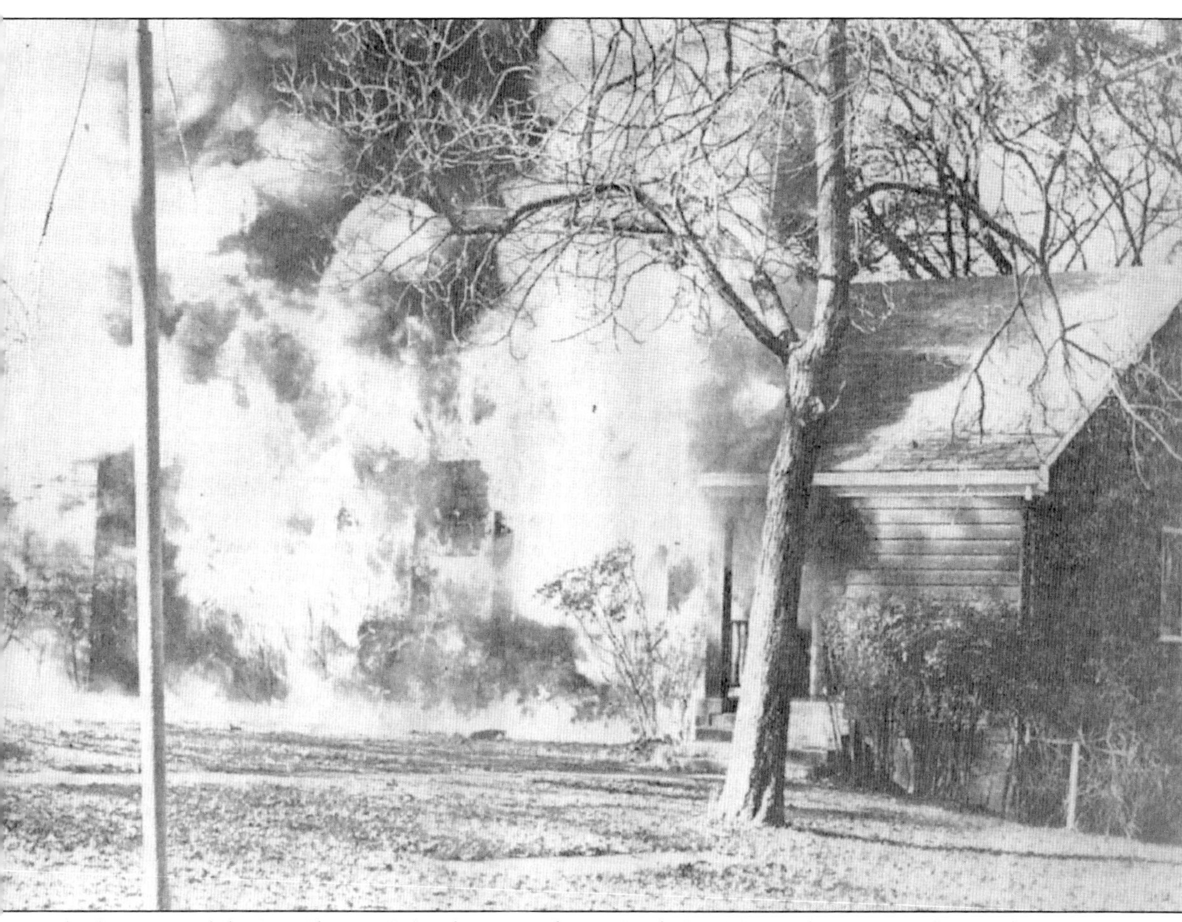

The burning of the Las Plumas School occurred on March 2, 1967. Early in 1967, the employees and their families began to move to new residences in surrounding communities. After the buildings were burned, the area was bulldozed, and all the surrounding vegetation was cleared. The equipment and machinery in the powerhouse were removed. Only some concrete foundations remained. (Courtesy of ER.)

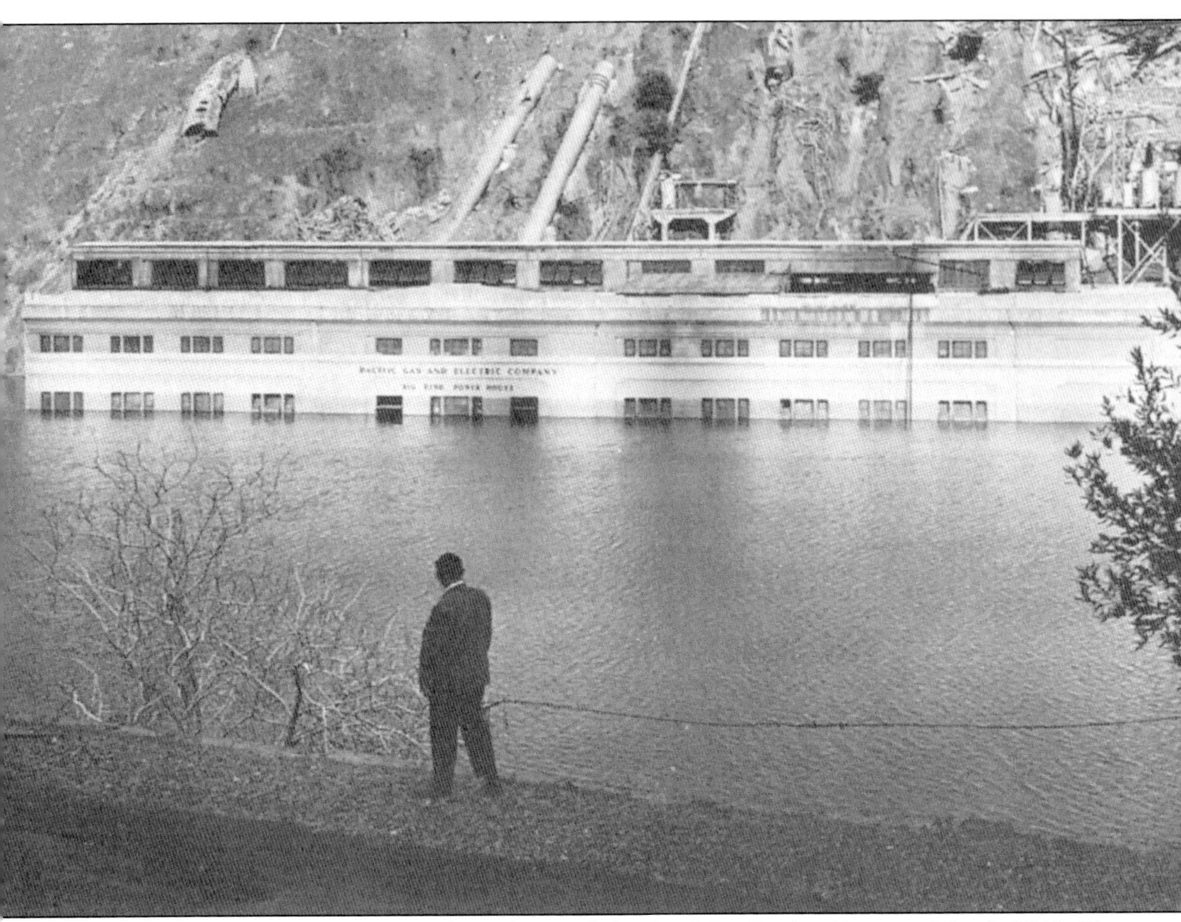

Bill Leeson is shown walking along the south bank of the Feather River in March 1968. He is watching the progress of the rise of the water on the Big Bend Powerhouse. The powerhouse was shut down at 11:59 p.m. on September 30, 1967, and on November 14, 1967, the gates on the Oroville Dam were closed, and the water that would create Lake Oroville began to rise. At the time, Leeson was vice president of the Butte County Historical Society. He left a great legacy of research on Las Plumas and the Big Bend Powerhouse. Much of the information in this chapter was based on his research. (Courtesy of Pacific Gas and Electric Company.)

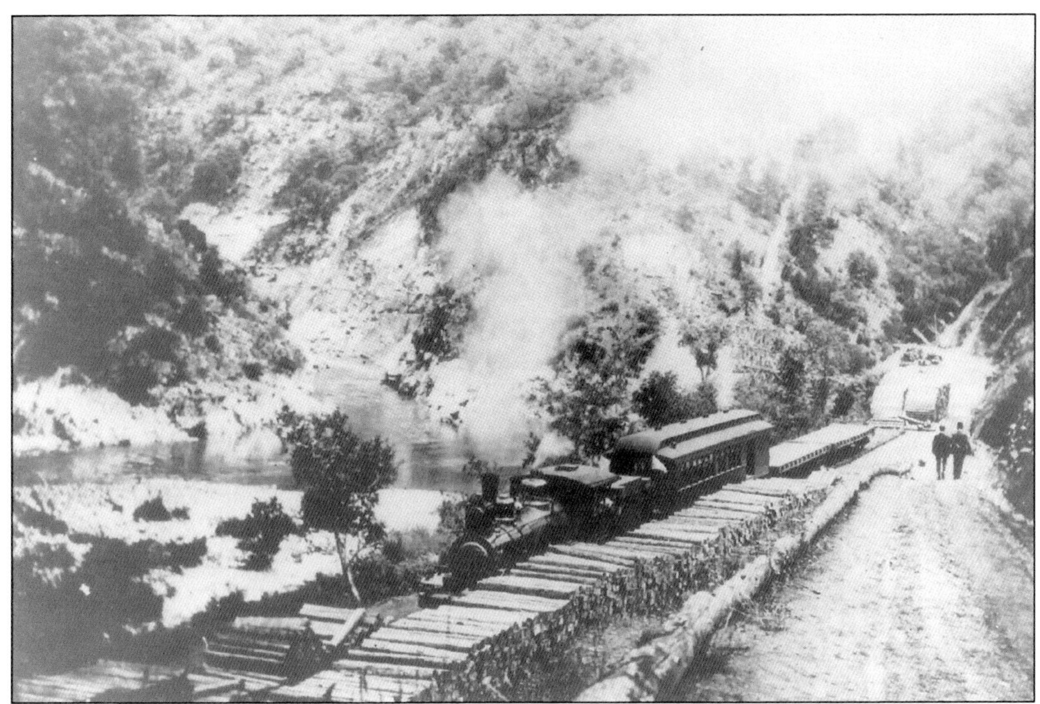

The Western Pacific Railroad first began venturing into the mountains in 1909 and made daily runs from Oroville to Salt Lake City beginning in 1910. The first 16 miles stretched from Oroville to the Las Plumas station and then another four miles to the Berry Creek station. Above is the construction of the Western Pacific track at Berry Creek station in 1908. Massive amounts of wood and rock were used in cribbing the walls to support the railbed on the Feather River route. Some of the bridges were more than 1,000 feet long and were made of wooden timbers that had to be muscled into place by manpower. Below is the Berry Creek station, built in 1927 to replace an older depot. It measured 80 by 30 feet. (Above, courtesy of BCHS; below, courtesy of Steve Hayes.)

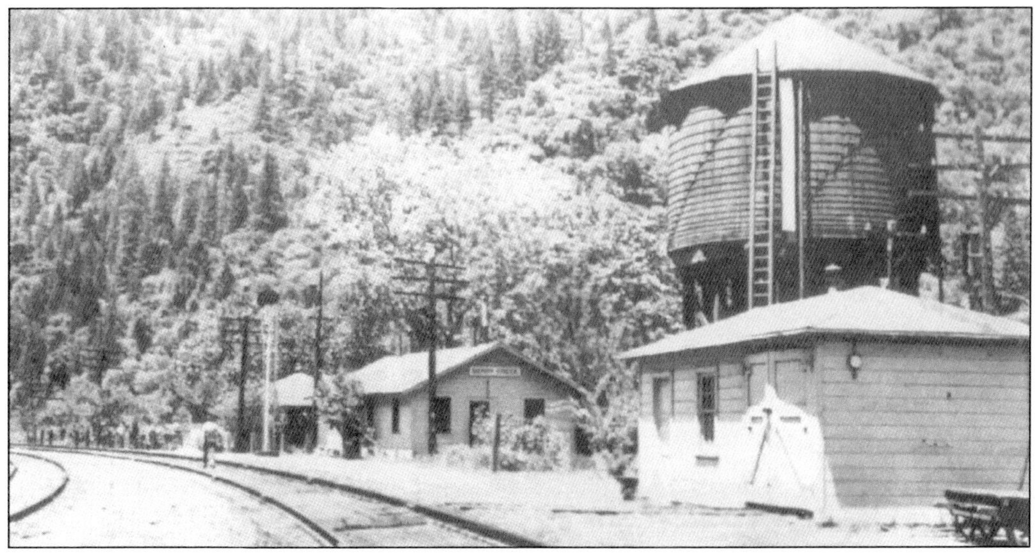

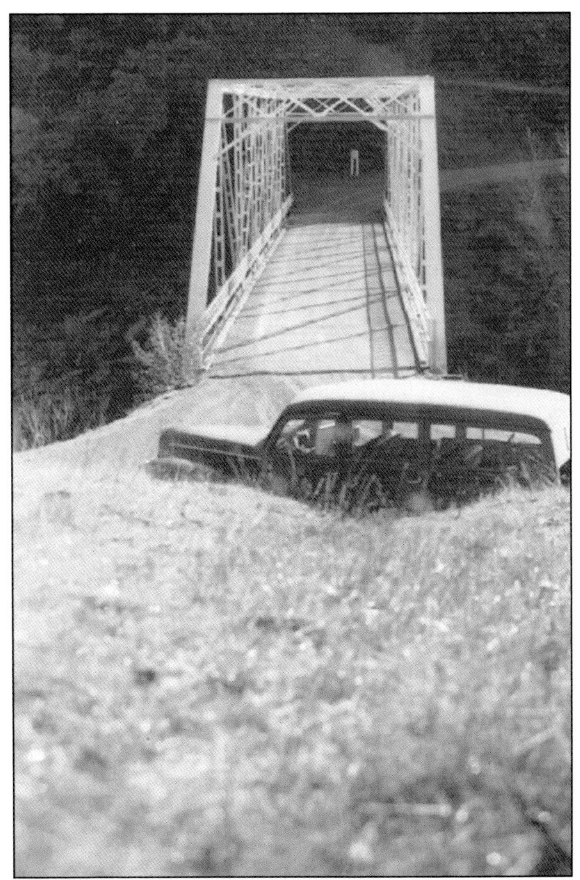

The Nelson Bar Bridge is seen at left as it appeared in 1947. The T.H. Polk Company built the bridge from August to October 1911. It was 140 feet long and was posted as a one-lane bridge. It was disassembled and removed prior to the area being flooded by Lake Oroville. Nelson Bar was a mining town located about one mile north of the present-day Lime Saddle Marina. The town was established when Benjamin Nelson found gold there in 1850. The town spanned both sides of the river, and its ferries and bridges were destroyed several times by high water. Below is the old covered bridge at Nelson Bar that was replaced by the 1911 bridge. (Left, courtesy of BCPW; below, courtesy of BCHS.)

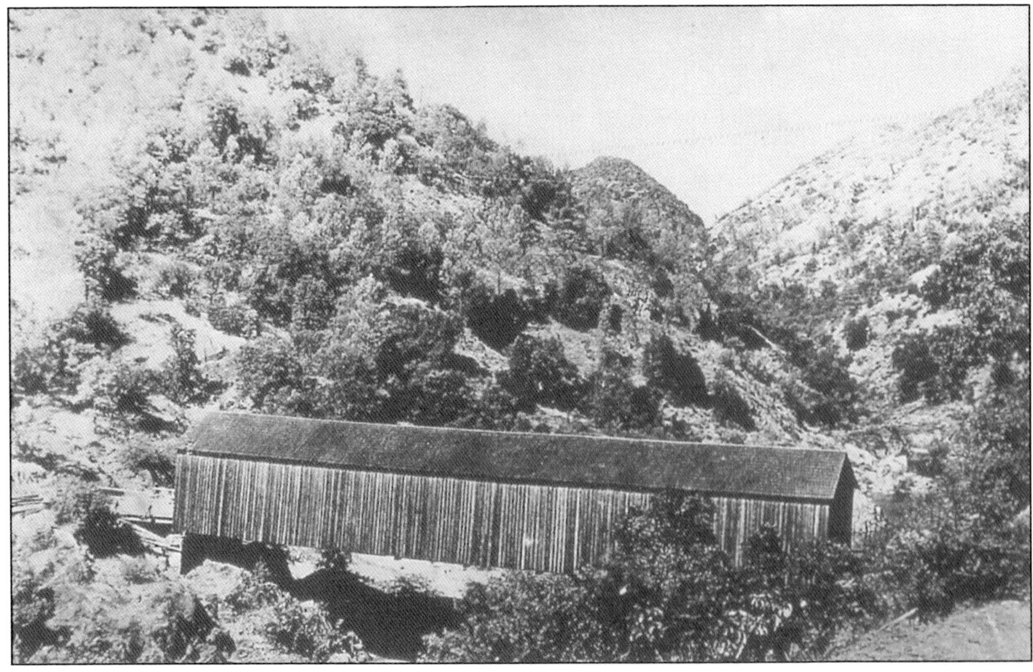

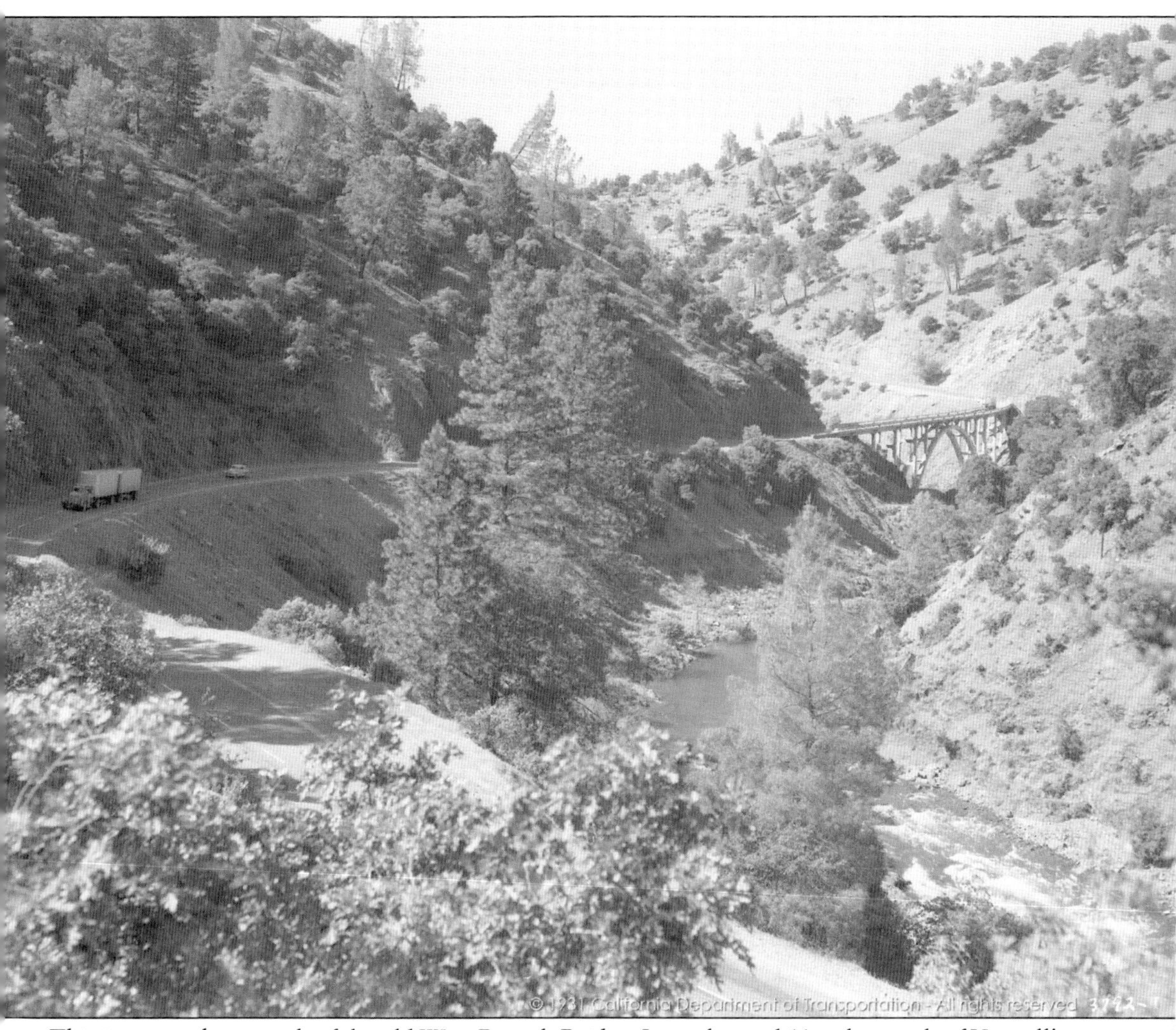

This is a rare photograph of the old West Branch Bridge. It was located 11 miles north of Hansell's Bridge on Highway 24. Both reinforced-concrete-arch bridges were built in 1931 and looked very similar. From this point, traffic climbed the hill and continued north through the Feather River Canyon. Today, that upper stretch of road is known as Dark Canyon Road, and its south end terminates at the Dark Canyon boat ramp. Of the 17 miles between the site of the old Hansell's Bridge and Jarbo Gap, 12 of those miles are under Lake Oroville. (Courtesy of California Department of Transportation.)

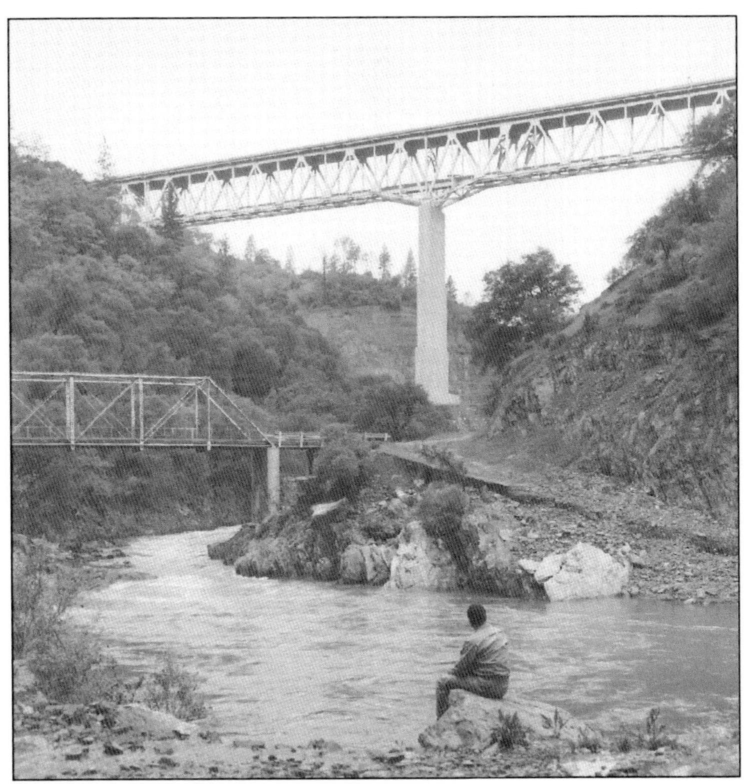

The old meets the new in this photograph of the Oroville-Concow Bridge on the West Branch of the Feather River. The Clark and Henery Company built the 96-foot-long Pratt truss bridge in 1903. This view from late 1961 also shows the just completed span of the new West Branch Bridge. The man sitting on the rock is writer and historian Bill Talbitzer, who documented much of the history of the Feather River country. (Courtesy of BCHS.)

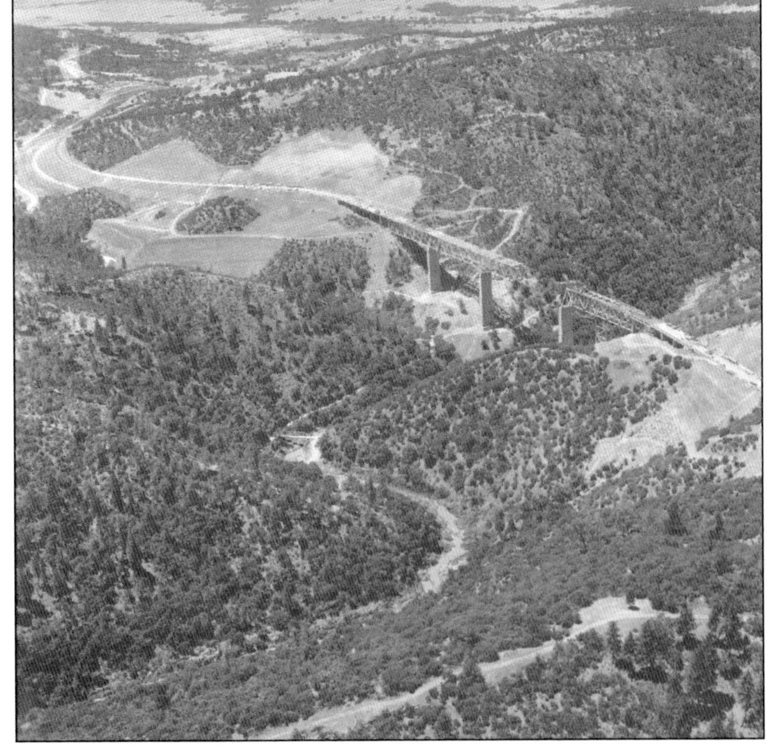

This aerial view shows the construction of the new West Branch Bridge on July 6, 1961. The construction of Highway 70 up to the Feather River Canyon was necessary due to the fact that Lake Oroville would be flooding the old Highway 24. The cantilever double-deck bridge is 450 feet high and 2,731 feet long. The new bridge replaced the old West Branch Bridge and the Oroville-Concow Bridge. (Courtesy of CDWR.)

Two

The Middle Fork

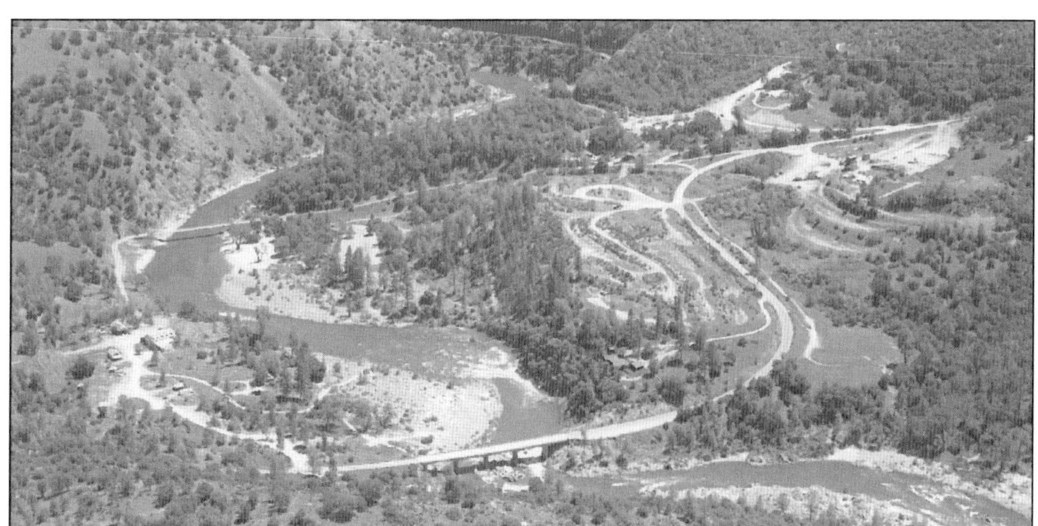

This chapter includes the Feather River Bridge on Highway 24, otherwise known as Hansell's Bridge. It was ground zero for the construction of Oroville Dam. Also included is the community of Bidwell Bar that was located about nine miles northeast of Oroville. The maximum depth of Lake Oroville at Bidwell Bar is around 600 feet. This photograph shows Bidwell Bar in the spring of 1964. The old Bidwell Bar suspension bridge is seen at left, and just downstream is the concrete bypass bridge. (Courtesy of CDWR.)

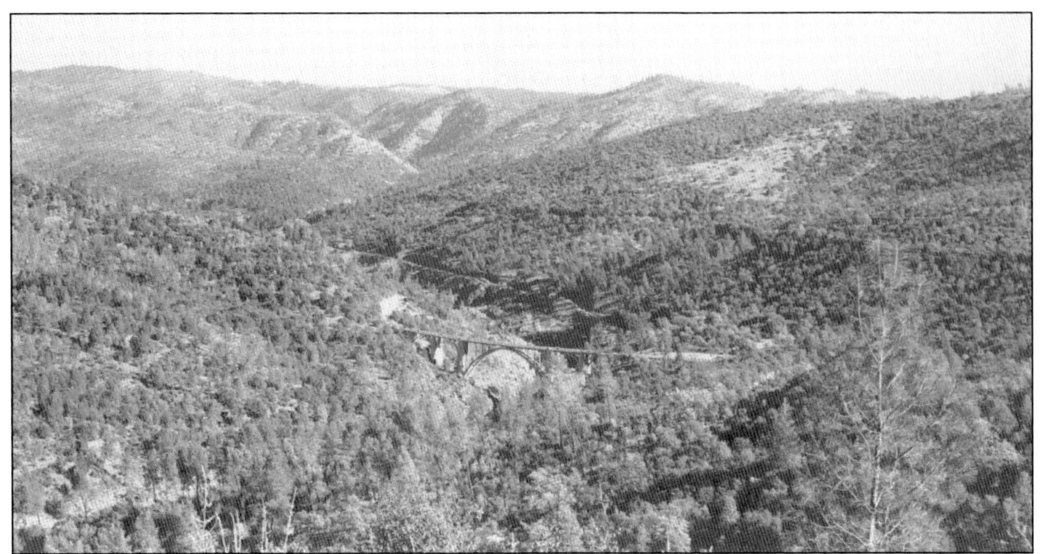

Above is an eastward view of the Feather River Bridge, aka Hansell's Bridge, as it crosses the Middle Fork of the Feather River on Highway 24 in 1955. Highway 24 brought traffic from the Oroville area through the canyon. Once the Feather River highway was completed in August 1937, the route went on to Plumas County and parts east. Below is an image taken during construction of the bridge in 1930. Built by a contractor using convict labor, the bridge was also known by the names the Gateway Bridge and the Rainbow Bridge. It was 270 feet long and stood 145 feet above the river. (Above, courtesy of BCHS; below, courtesy of JL.)

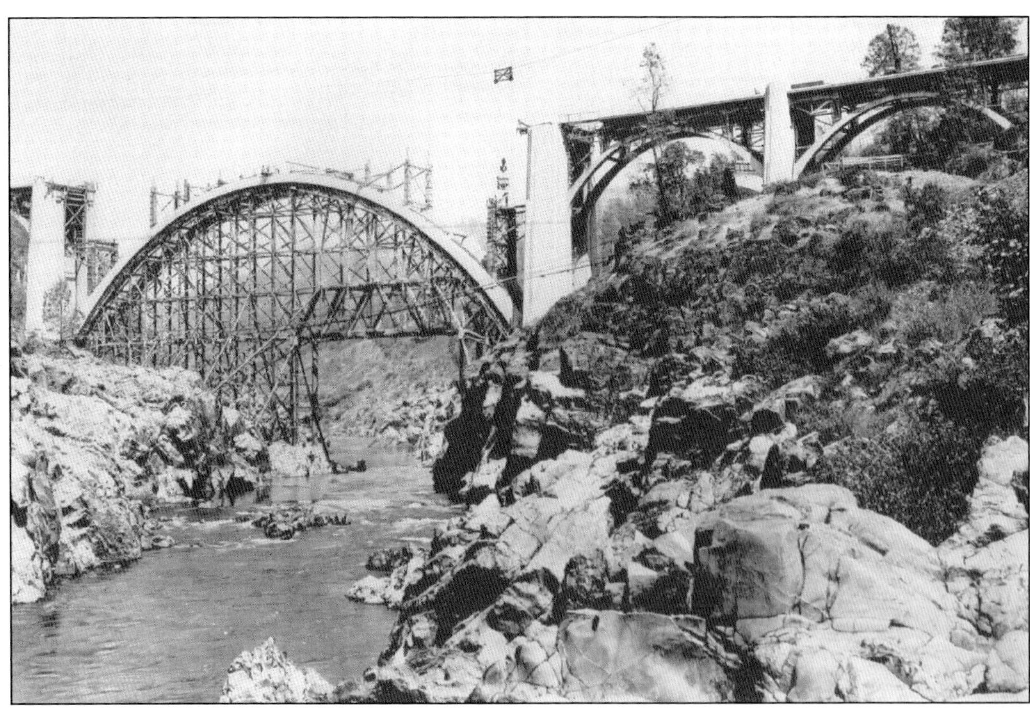

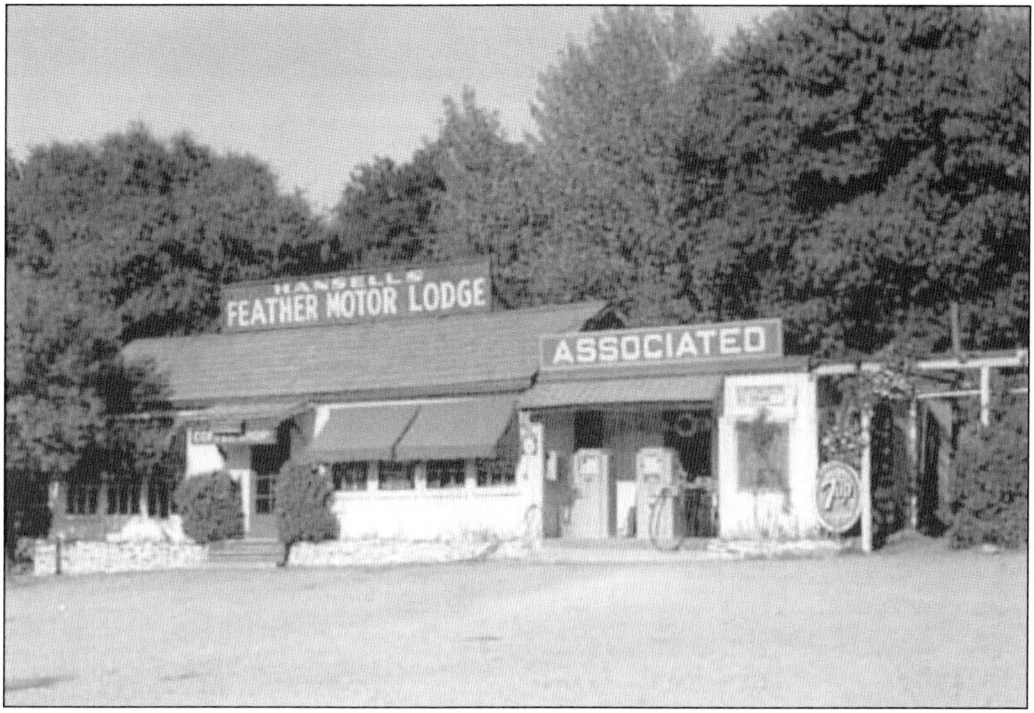

Hansell's Feather Motor Lodge opened for business on the same day that the Feather River Highway opened in 1937. Jack and Grace Hansell lived and worked in Las Plumas and wanted to start their own business. Their combination restaurant, gas station, and auto court was located in a level area on the south end of the Feather River Bridge. From that day forward, the bridge was unofficially known as Hansell's Bridge. Hansell's Feather Motor Lodge had the only telephone for the 45 miles between Oroville and Belden. The business survived for a quarter of a century and served thousands of travelers until the early 1960s, when the site of the business was sold to the state. Jack Hansell is pictured at right. (Both, courtesy of JL.)

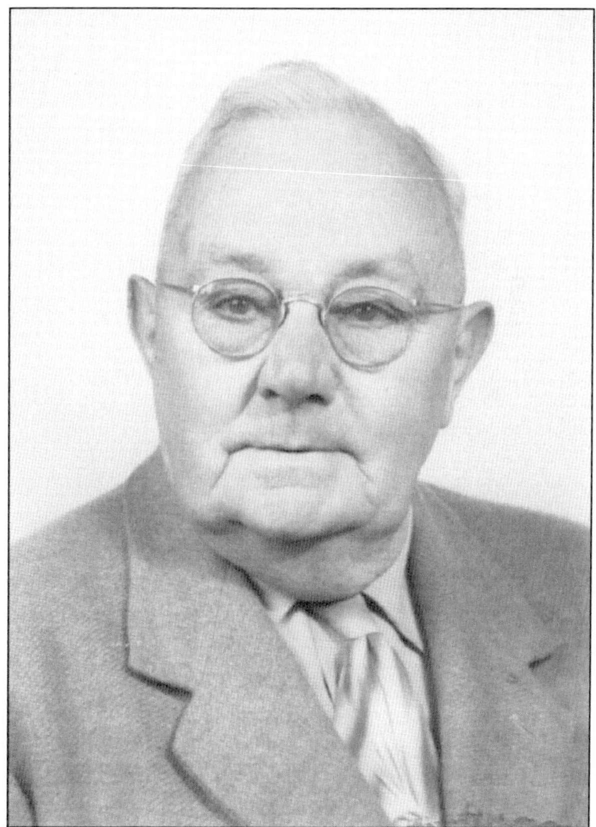

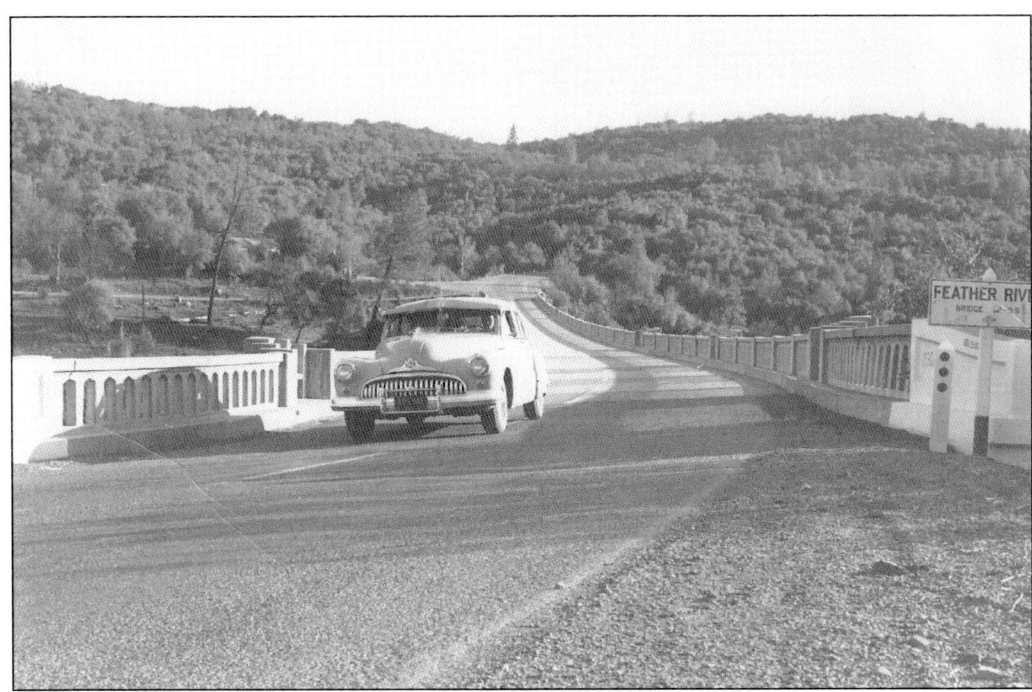

Above, Ron Turner photographed his wife, Marlene, as she drove a 1948 Buick Roadmaster across Hansell's Bridge in 1952. Hansell's Feather Motor Lodge can just barely be seen on the other side of the river in the trees toward the left. Below, the California Zephyr Domeliner crosses beneath the bridge on its way south toward the Sacramento Valley. The original California Zephyr trains ran from Chicago to Emeryville, California, beginning on March 19, 1949, until they ceased operation in 1970. On June 1, 1957, Gov. Goodwin Knight arrived at this location by special train. He made a speech from the caboose and announced the construction of Oroville Dam at this site. (Both, courtesy of RT.)

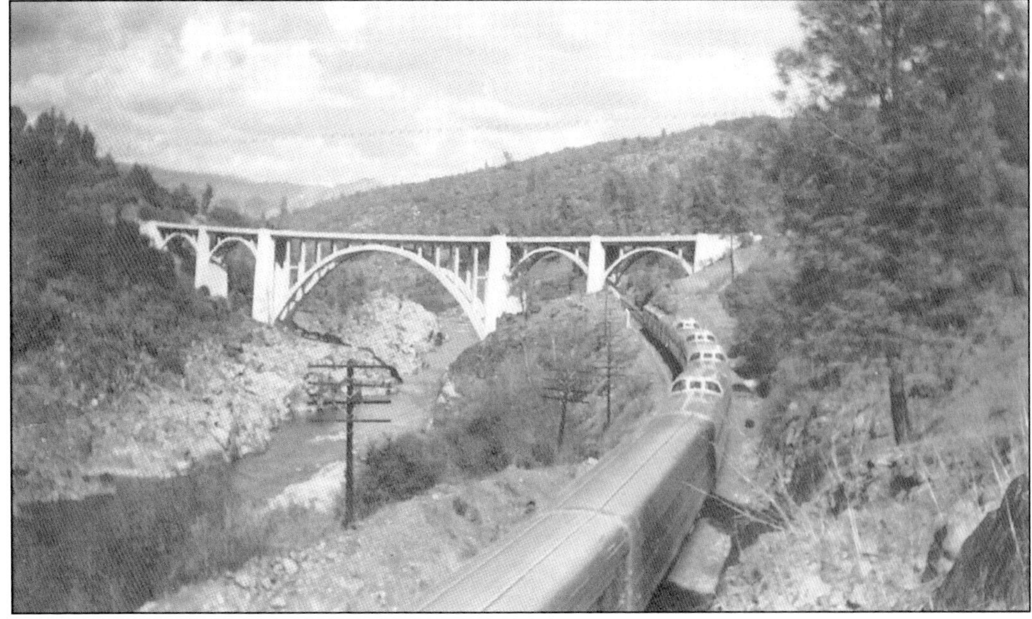

Hansell's Bridge is now part of the Oroville Dam project in this southeast view from February 2, 1963. The area where Hansell's Feather Motor Lodge had been is shown crowded with parked vehicles. Also, the old Western Pacific Railroad tracks have been removed. The bridge continued to serve as an access bridge for the project until April 1965, when it was blown up in three stages. The embankment of Oroville Dam was then beginning to encroach on its northern supports. (Courtesy of CDWR.)

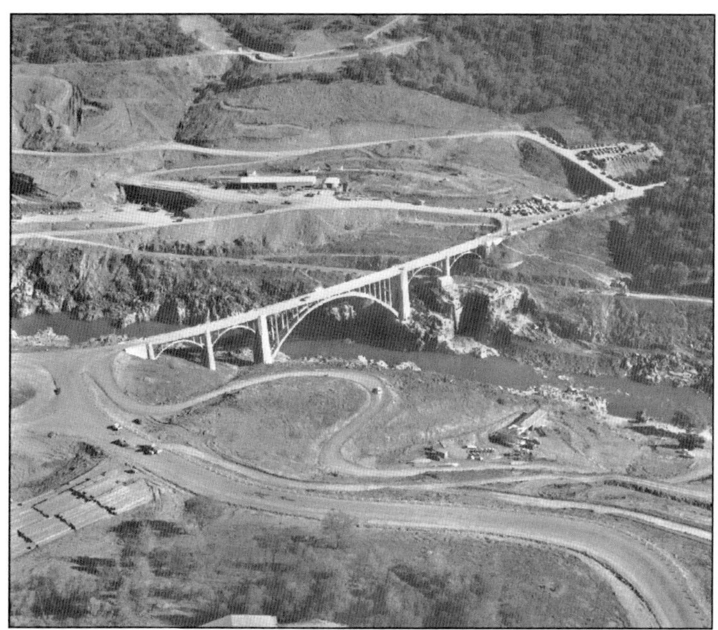

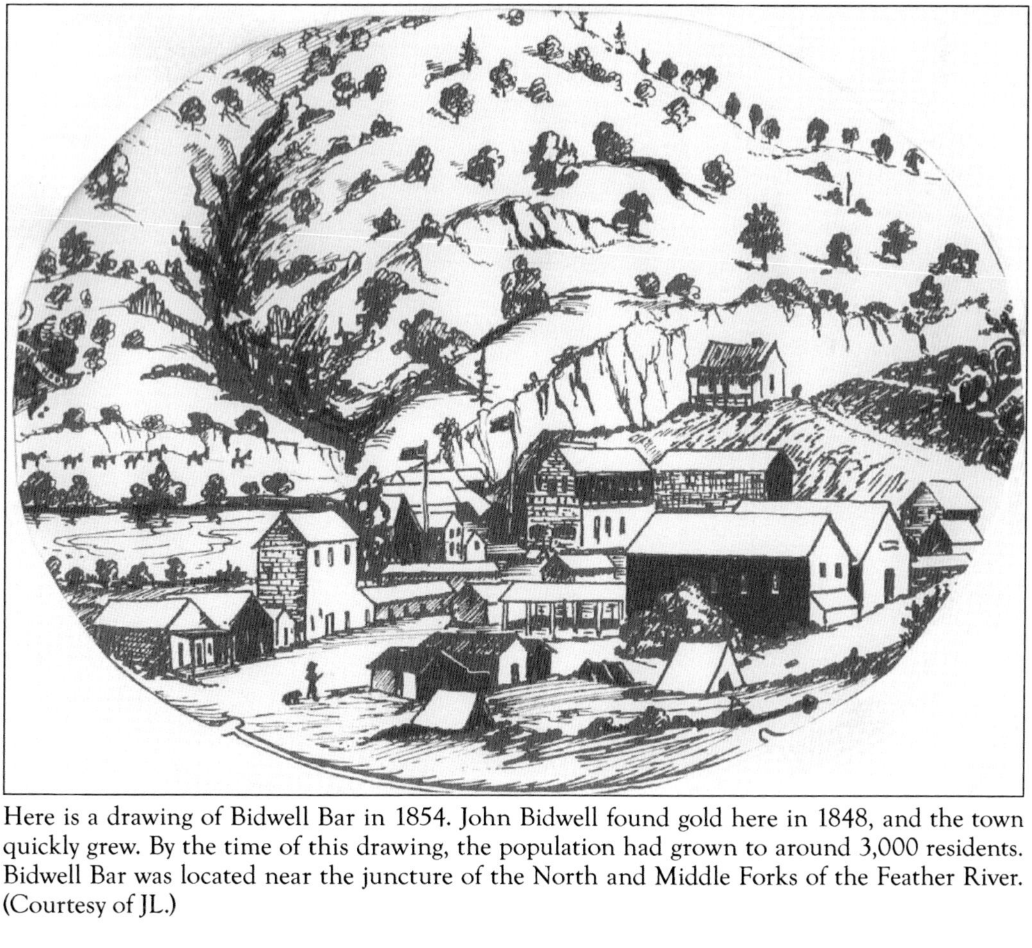

Here is a drawing of Bidwell Bar in 1854. John Bidwell found gold here in 1848, and the town quickly grew. By the time of this drawing, the population had grown to around 3,000 residents. Bidwell Bar was located near the juncture of the North and Middle Forks of the Feather River. (Courtesy of JL.)

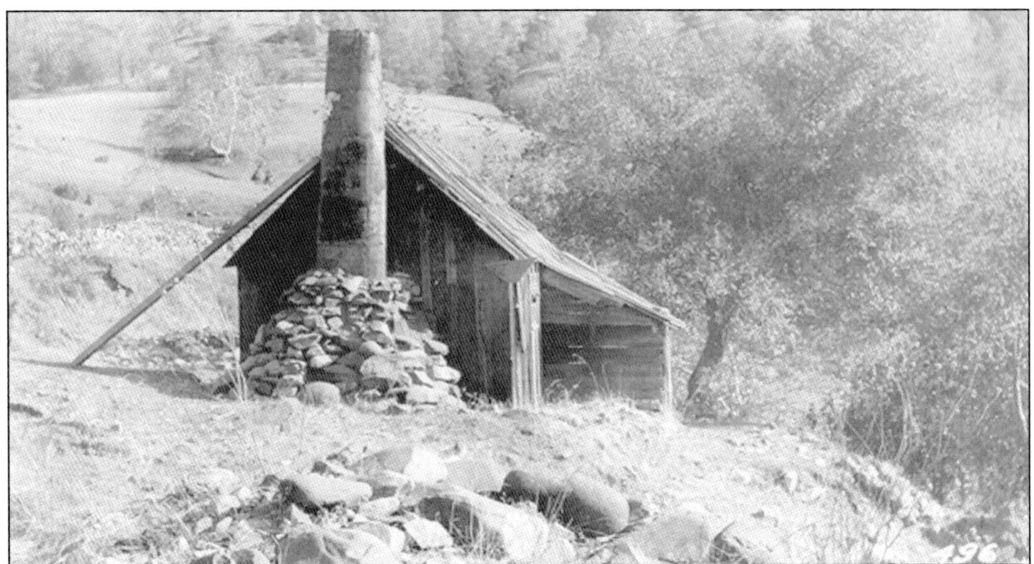

This is a miner's cabin in Bidwell Bar in 1906. Fire destroyed the town on August 2, 1854, but it was rebuilt because of a high expectation that a bonanza of gold had yet to be found. By December 1856, however, the gold had run out. The population dropped to 200 in 1857 and to 30 in 1882. This photograph shows that miners were still trying to find their fortunes in the 20th century. (Courtesy of YFM.)

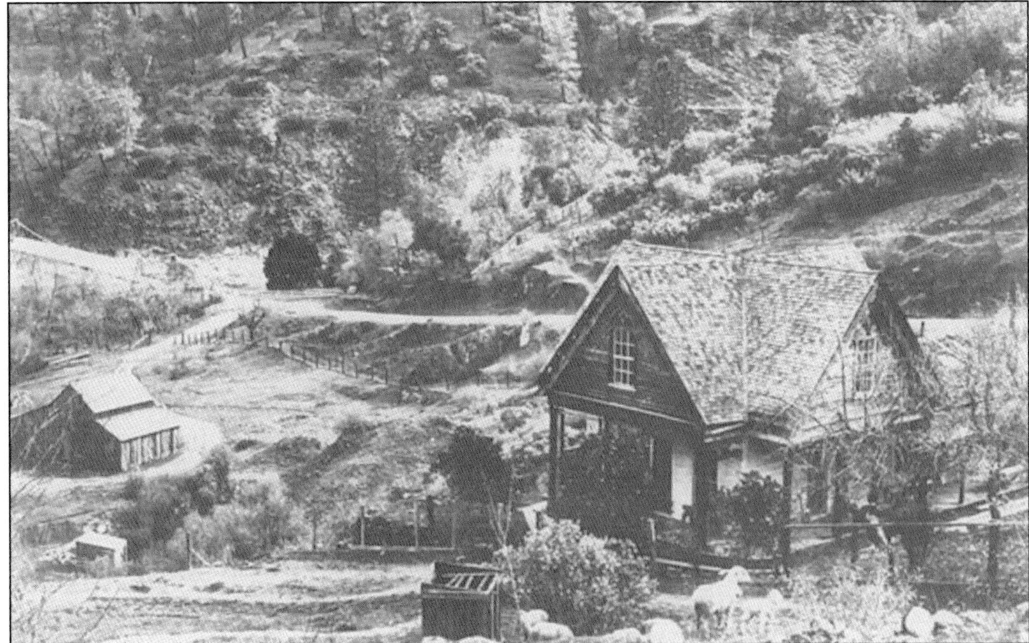

John Bendle's home is pictured here in 1903. The Bidwell Bar suspension bridge can be seen just a short distance away. Joseph Gluckauf built the first stone store in Bidwell Bar in 1855. Bendle bought the Gluckauf store on July 5, 1859, changed its name to Bendle's Store, and ran it for many years. Bendle later gained fame when he participated in the capture and killing of George Sharkovich at Bidwell Bar on the evening of June 4, 1871. Sharkovich had murdered young Susie McDanel of Cherokee three days before. (Courtesy of MLCSUC.)

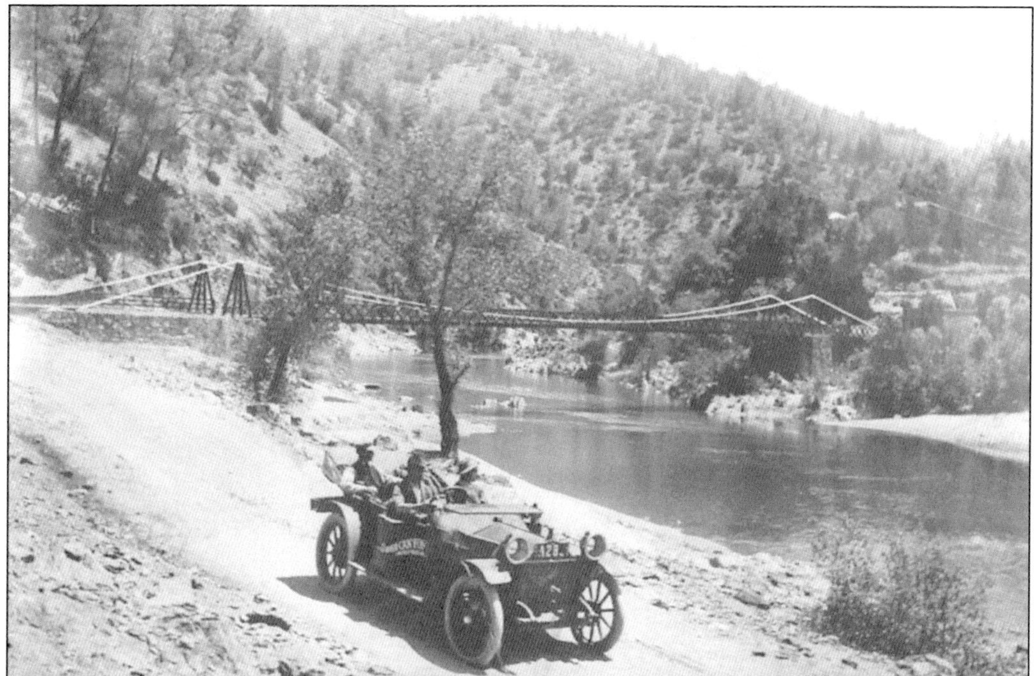

A Hupmobile Roadster rolls along the north shore of the Feather River after crossing the Bidwell Bar suspension bridge in 1914. At that time, the Hupp Motor Company was involved in its Nobby Tread Pathfinder Tour to prove the toughness of its automobiles. It had been participating in similar events since 1910. The California tour also included promotions to extend the Lincoln Highway through the Feather River Canyon. (Courtesy of BCHS.)

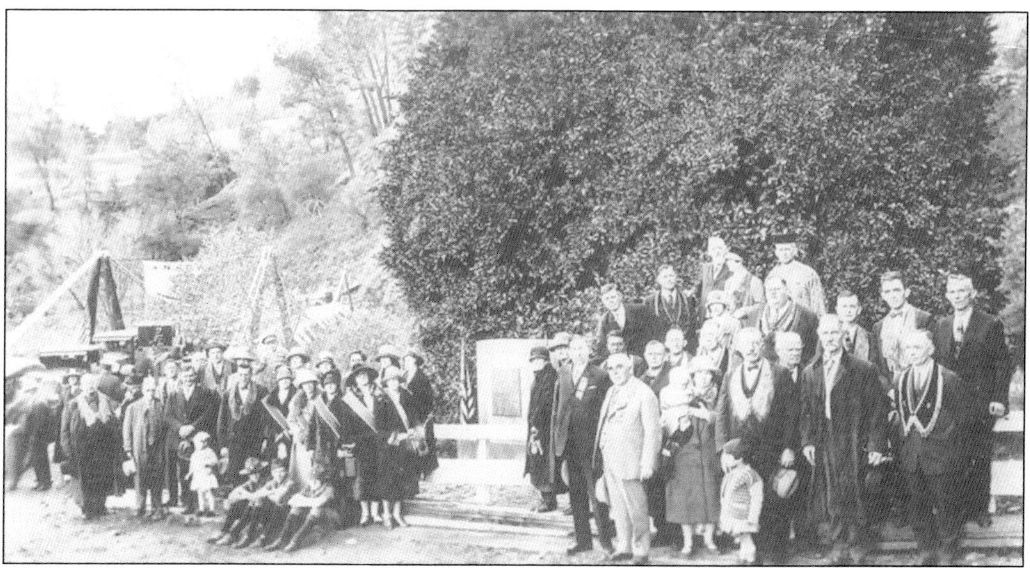

On November 27, 1926, a dedication ceremony commemorated the 70th anniversary of the planting of the Mother Orange Tree and the completion of the Bidwell Bar suspension bridge. Both historic events occurred in 1856. The plaque, along with several other historic monuments, is now located at the new site of the Bidwell Bar Bridge. (Courtesy of BCHS.)

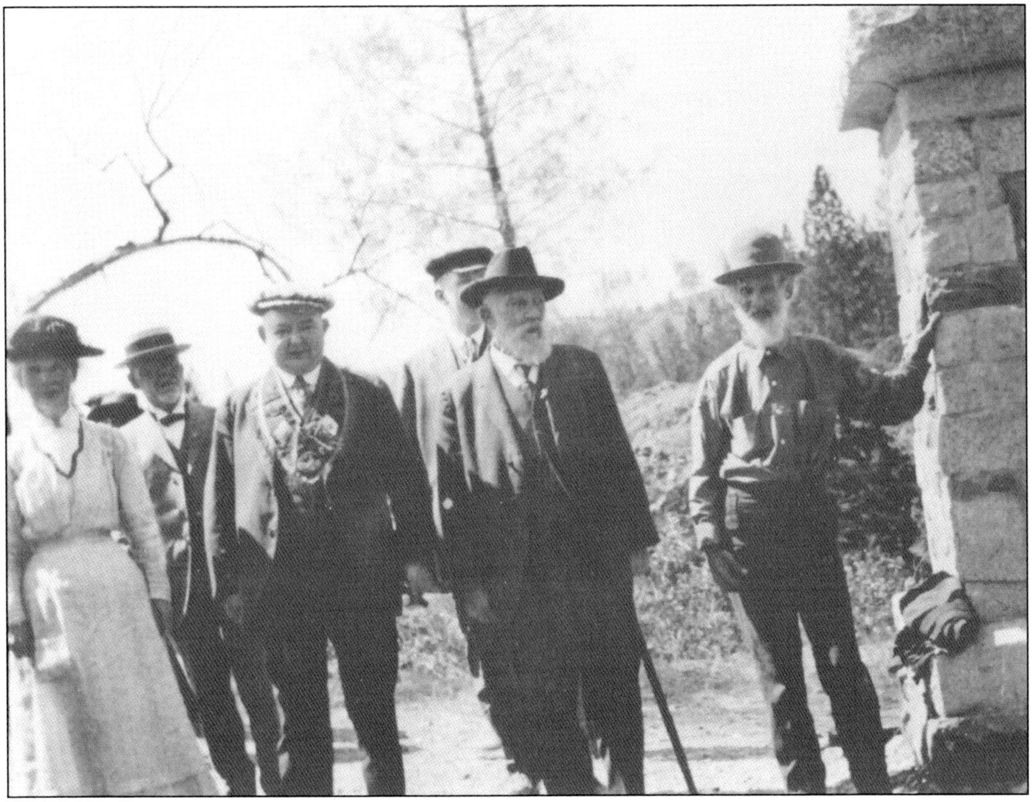

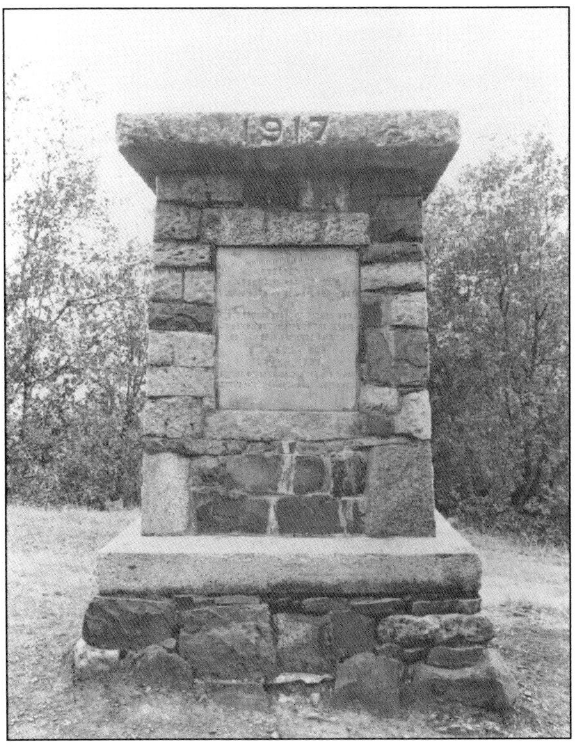

In 1914, work began on establishing a monument at Bidwell Bar to memorialize the fact that, between 1853 and 1856, Bidwell Bar had been the second county seat of Butte County. The monument is dated 1917, but the dedication ceremony was not conducted until May 12, 1918. Above, Robert Strange is seen in the back row. The man on the right is unidentified. In the front row are, from left to right, Kate Bendle, Joseph V. Snyder, Robert A. Moore, and John Bendle, who remembered where most of the buildings had been. Thus, he was chosen to decide where the monument would be placed. Bendle passed away at age 85 on December 30, 1918. He was buried in Bidwell Bar Cemetery. At left, the monument is pictured in 1964, just prior to its removal from the canyon. The monument now is displayed near the new location of the old Bidwell Bar Bridge. (Above, courtesy of BCHS; left, courtesy of JL.)

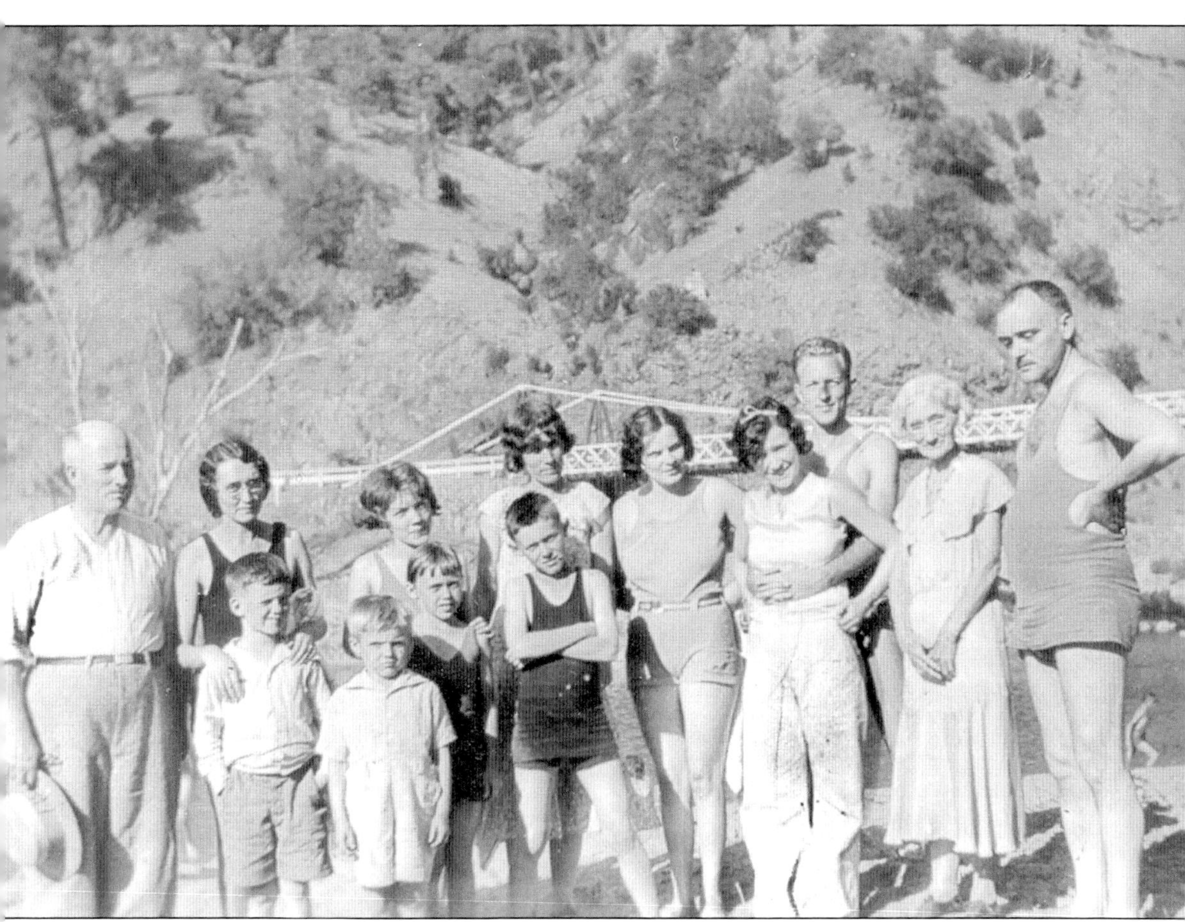

Even as early as the 1920s, the Feather River near the Bidwell Bar suspension bridge was a very popular swimming location. In this 1932 photograph are, from left to right, (first row) Eugene Foley Jr., William Roger Gray, Dorothy Gray, and Philip Gray; (second row) Eugene Foley, Rose Sharp Foley, Carol Gray, Alice Sharp Gray, Lois Sharp, Dorothy Sharp Harlan, Wilton Harlan, Amanda Rogers Sharp, and Frank Sharp. Wilton Harlan was an Oroville pharmacist and some of his descendants have remained in that vocation. Carol Gray later married John Williams of Williams TV. The family business that began in 1946 is still located on Myers Street in Oroville and is owned by Carol's son Greg. Carol did the accounting for the business until she was 89 years old. (Courtesy of Diane Lloyd.)

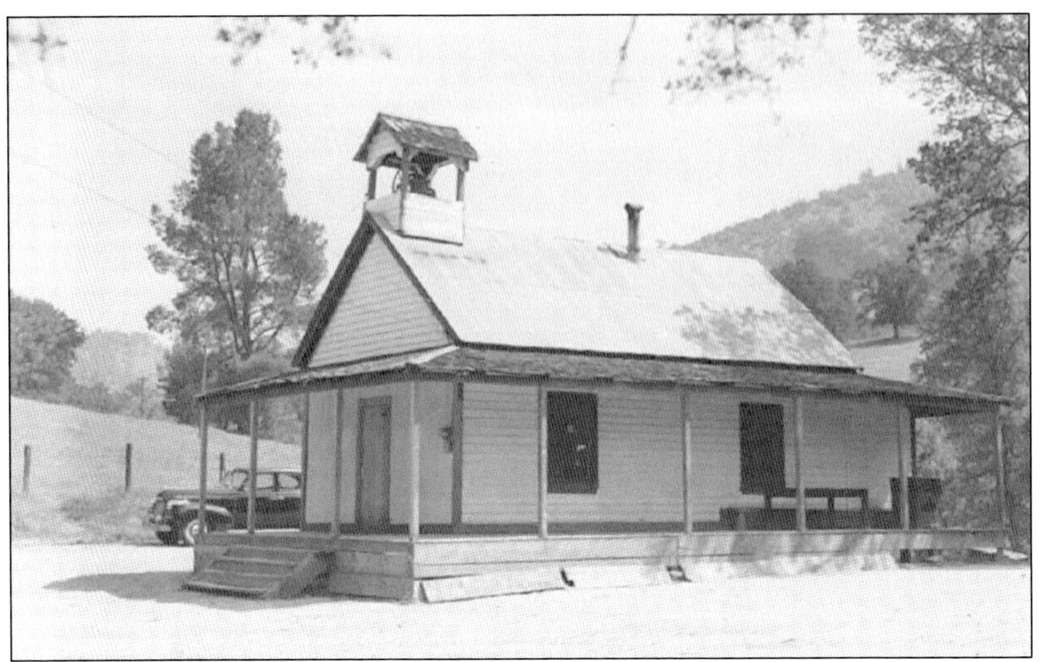

The first Bidwell Bar School was built in 1855 and served for more than 40 years. When that school was torn down, the lumber was reused to build a woodshed and a shed for horses. These photographs show the second Bidwell Bar School that was built about a half mile north of the old suspension bridge in January 1899. Above, the school is pictured around 1940. The car in the photograph might have belonged to Helen Grein, who taught at the school for 34 years. The image below was taken in the late 1950s. By that time, an addition had been made to the school. (Above, courtesy of BCHS; below, courtesy of MLCSUC.)

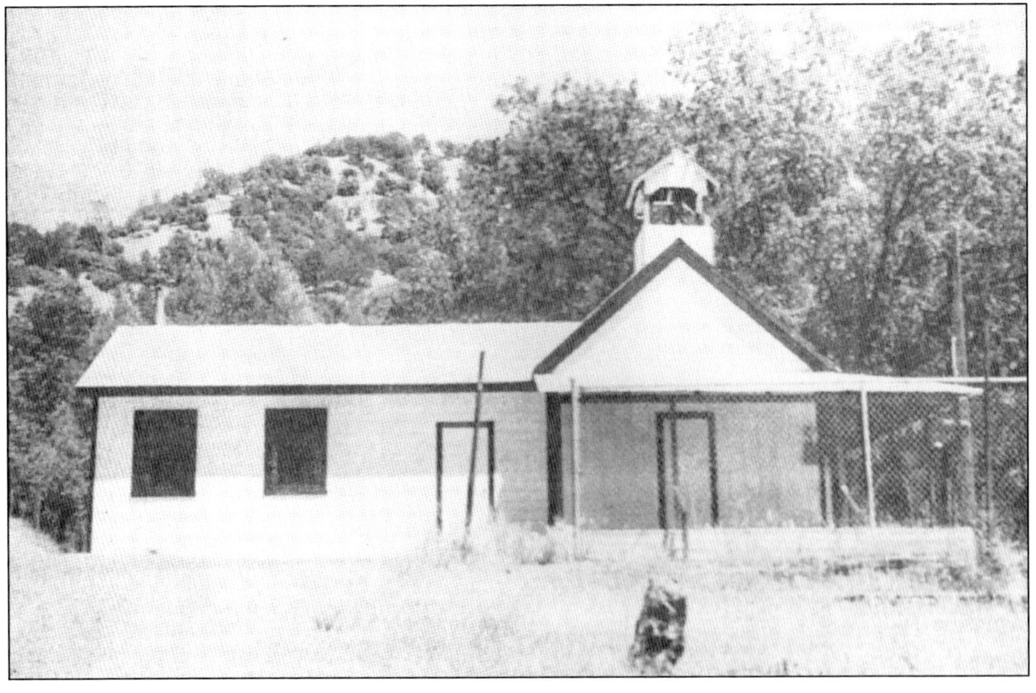

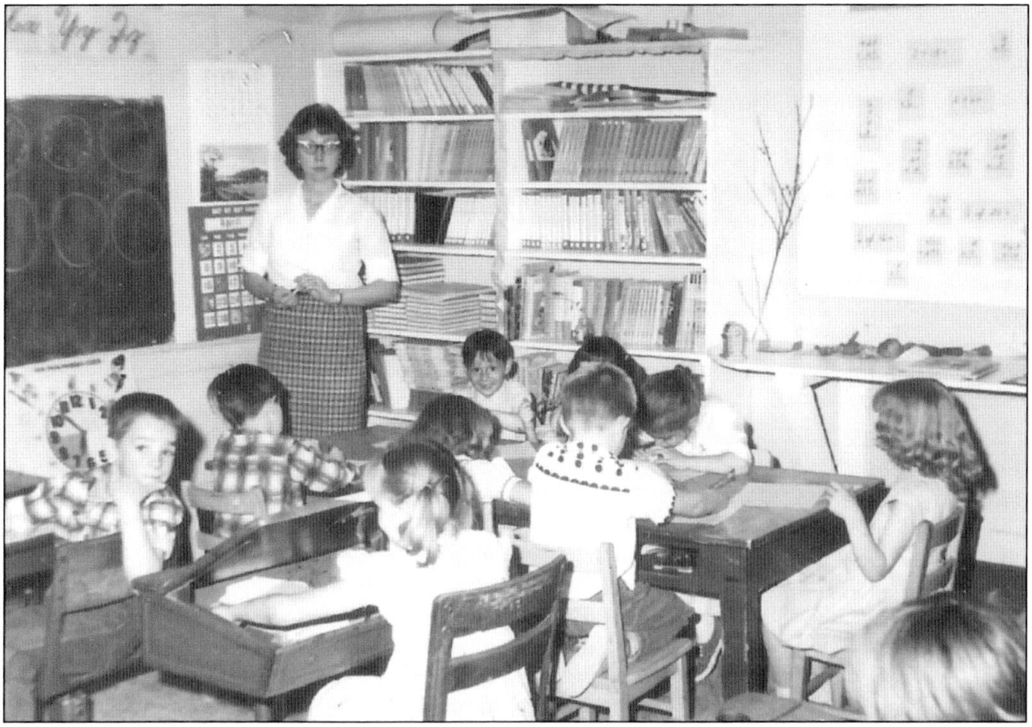

The interior of the Bidwell Bar School is seen in these class photographs, both taken in 1962. The school provided an education for students from kindergarten through eighth grade. High school students were bussed to Oroville High School. The route from Bidwell Bar went southwest on Old Quincy Road about four miles to the present-day Saddle Dam area. The Oroville-Quincy Highway then ran toward the west into Oroville for another five miles. That section of road from Saddle Dam to Bidwell Bar now runs underwater through the area of Bidwell Marina. (Above, courtesy of BCHS; below, courtesy of MLCSUC.)

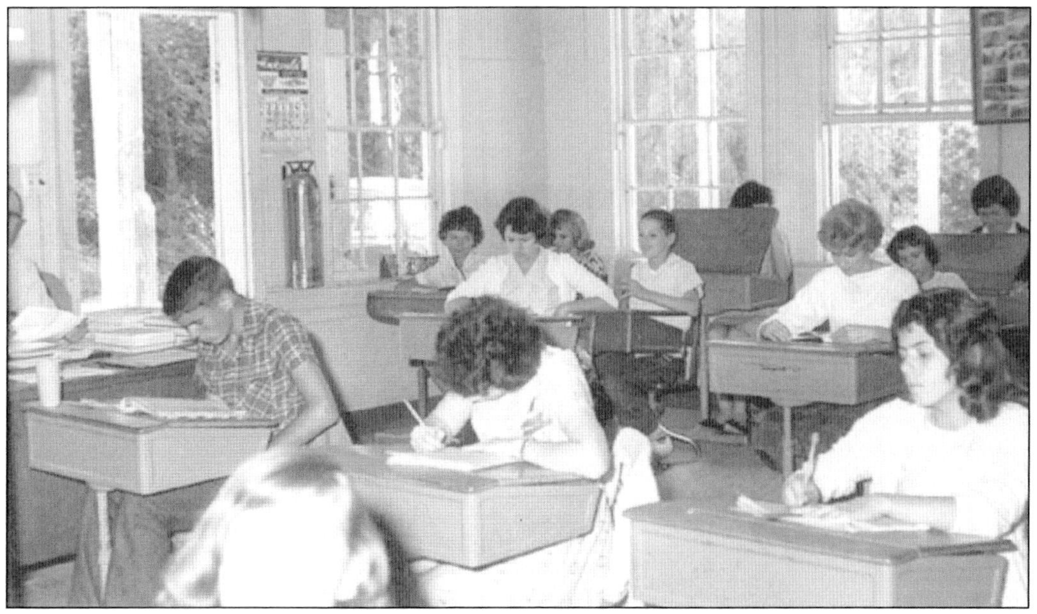

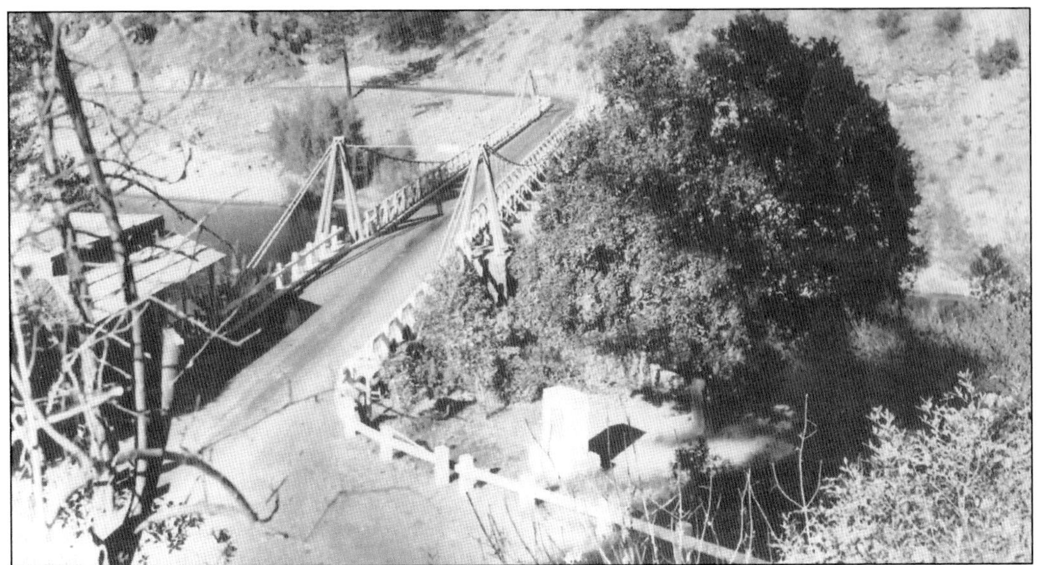

These are two views of the Bidwell Bar suspension bridge. Both were taken prior to 1954 when the road was gated and the bridge was restricted to only foot traffic. It was felt that the old bridge had deteriorated to the point that it was a danger to heavy traffic. Beginning that year, all vehicle traffic was rerouted to a concrete bridge that was located just downstream from the old bridge. The view in the photograph above looks north and includes the old tollhouse on the left and the Mother Orange Tree on the right. The photograph below shows the bridge with a view to the south. During 1852, the town's first bridge had been wiped out by high water, and the residents of Bidwell Bar ordered a new bridge. It was the first suspension bridge west of the Mississippi River. (Above, courtesy of BCHS; below, courtesy of BCPW.)

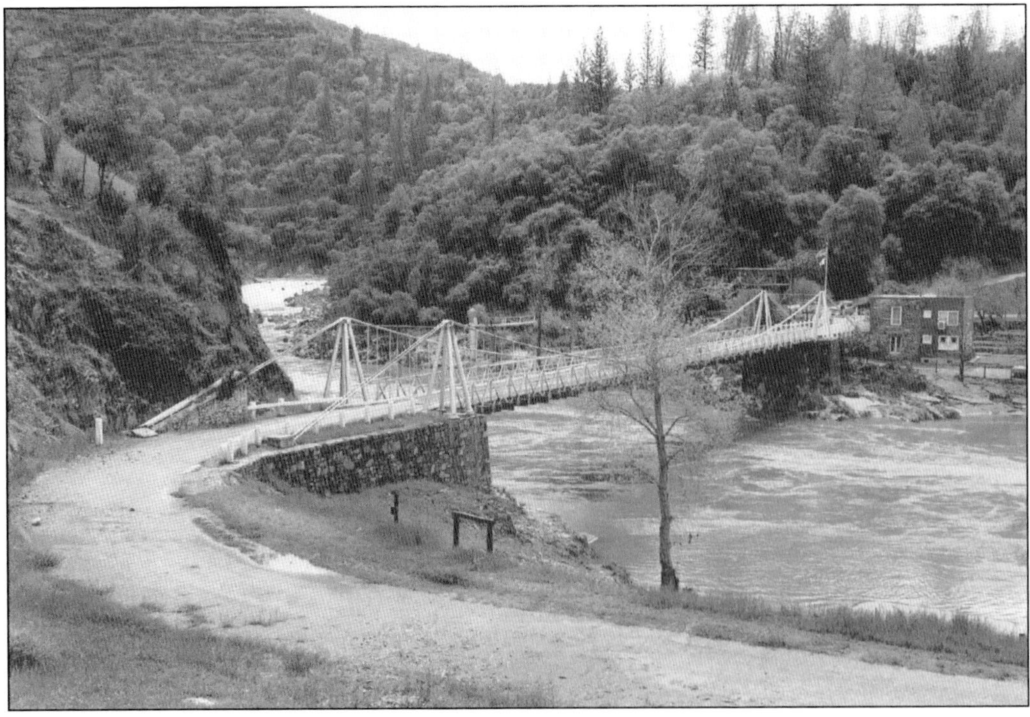

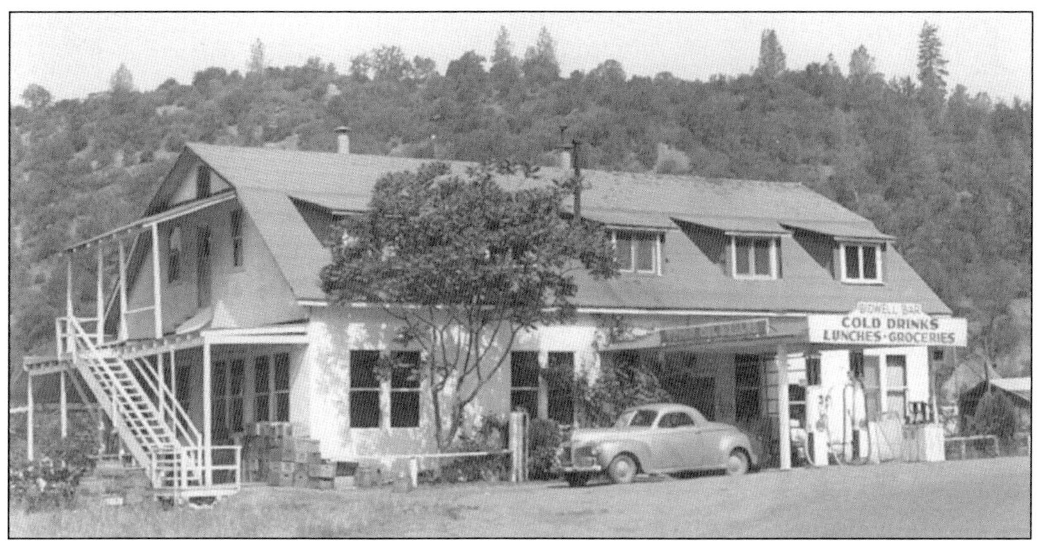

Mooney's Tavern is pictured above in 1940. John N. Mooney built this combination dance hall, hotel, café, and bar around 1935. It was located on the north side of the Middle Fork and was not part of the original town of Bidwell Bar on the south side. In the 1950s and 1960s, Derrald and Helen Buis operated the business. The local media called November 20, 1964, the day Bidwell Bar "ceased to exist as a town." That was the day all the buildings were burned to the ground. Below is a matchbook cover from 1962 advertising the restaurant and tavern. (Above, courtesy of MLCSUC; below, authors' collection.)

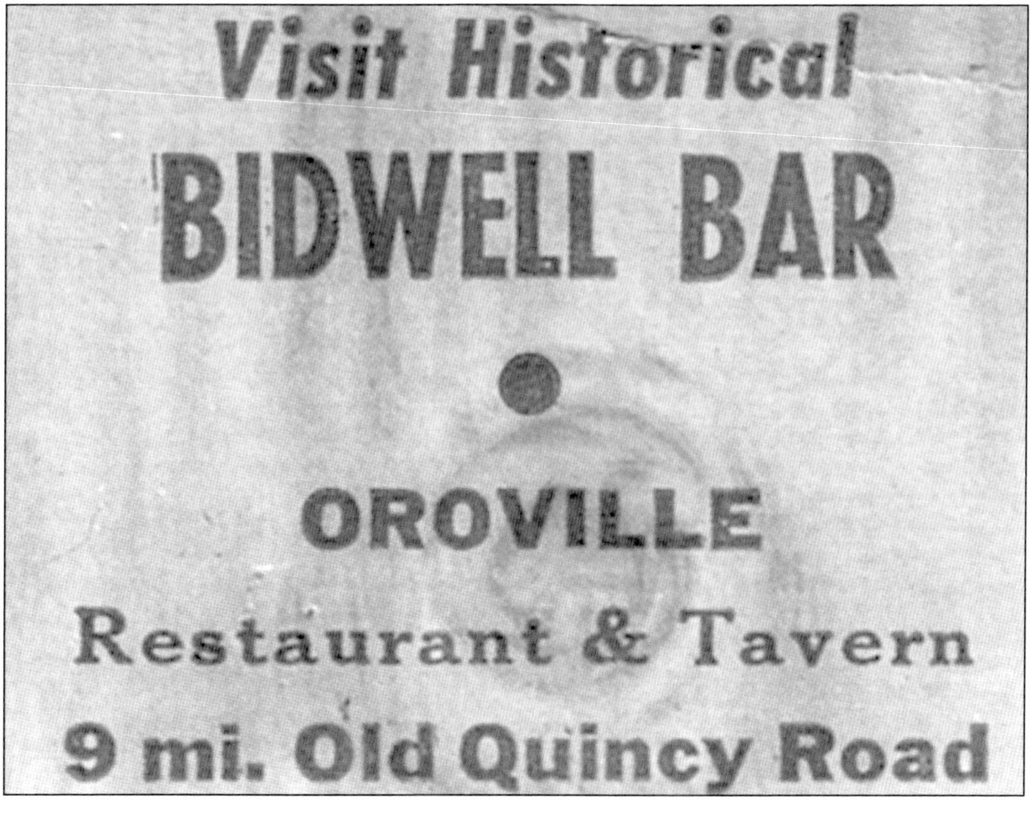

Visit Historical

BIDWELL BAR

OROVILLE

Restaurant & Tavern

9 mi. Old Quincy Road

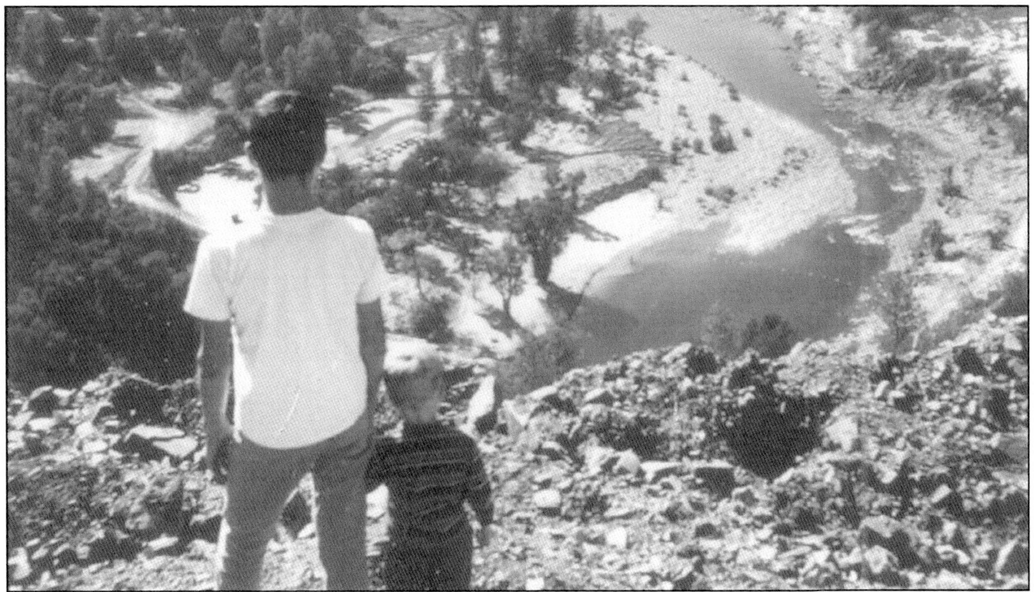

Gary E. Johns and his little brother Joseph gaze down on the Curry-Bidwell Bar State Park during the late summer of 1964. The very busy parking lot of the park can be seen below on the other side of the river. Gary later became a teacher and spent 30 years teaching and coaching at Palermo Union School and Las Plumas High School. He retired in 2013. Joseph owns K-Gas, Inc. Propane in Oroville. (Courtesy of Gary E. Johns.)

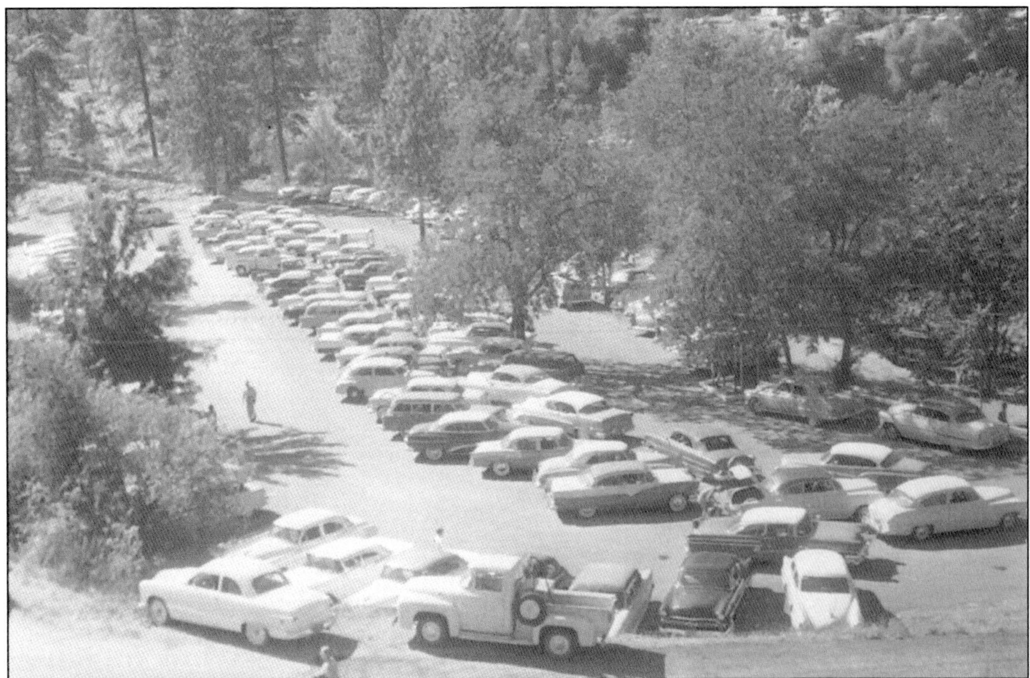

The packed parking lot of the Curry-Bidwell Bar State Park indicates the popularity of the park on summer weekends. Hundreds of people would make the trip into the canyon to swim in the cool waters of the Middle Fork of the Feather River. It was also a great place for a barbecue and to visit some of the historic sights of the park. This view is from about 1958. (Courtesy of SS.)

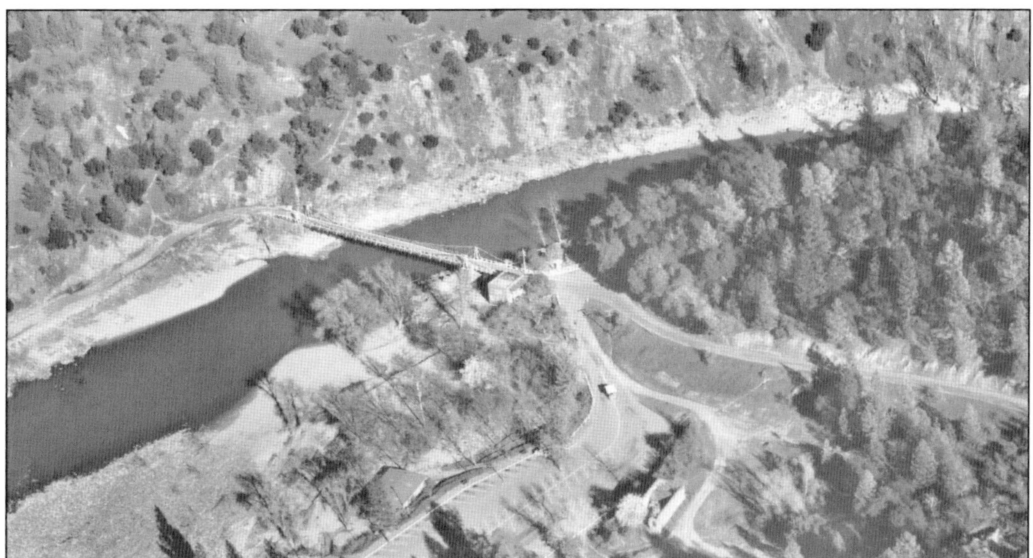

This is a view looking down on the Curry-Bidwell Bar State Park on February 27, 1963. The off-season was a good time to hike the hills and visit the historic bridge, tollhouse, and Mother Orange Tree with a bit of quiet solitude. William T. Curry had been the toll keeper and landowner and had expressed an interest in saving the land for park purposes. The local Fellows Club negotiated with Curry, and the Bidwell Bar Park Association was formed. Curry deeded the land to the state for $5 in March 1925. Bill Curry died in August 1928. The park commission decided to name the area the Curry-Bidwell Bar State Park, which was established in 1947. (Courtesy of CDWR.)

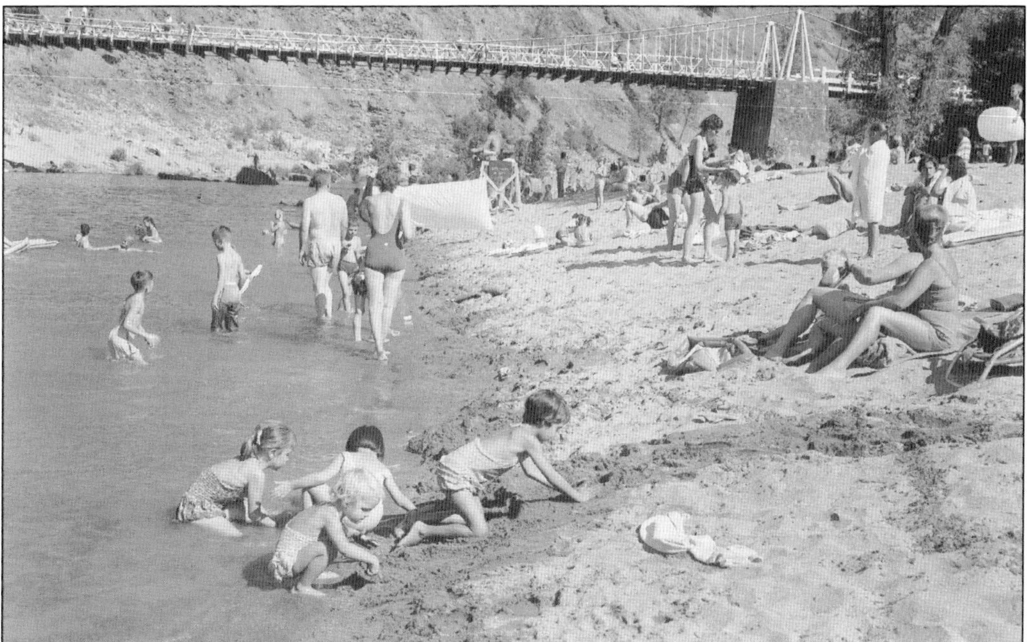

This view of the Curry-Bidwell Bar State Park is from August 18, 1962. Note the little boy on the right side of the photograph with an inflated pillowcase in his hands. The more adventurous park visitors would wet down pillowcases and fill them with air, then run and take a flying leap to skim across the river. The park was a popular recreation destination for 17 years. (Courtesy of CDWR.)

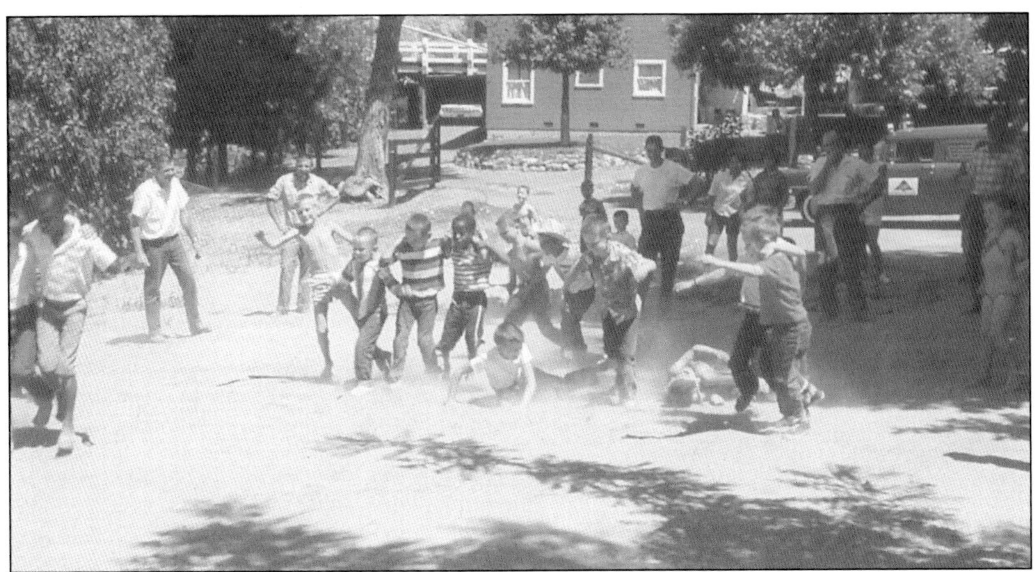

Travelers from other local mountain communities would also visit Bidwell Bar. These photographs from the summer of 1961 show residents from Feather Falls Village who came by train to enjoy the day. The Georgia-Pacific Corporation had arranged the train trip for its employees. The journey from Feather Falls to Bidwell Bar was about 18 miles and took around two hours. Above, the visitors enjoy a three-legged race. The tollhouse and suspension bridge appear in the background. Below, visitors enjoy the water and sand on the south side of the river. (Above, courtesy of YFM; below, courtesy of WFC.)

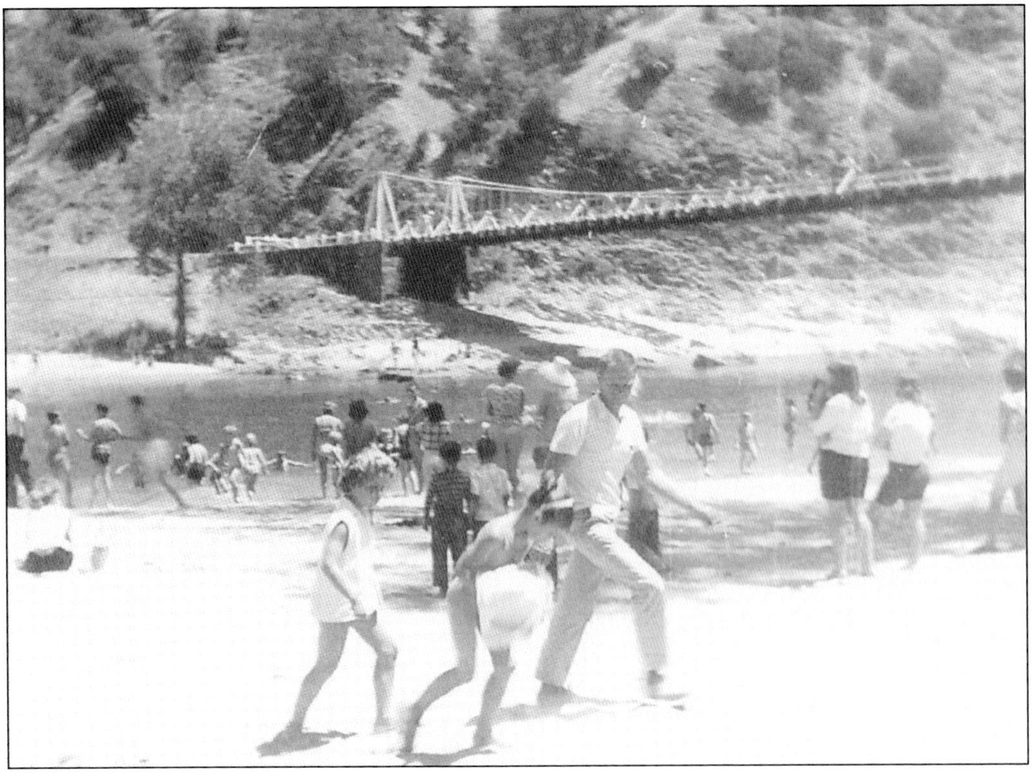

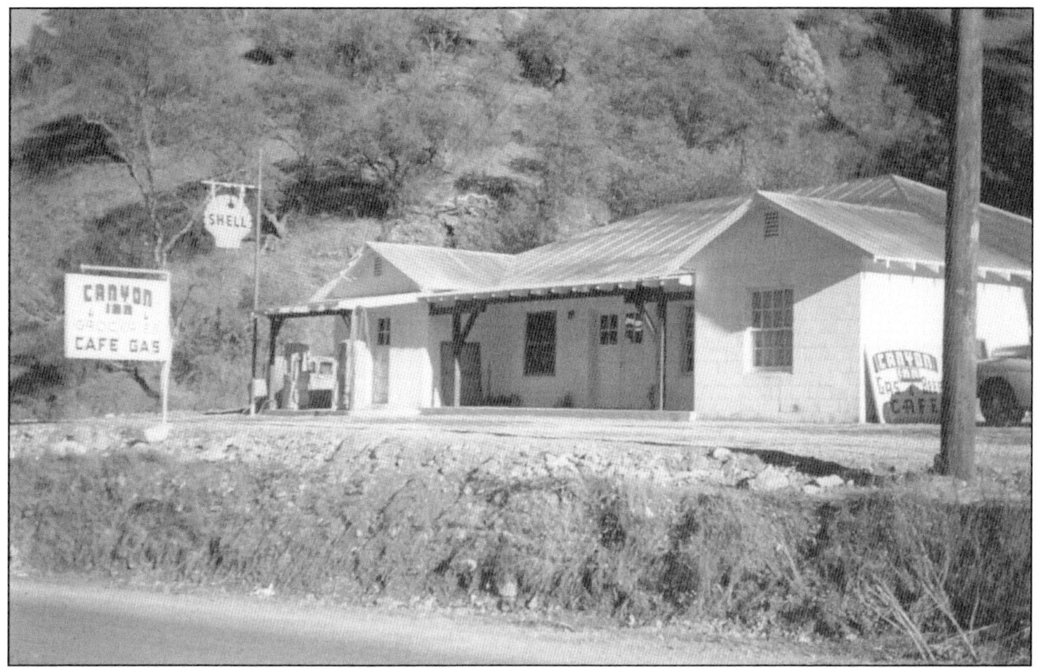

A well-known landmark on Old Quincy Highway between Bidwell Bar and Saddle Dam was the Canyon Inn. The inn, located about two miles south of Bidwell Bar, was one of the few places to get gas and groceries in the area. This photograph is from 1958. (Courtesy of SS.)

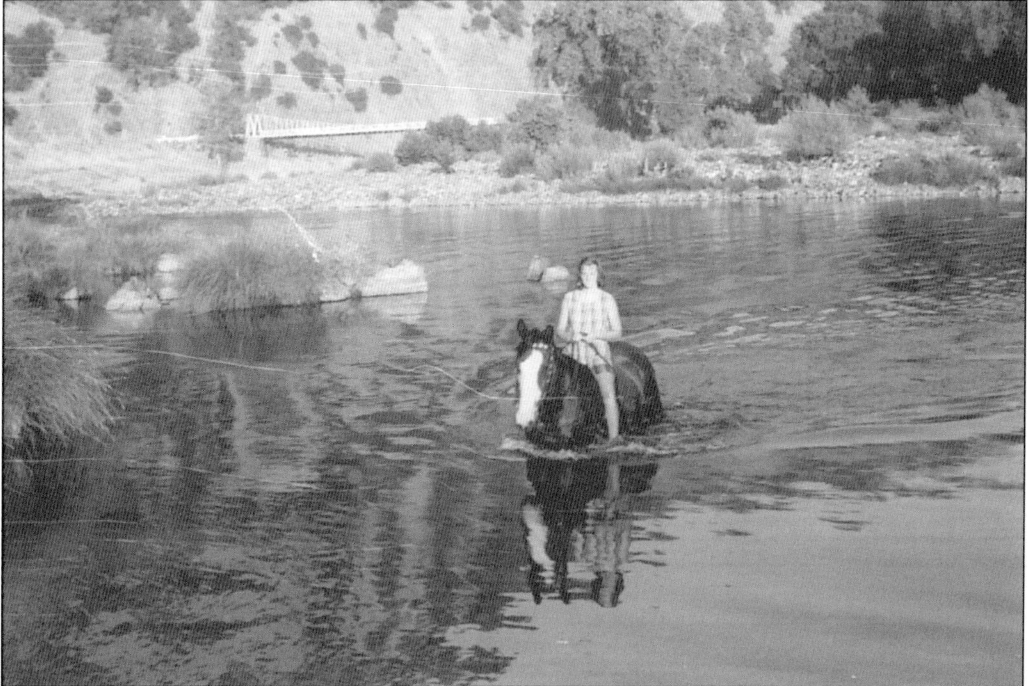

Sue Soderberg is shown riding her horse Rocky across the Feather River in August 1960. The Bidwell Bar suspension bridge can be seen in the background. The view is looking east from the north shore of the river, between the old suspension bridge and the concrete bypass bridge. (Courtesy of SS.)

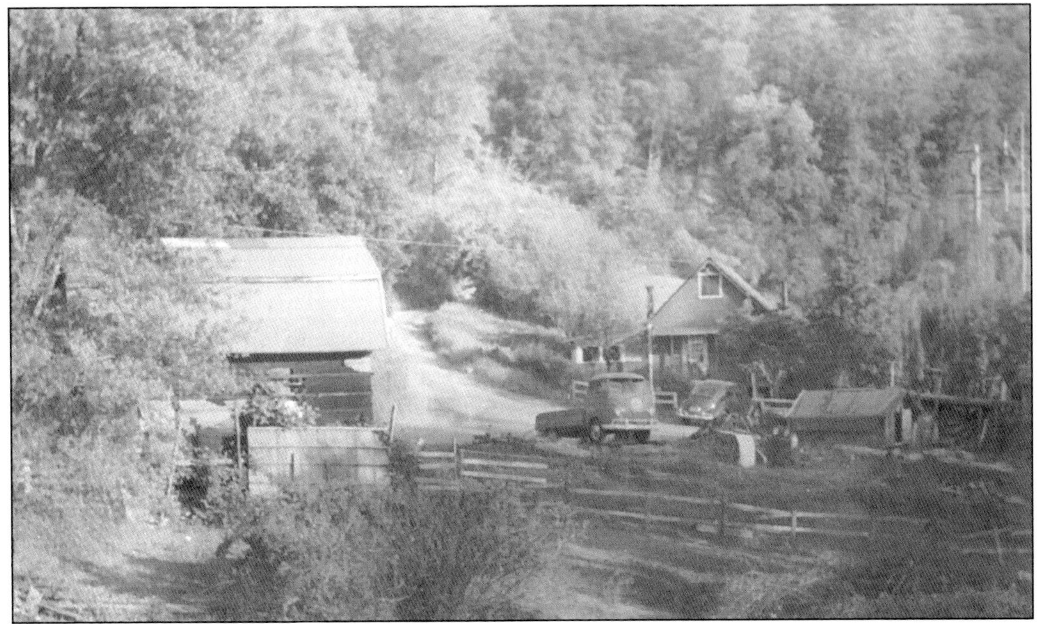

This is the Soderberg home in 1956. It was located a half mile south of the Bidwell Bar suspension bridge. Clarence and Lillian Soderberg resided in Bidwell Bar with their sons, Jerry and Pat, and their daughters, Marion and Sue, from 1930 to 1960. Clarence worked in the Feather River Pine Mills at Bidwell Bar and served as a sheet metal worker. He built the majority of school lockers in the area. (Courtesy of SS.)

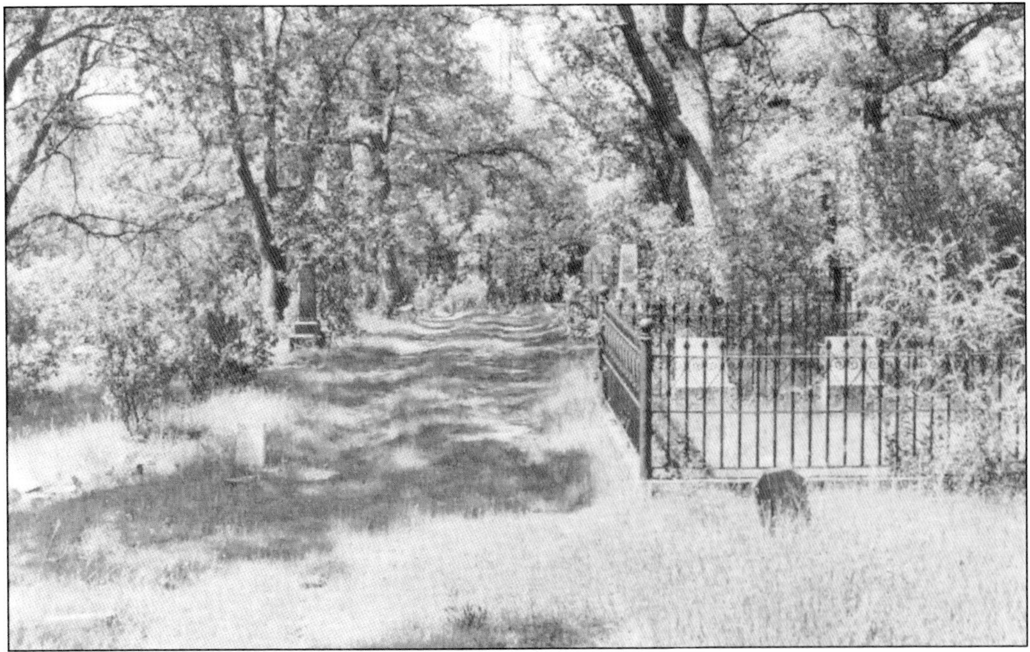

Just north of the Soderberg home was the Bidwell Bar Cemetery, where residents had been buried since 1850. This photograph is from about 1950. Prior to the area being flooded by Lake Oroville, all the graves from Bidwell Bar and Enterprise, as well as six family plots, were relocated to the Pioneer Cemetery next to the Thompson Flat Cemetery near Cherokee Road. (Courtesy of BCHS.)

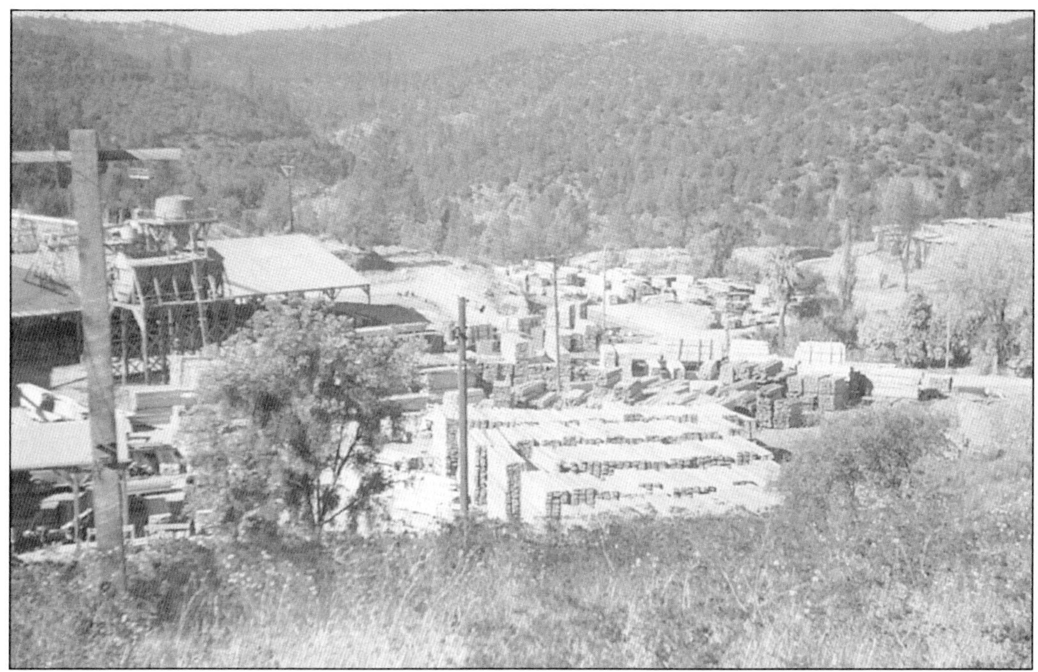

The Feather River Pine Mills Manufacturing Mill is pictured above in 1948. Located just north of the Bidwell Bar Cemetery, it was the main employer for the area. The photograph below was taken in February 1965, and it shows the debris of some of the old mill. Towering in the background is the new Middle Fork Bridge, also known as the new Bidwell Bar Bridge. The new bridge would reach completion in late 1965. It is 1,108 feet long and is suspended 627 feet above the canyon. All the traffic that had been going through Bidwell Bar would now be routed to the new road and bridge. (Both, courtesy of SS.)

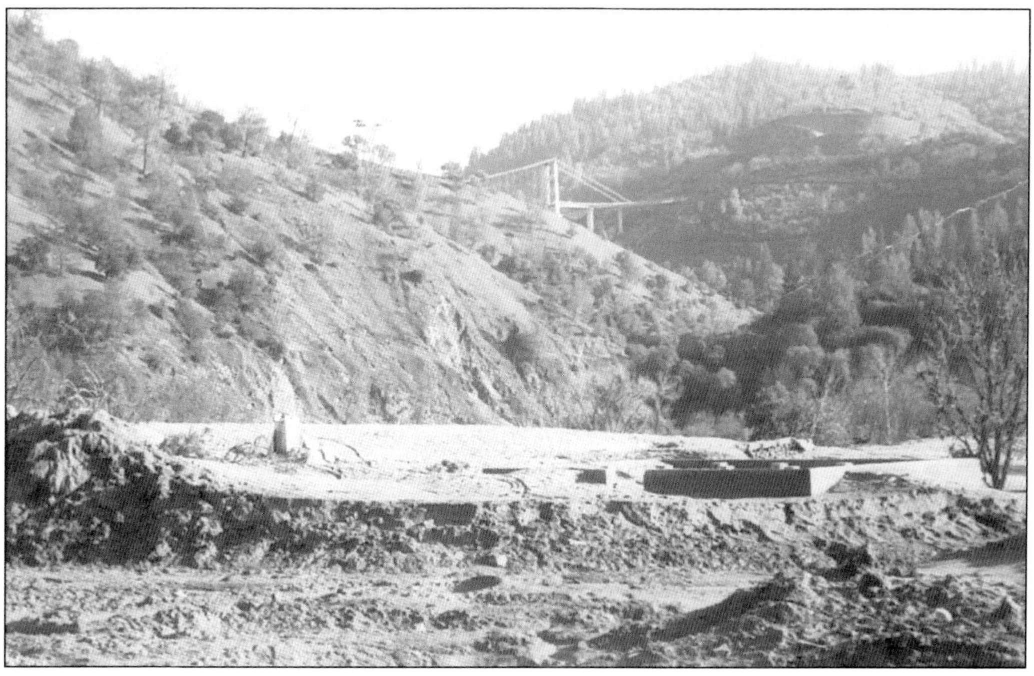

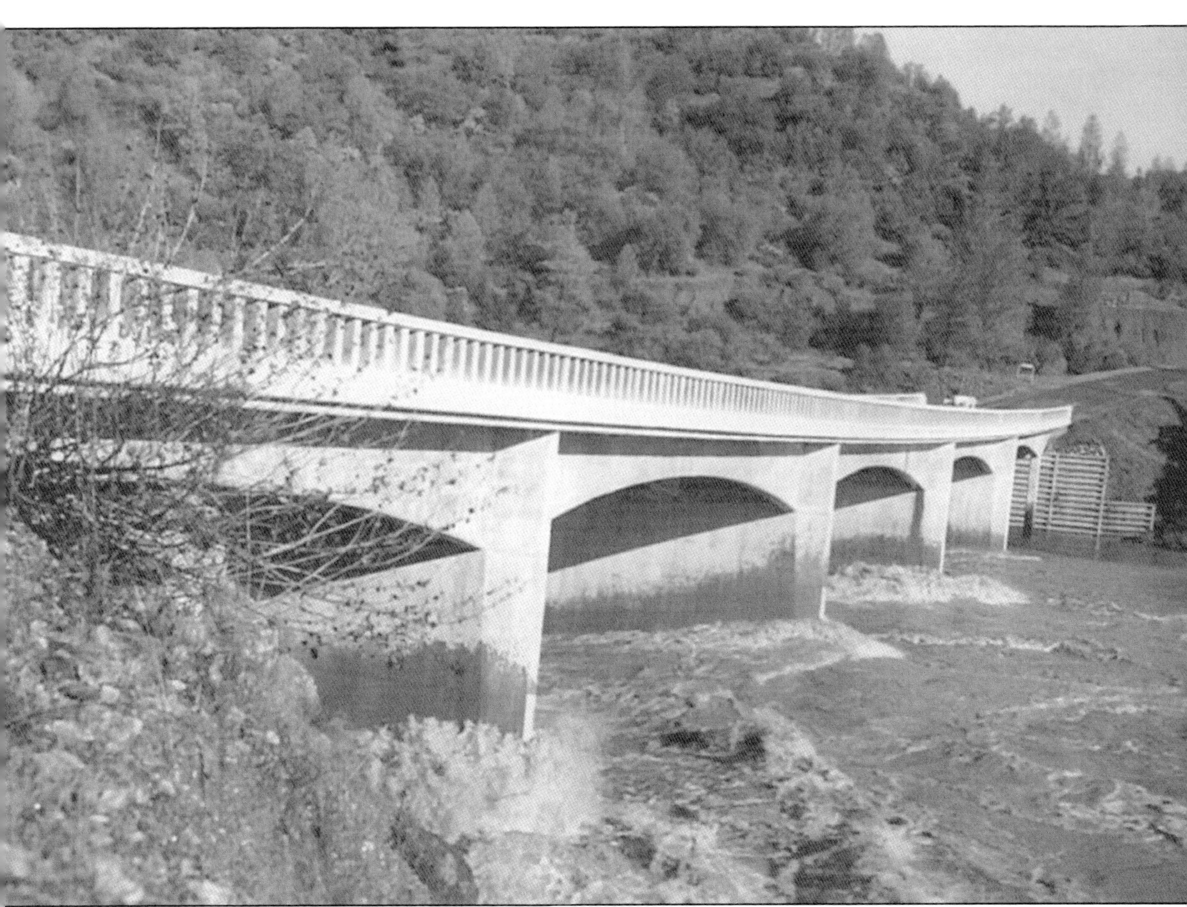

The Bidwell Bar bypass bridge is pictured here in December 1951. It was built in 1947, and all vehicle traffic was rerouted across this bridge when the Bidwell Bar suspension bridge was restricted to foot traffic in October 1954. The bridge was located a quarter of a mile west of the old suspension bridge. In November 1967, this bridge was the first landmark to be flooded by Lake Oroville, as Bidwell Bar is in one of the deepest parts of the canyon. It took only about a week and a half for the lake level to rise to 100 feet and for this bridge to be under 8 feet of water. This is one of the few bridges that was not destroyed or removed from the canyon prior to flooding. (Courtesy of BCPW.)

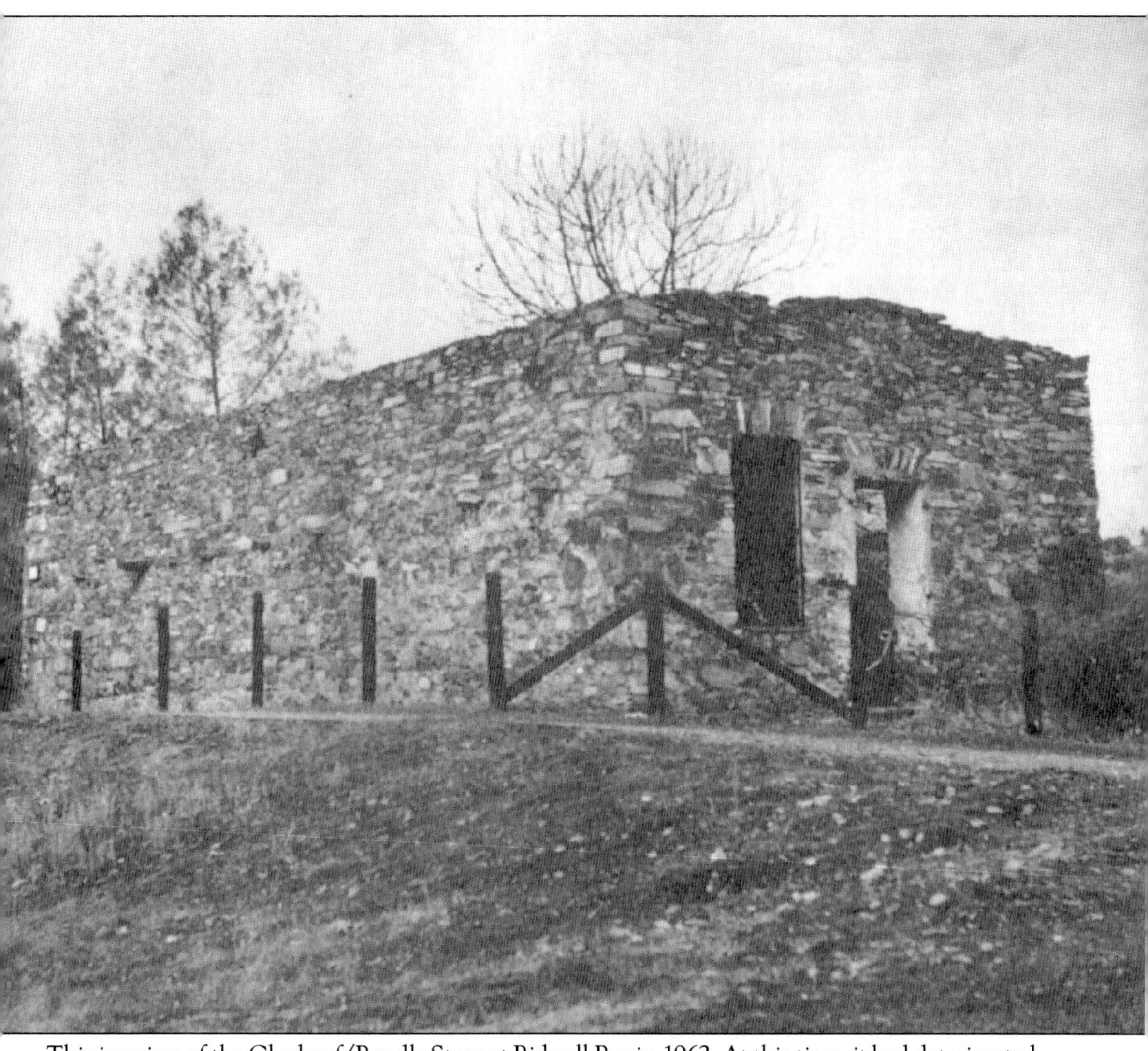

This is a view of the Gluckauf/Bendle Store at Bidwell Bar in 1962. At this time, it had deteriorated to a shell of what it had once been. It had lost its roof, and a tree was growing out of the middle. Constructed of rock material mined from the local area, it stood for 110 years and was the last building left standing in Bidwell Bar. It too was leveled prior to the area being flooded. (Courtesy of BCHS.)

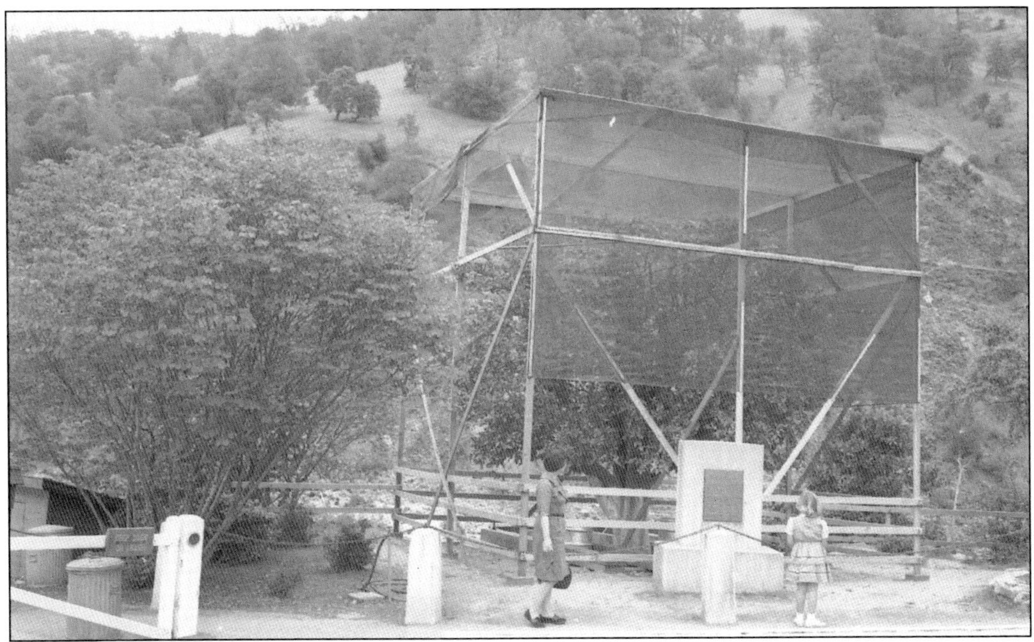

Here are two photographs of the Mother Orange Tree at Bidwell Bar in April 1963. It was already being protected and prepared for its eventual move out of the canyon. Judge Joseph Lewis purchased the tree in Sacramento in 1856, and it was planted north of the Feather River. In the winter of 1862, bridge tender Isaac Ketchum saved the tree from flooding by moving it to a higher location near the suspension bridge on the south side of the river. Ketchum tended the tree until his death in 1905. He was buried beneath it, and his body was later reinterred at the Pioneer Cemetery off Cherokee Road. He had been the bridge tender for 46 years. (Both, courtesy of BCHS.)

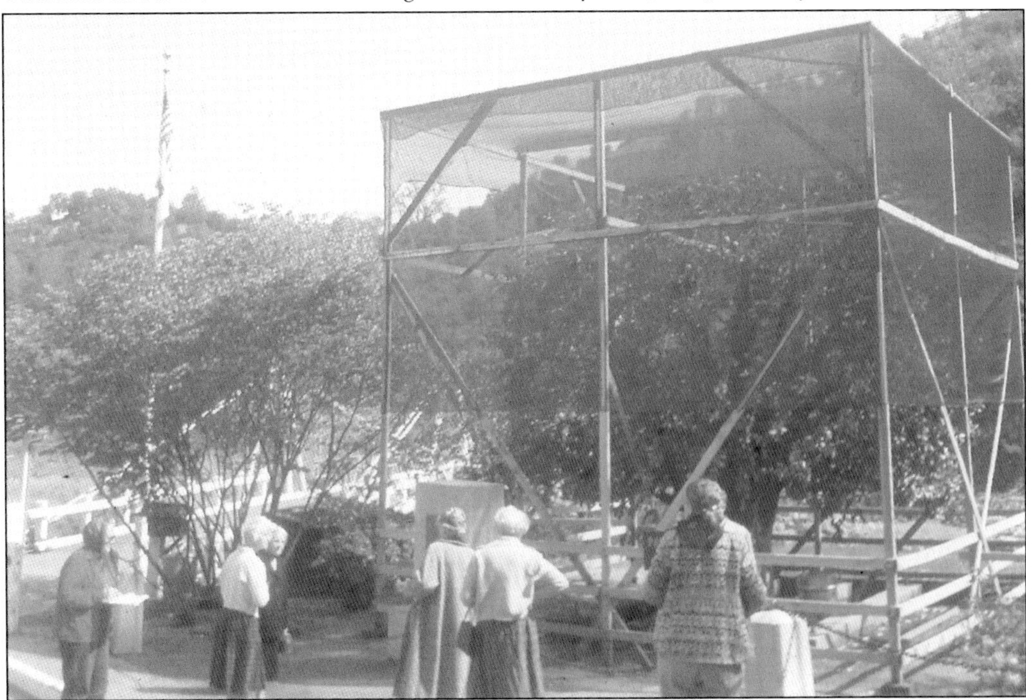

Three

The South Fork

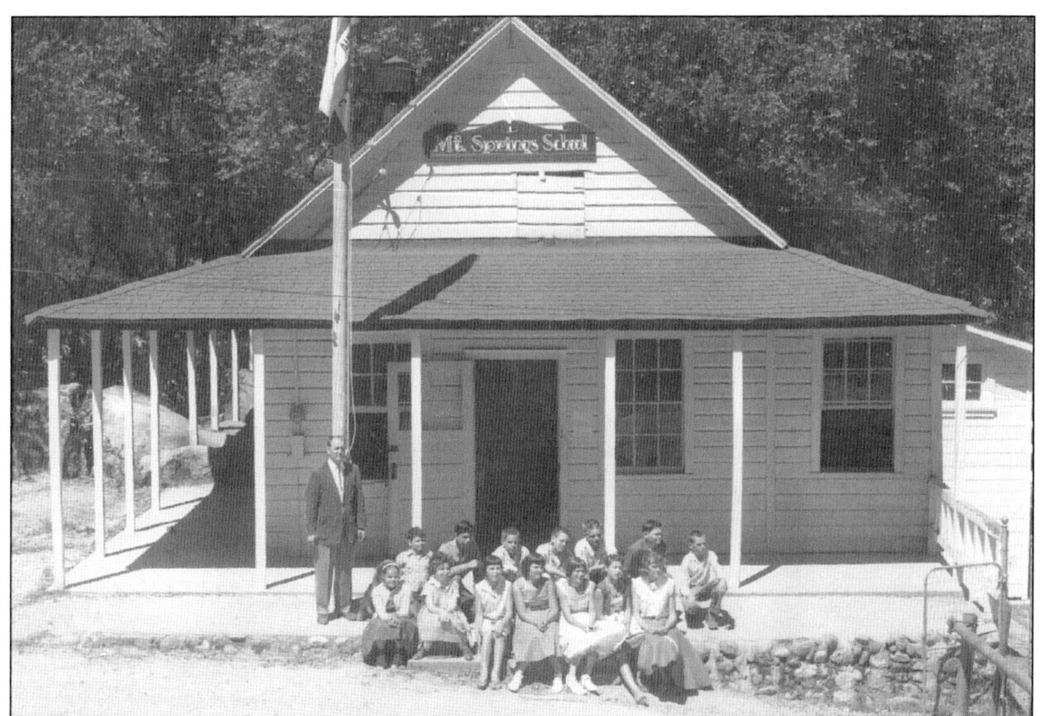

This chapter includes the area around Enterprise, which was located about 10 miles east of Oroville. Established in 1852, it was originally called Mountain Springs. It was a construction camp and supply center for nearby mining operations. The Mountain Springs School is seen here with teacher Richard Pryor and his class in 1960. This area is under about 280 feet of water when Lake Oroville is at its height. (Courtesy of LSE.)

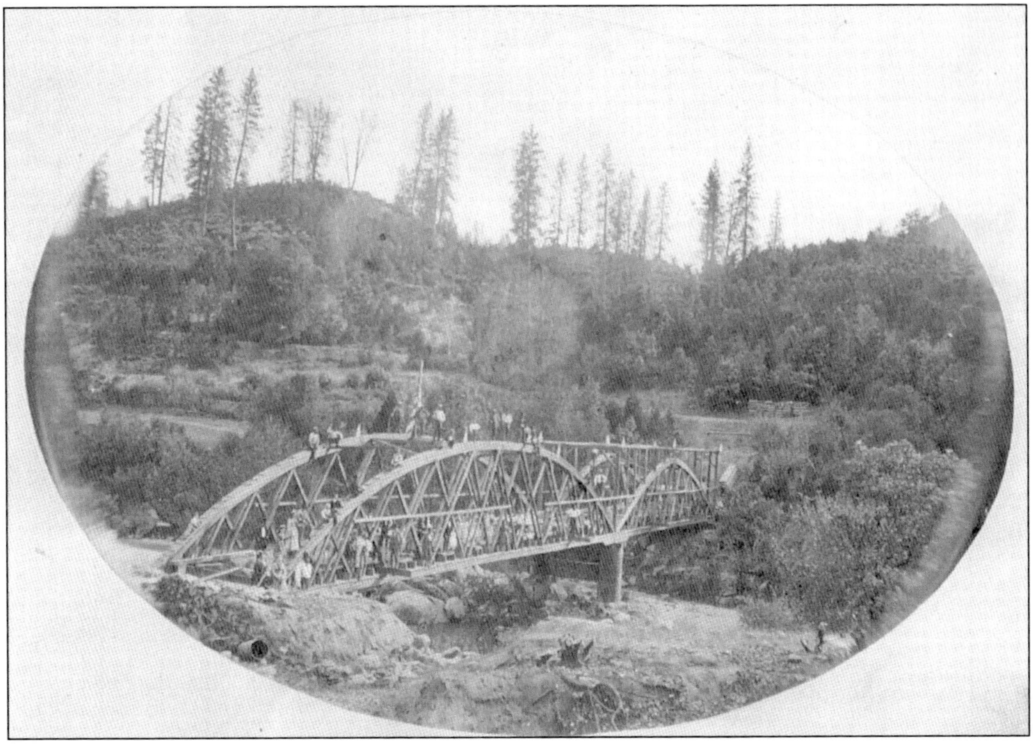

The Enterprise Covered Bridge is seen under construction in 1876. The American flag suggests that this photograph might have been taken in July during the celebration of the country's centennial. The bridge was a great addition to the canyon as stages and freight wagons could now keep to a schedule. Prior to the bridge's construction, it was questionable whether vehicles could ford the river. When the bridge was finished, people came from miles around and danced all night. (Courtesy of JL.)

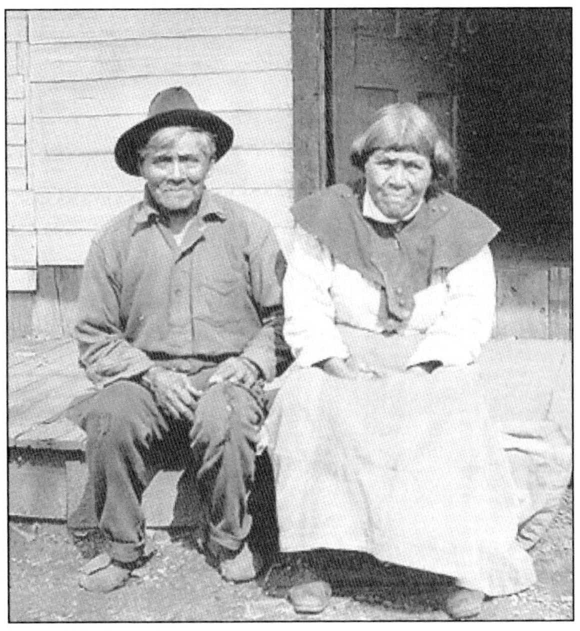

George and Lah, also known as "Eliza," Pinkey are shown sitting on their porch at Enterprise in 1910. The Gold Rush in 1849 brought thousands of miners to the area. The miners brought new diseases, and their mining practices destroyed the landscape. In 1851, negotiations with the Native American tribes led to 18 treaties that would have established a reservation in the areas of Oroville and Chico, but the Senate did not ratify the treaties. There were numerous violent incidents between the tribes and the government, and the tribes were rounded up and shipped off to reservations in 1853 and 1863. The 1863 incident was a brutal march to Round Valley that resulted in many deaths. Many later returned to South Fork and other Feather River areas to reside. (Courtesy of MLCSUC.)

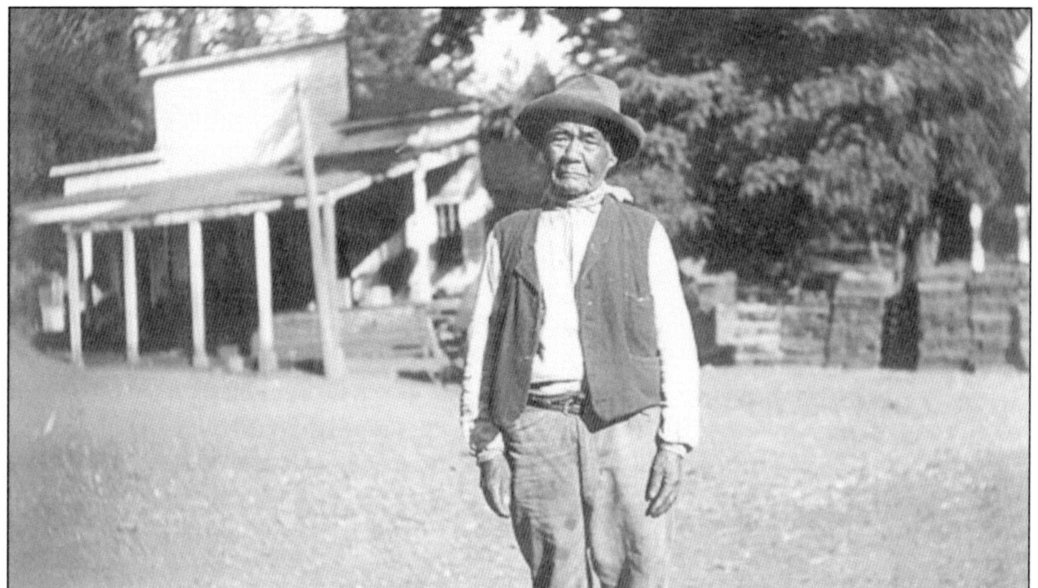

An unidentified Maidu man is pictured at Enterprise in 1890. The Maidu had resided in the Feather River canyons for hundreds of years. The Feather River offered a wealth of fishing resources, especially in the seasonal salmon runs. Fish could be dried, smoked, and canned. Hunting also provided ample food for the tribes. Deer were in great supply, along with elk, rabbits, squirrels, quail, and geese. (Courtesy of MLCSUC.)

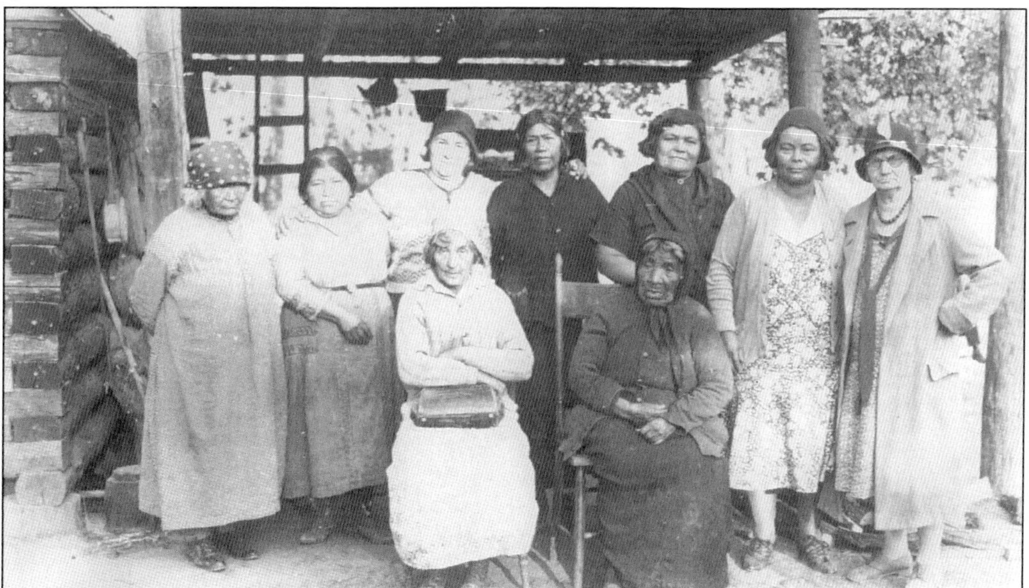

This group of Maidu ladies is gathered on the porch of a log building around 1910. From left to right are (first row) Lizzie Parker and Emma Parker; (second row) Nancy Martin, Sadie Martin, Ina Jackson, Selena Jackson, unidentified, Starry Edwards, and Ellen McCaully. In the late 19th and early 20th centuries, the Maidu adapted to new ways and many became ranch hands, lumber workers, and miners. Several rancherias were later established, which helped formalize the tribe's legal status with the American government. Enterprise became a social and shopping center for the Maidu. (Courtesy of YFM.)

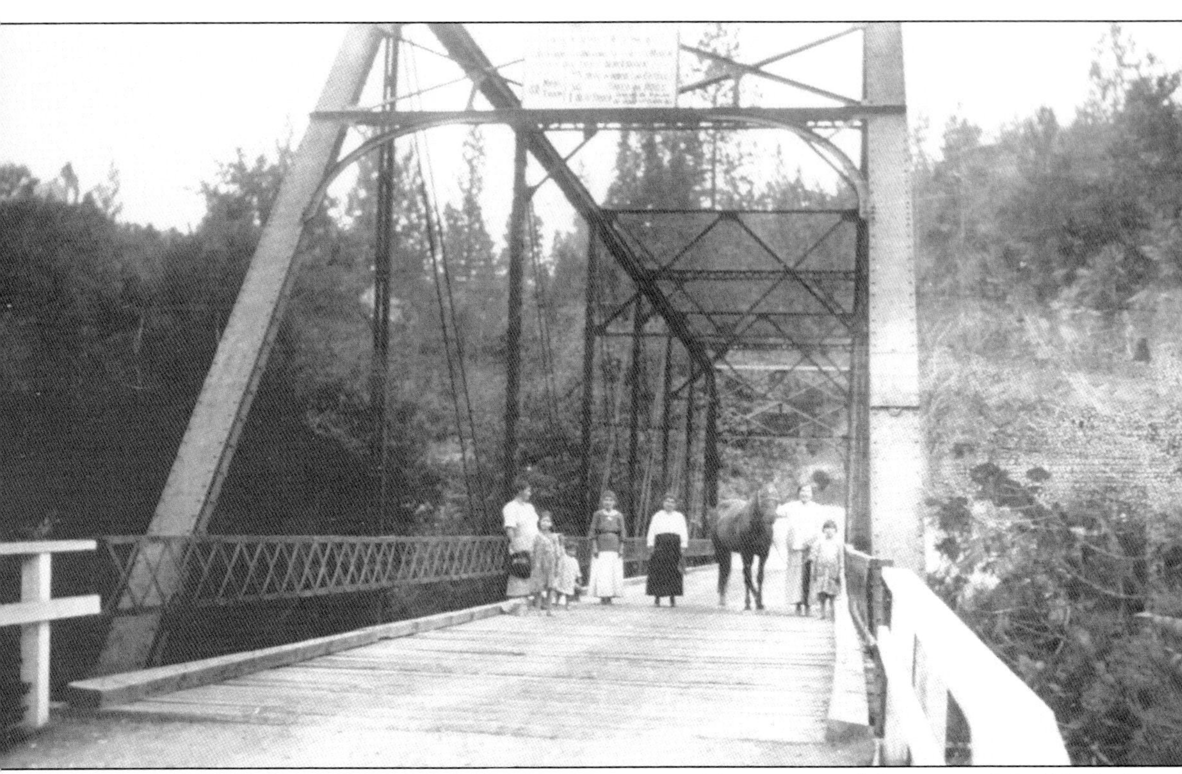

The metal Enterprise Bridge is pictured here in 1910. In 1907, a massive slide occurred that blocked the river. When the river broke through, a torrent of water, rocks, logs, and trees slammed against the 1876 wooden covered bridge, which gave way and collapsed. The enormous mass also took out a store and saloon. A cabin with two men was washed across the river. One man survived, but the other was never found. Construction of the new steel bridge began later that year. It was built a short distance upstream and at a different angle and grade from the old bridge. This photograph indicates that there were different tolls for chickens, cows, and hogs. It is not evident what the fee was for the people on the bridge. (Courtesy of YFM.)

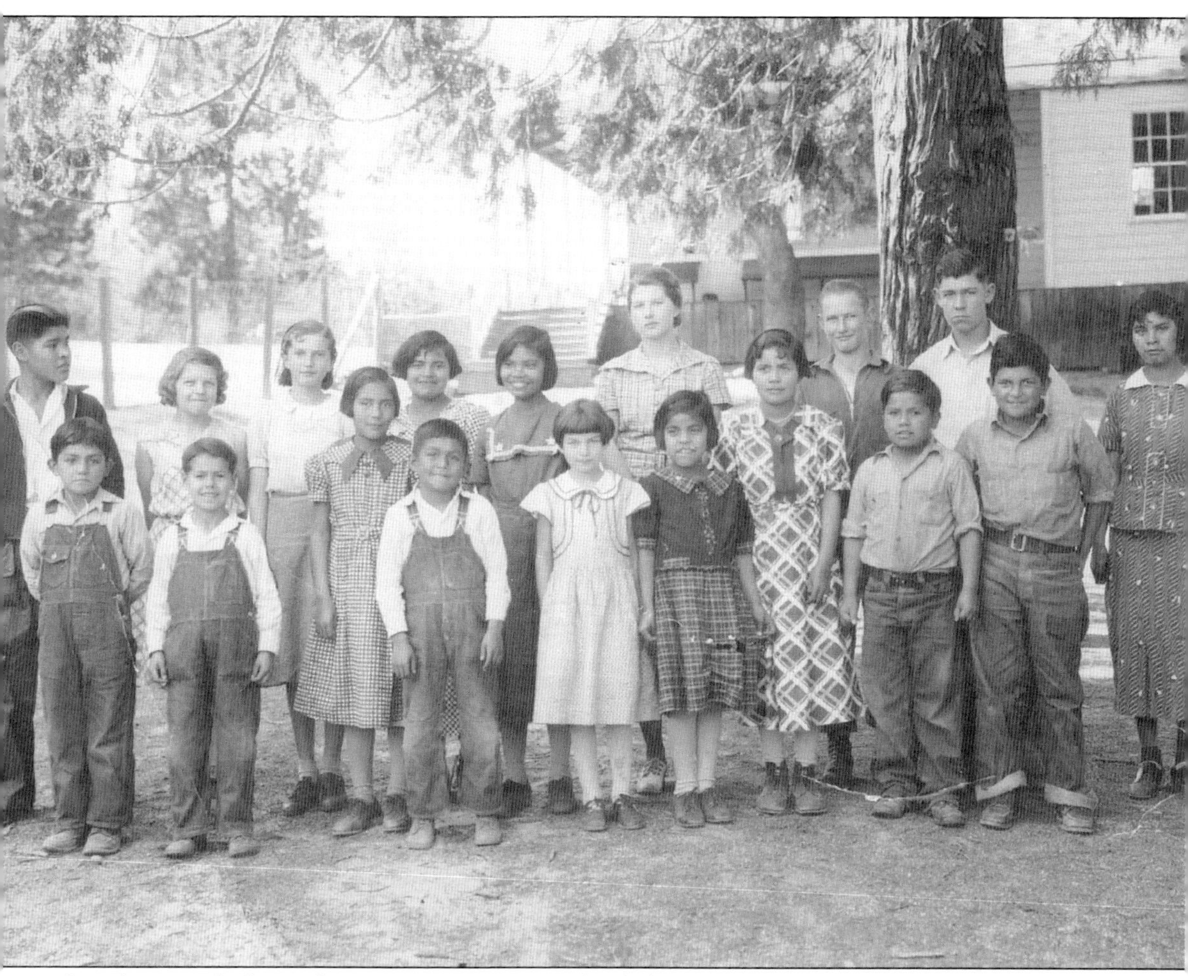

This photograph shows the Mountain Springs School class in 1935. From left to right are (first row) David Smith, Cecil Spencer, Grace Watson, Glen Watson, Clair Miller, Vera Martin, Irene Watson, Everett Smith, Richard Smith, and Thelma Wagner; (second row) Stanley Martin, Helen Bean, Ruth Leonard, Lillian Williams, Gladys Wagner, teacher Miss Dunlap, Billy Zirkle, and Robert Irvin. Years later, Spencer went on to own and manage Spencer's Lumber Mill at Enterprise. (Courtesy of LSE.)

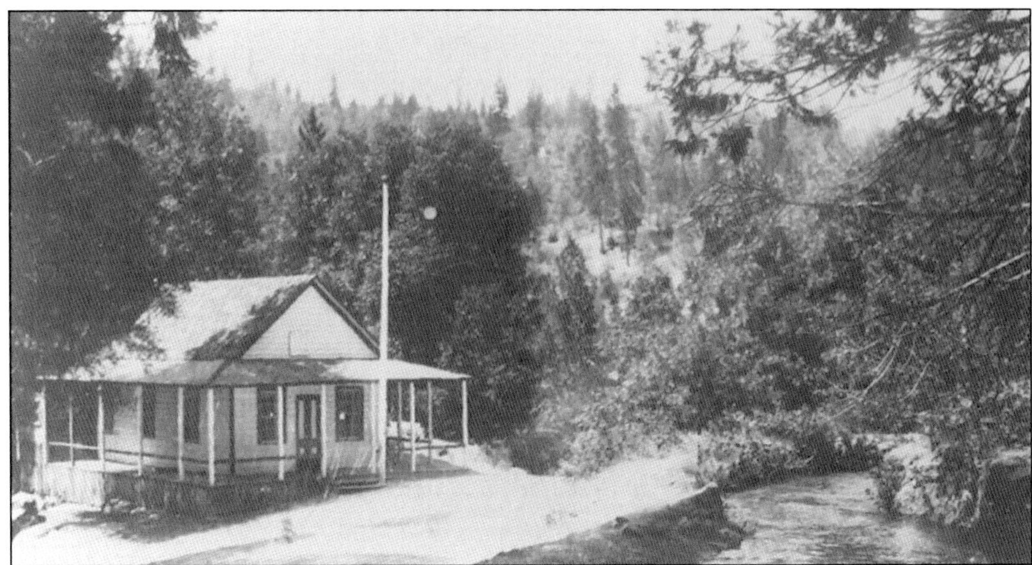

This very rare photograph from the 1940s shows the Mountain Springs School and the Palermo Canal that ran to the west from the OWID dam. It was also known as the OWID ditch. OWID stood for the Oroville Wyandotte Irrigation District. During its journey, the canal was crossed several times by Lumpkin Road, Enterprise Road, and several smaller routes. (Courtesy of BCHS.)

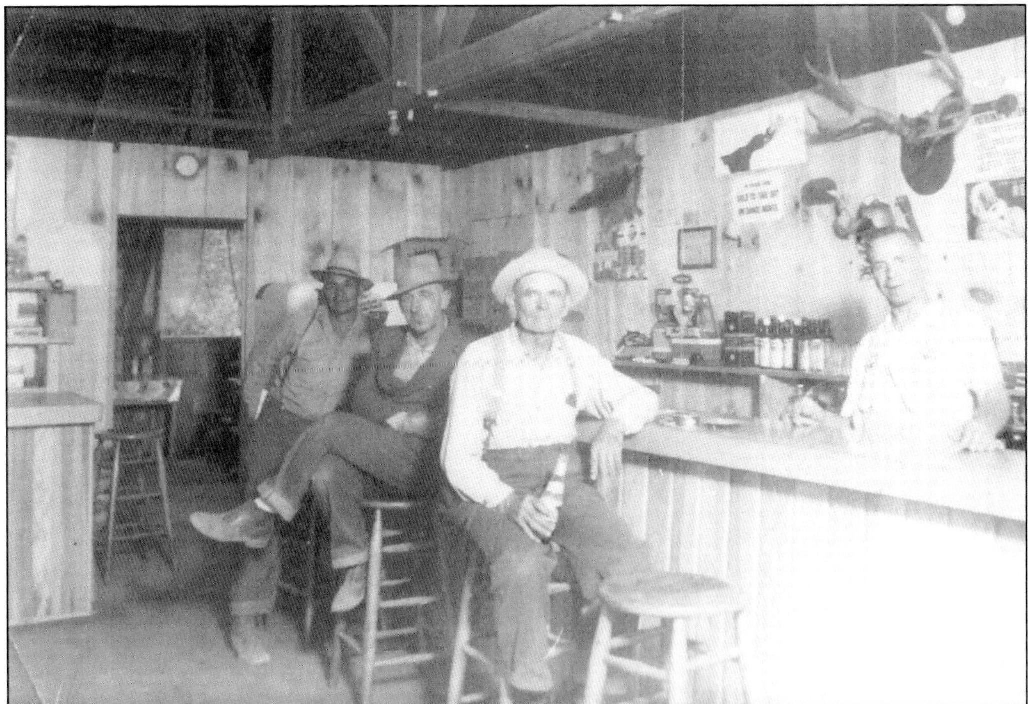

This is an interior view of Big Kate's Bar at Enterprise in the 1940s. These gentlemen are, from left to right, Dan Mullens, Art Slicker, Dick Harnett, and John Berger. Big Kate's was located just upstream from the Enterprise Bridge on the south side of the river. According to legend, Big Kate's physical size and personality were just as big as her name implies. Sadly, any photographs of Big Kate and the outside of her bar no longer exist. (Courtesy of MW.)

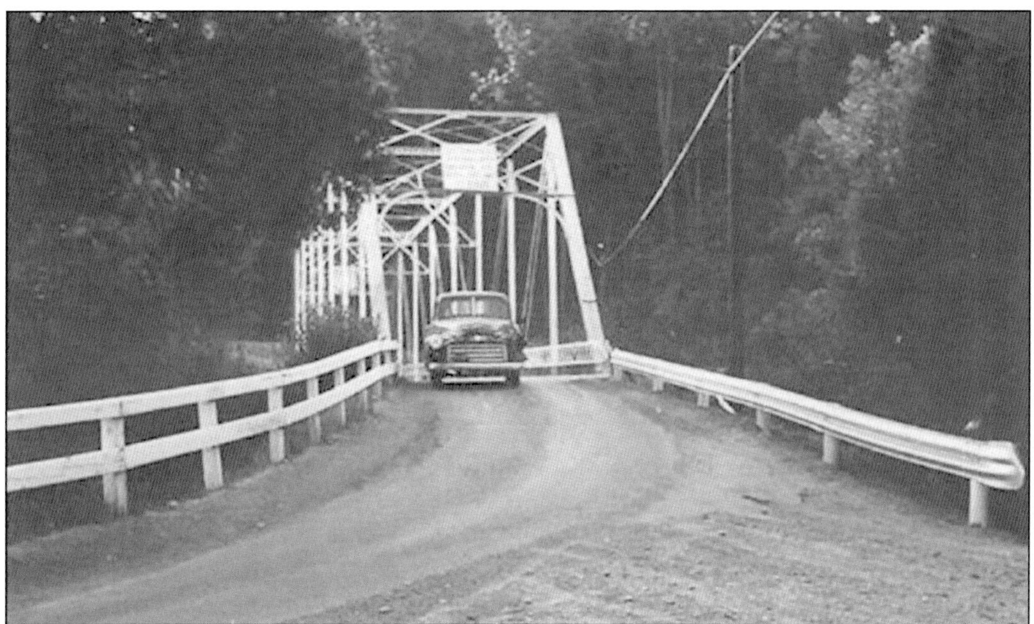

Both of these photographs depict the north side of the Feather River. Above is a 1953 GMC truck that has just crossed the Enterprise Bridge after passing Big Kate's Bar on the far side of the span. Below is the fork in the road after leaving the bridge. The road on the right continues up the hill toward Feather Falls Village. The road on the left heads east along the north side of the river to the logging truck bridge. Over the years, more than one vehicle has lost its brakes coming down the hill and slammed into the guardrail while attempting to cross the bridge. (Both, courtesy of AS.)

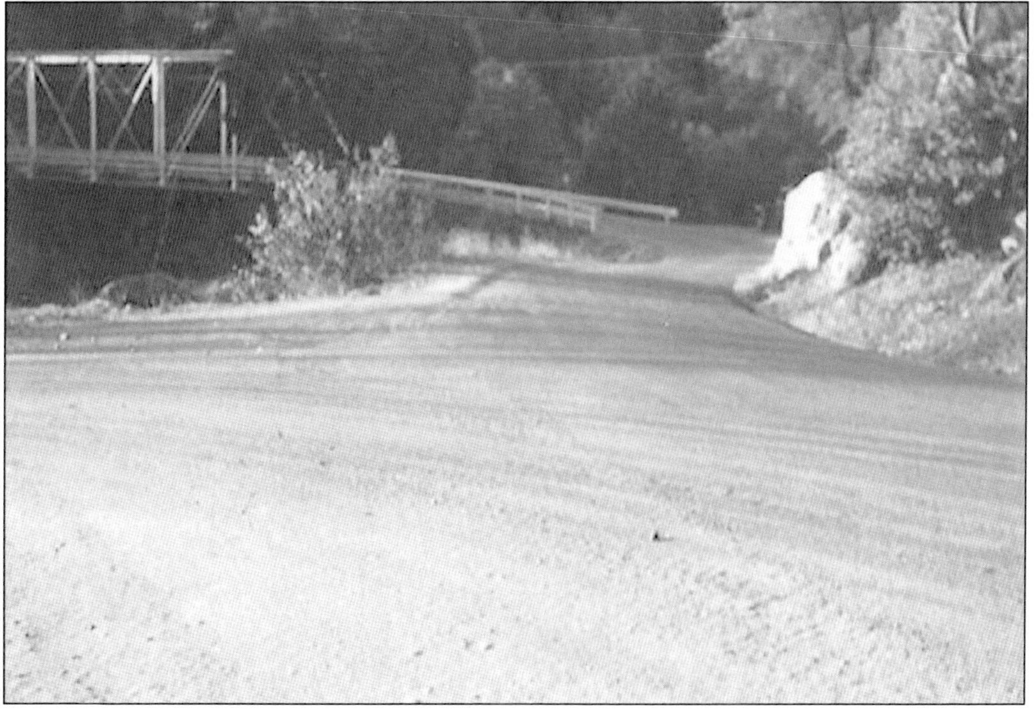

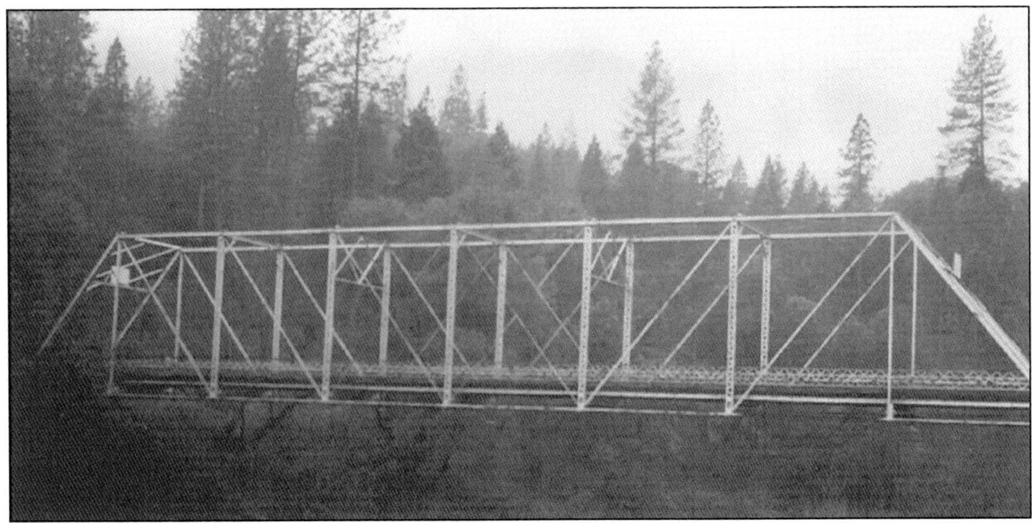

This is a side view of the Enterprise Bridge on January 30, 1947. One source says that it was completed the summer after the wooden covered bridged had washed out in 1907. Another source says it was completed in 1909. Either way, the 152-foot span was built by the American Bridge Company. Residents must have been glad to see its completion, because from the time of the old bridge's destruction, people had gotten across the bridge by a basket, a "Flying Dutchman," which was suspended by a cable. (Courtesy of BCPW.)

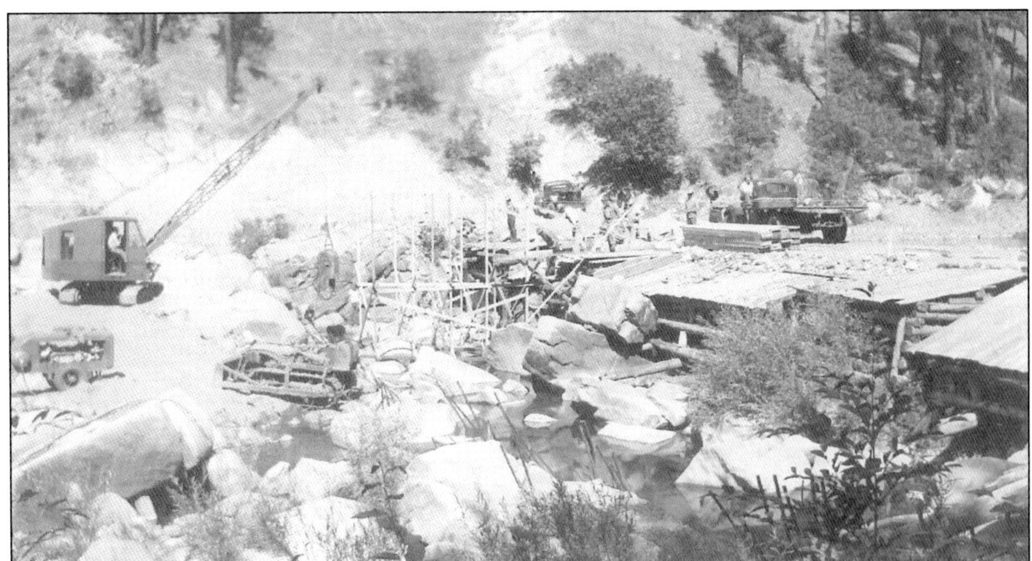

The OWID diversion dam is seen under construction in 1948. It was located upstream from the community of Enterprise, and it provided water for the Palermo Canal. The canal ran down the south side of the river, through parts of Oroville, and terminated in Palermo. This concrete dam replaced an earlier rock dam just downstream from this location. (Courtesy of South Feather Water and Power Agency.)

At right, Mary Killstoff Pappas and her grandson Bill Wilson are shown gold panning near Enterprise. Mary moved to Enterprise from San Francisco with her second husband, Jimmy Pappas, in 1928. They bought 40 acres on the south side of the river, about one mile upstream from the Enterprise Bridge. There, they built their first home, a rustic 20-by-30-foot cabin. Those who had been displaced by the Depression were allowed to camp on their property and do some gold mining. After some time, an extensive tent settlement developed along the river. Jimmy and Mary eventually built a larger, more modern home with indoor plumbing and electricity. Below, Bill Wilson is shown doing some shooting at the old OWID diversion dam. This view is looking east from the south side. Both photographs are from 1954. (Both, courtesy of EW.)

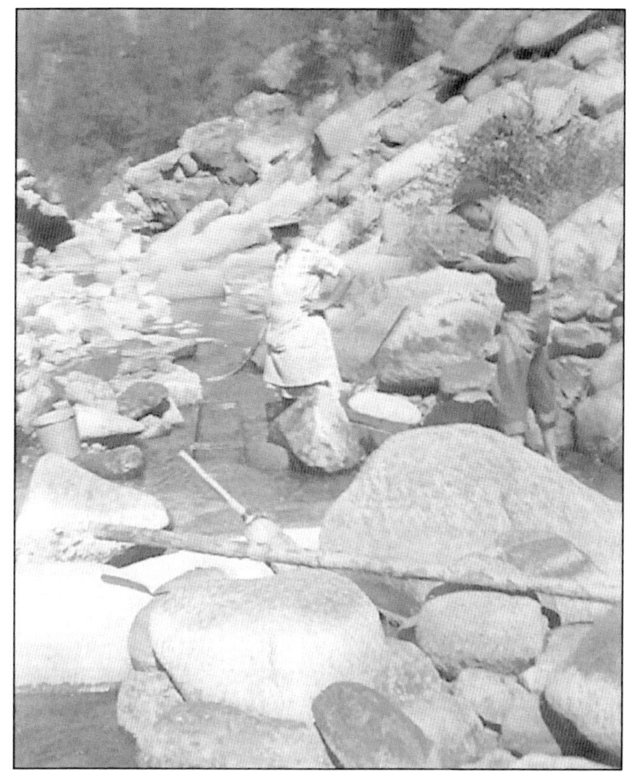

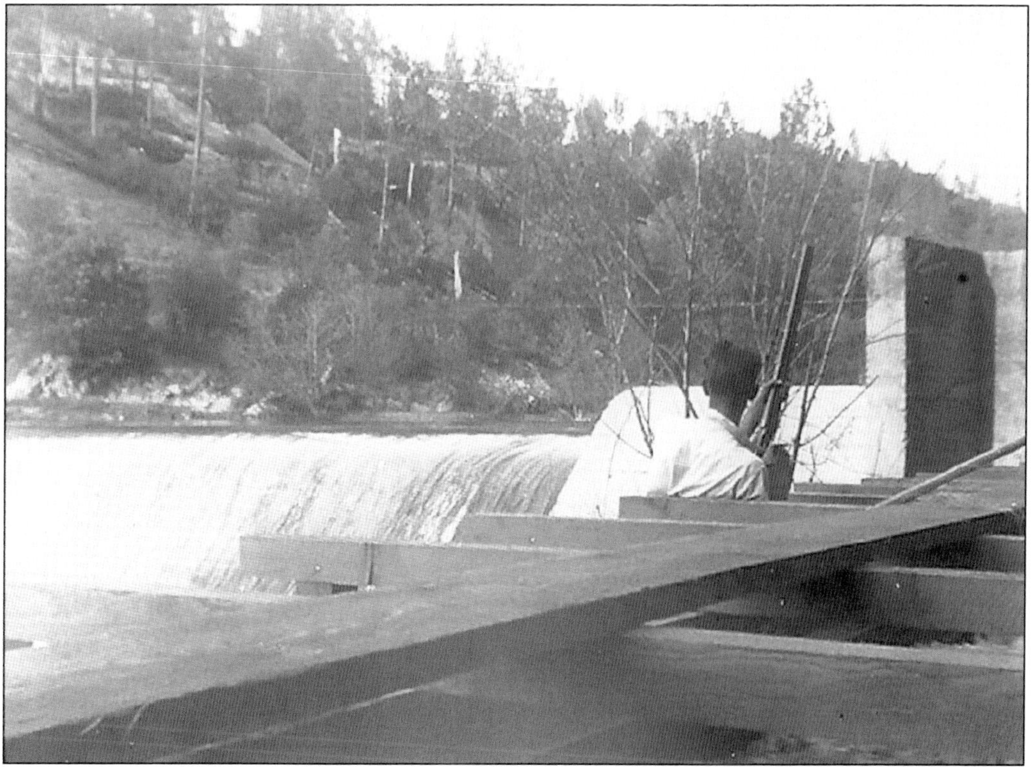

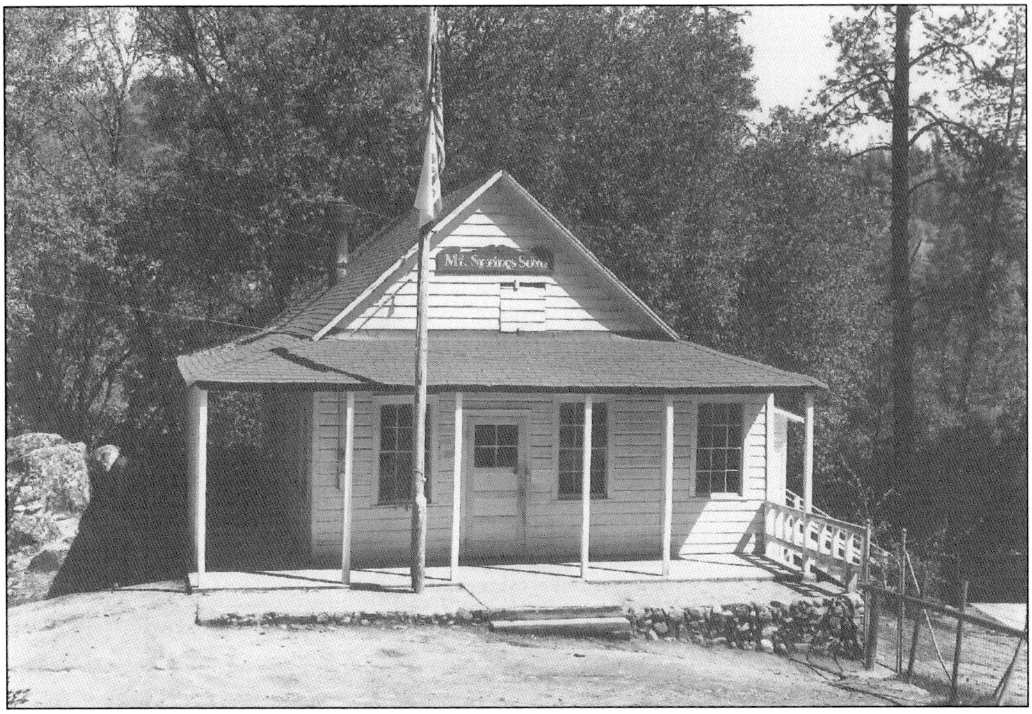

The Mountain Springs School is shown in January 1963. The school was established in 1863 and held classes until 1963. The school consisted of one room with one teacher and served grades from kindergarten through eighth. The number of students varied greatly at times, from 12 to over 30. In January 1964, a gentleman by the name of Kenneth A. Mather offered to provide a location for the school if someone would buy it and have it moved. Mather called it "the most attractive country school I've seen". He indicated that the Division of Beaches and Parks had told him that the state would have sold it for a dollar. Sadly, the school was not saved. (Courtesy of BCHS.)

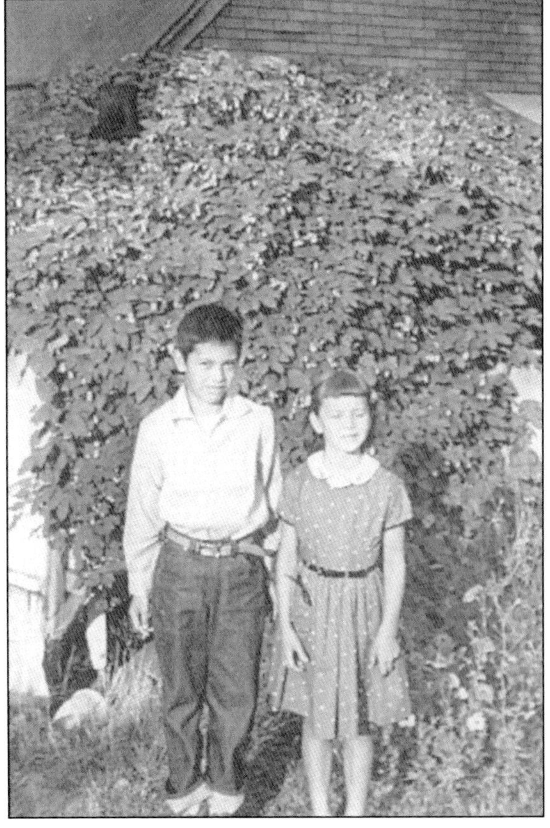

Frank Spencer and his sister Lois are pictured in front of their home at Enterprise in 1958. Their parents were Cecil and Cecilia Spencer. Cecil owned Spencer's Lumber Mill. The home was located quite close to the mill that was southeast of the school. (Courtesy of LSE.)

This may be the only existing photograph of the Sunnyside House Hotel. Built by George Drown in 1876, it served as a major stage and freight stop. The wagons and stages traveling the steep road from Oroville to Lumpkin would change horses at this location, which was situated on the north side of the Feather River on the road between Enterprise and Mooretown. When the hotel burned down in 1947, the only thing that survived was the cement watering trough. (Courtesy of BCHS.)

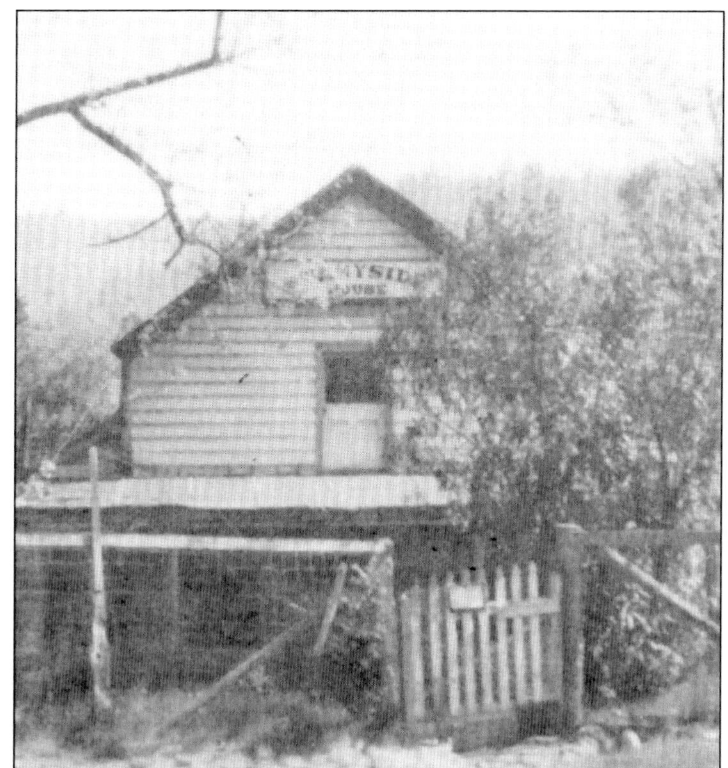

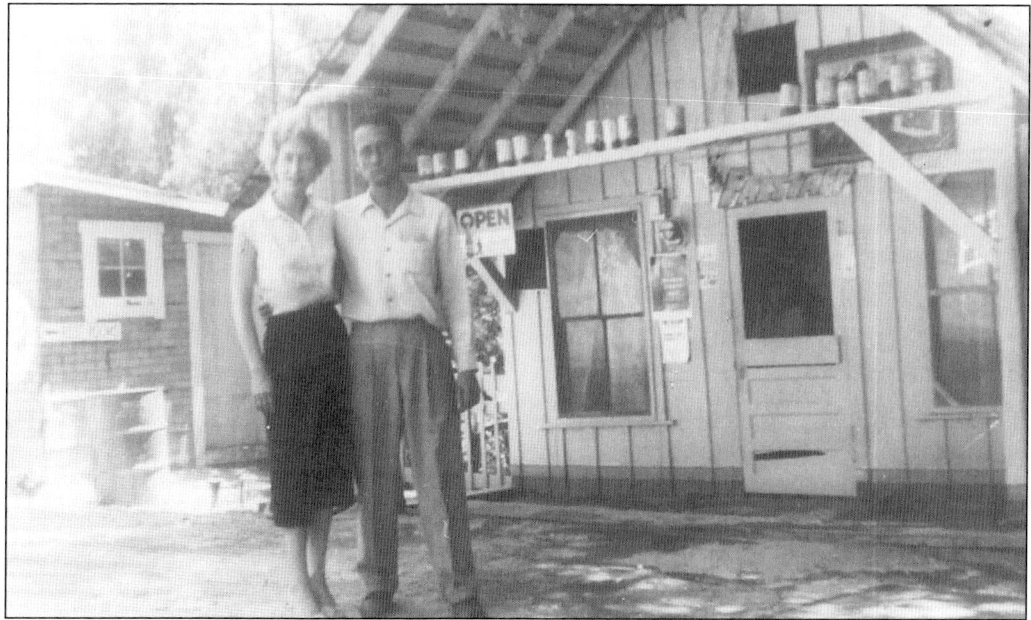

A couple stands in front of the Sunnyside Market in the 1940s. The market was located on the north side of the river, just a short way up Lumpkin Road from the bridge. The Sunnyside House, a major stage stop on the route, stood near that location during the 19th and early 20th centuries. Crofoot's Bar was situated across from the market in the 1950s. The market was later turned into a bar. The Sunnyside Market/Bar burned down in December 1958. (Courtesy of MW.)

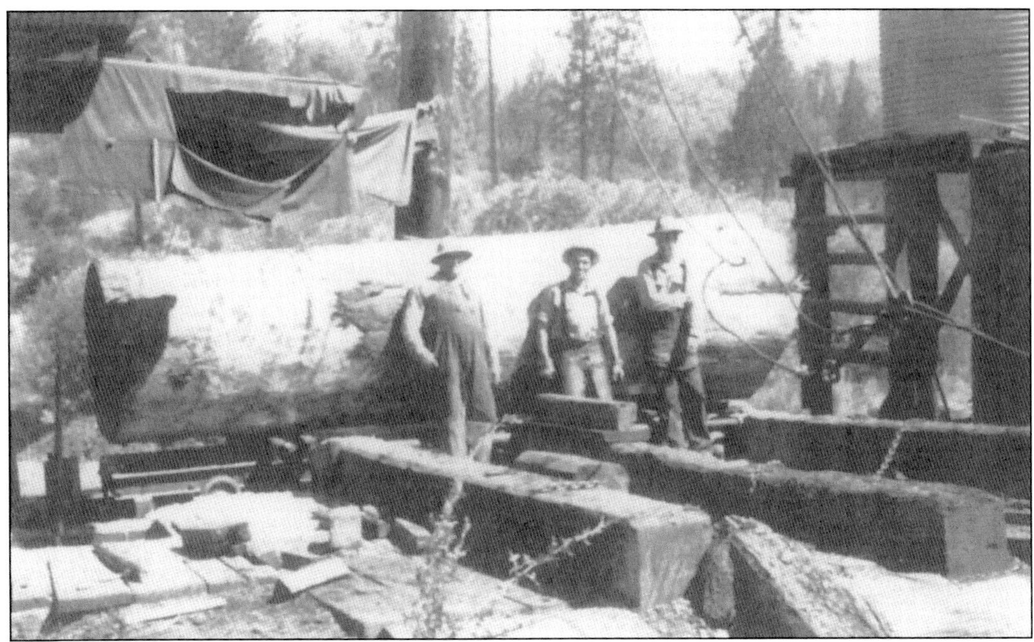

Both of these views are from 1956. Above is a photograph of Spencer's Lumber Mill at Enterprise. The men are, from left to right, Frank Swakea, Orrin Lee, and owner Cecil Spencer. Below is Lois Spencer sitting on the hood of one of her dad's logging trucks. Lois was born in Oroville in 1948 and lived in Enterprise until 1963. Her ancestors on the Maidu side of the family had lived in the canyon for hundreds of years. (Both, courtesy of LSE.)

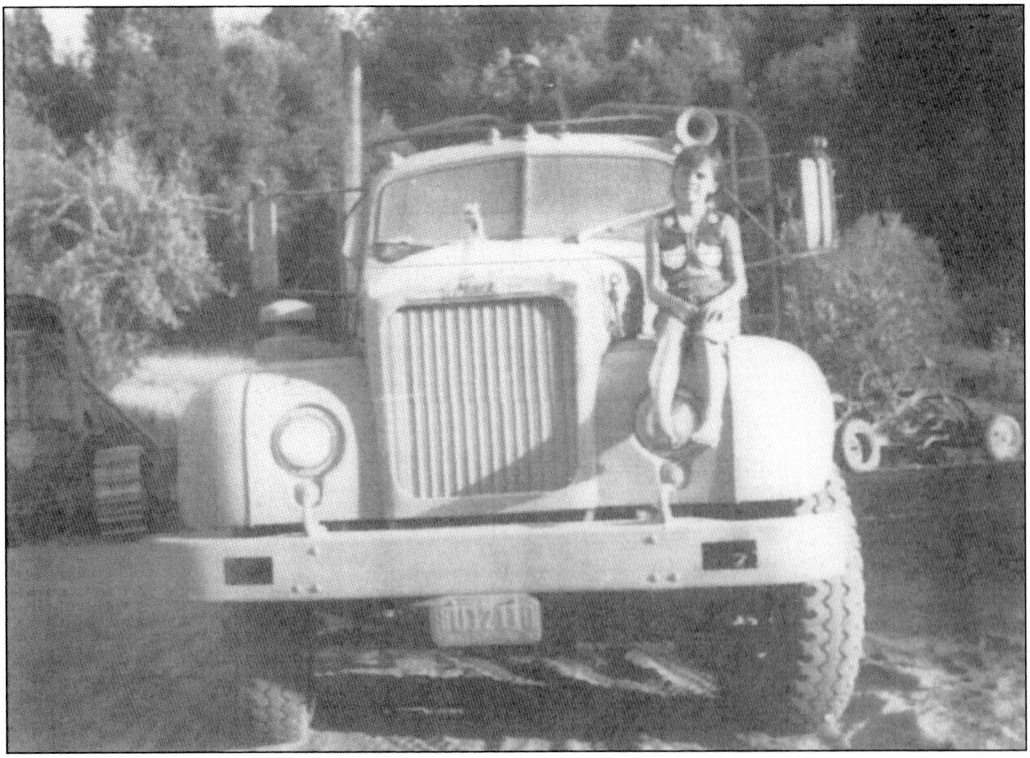

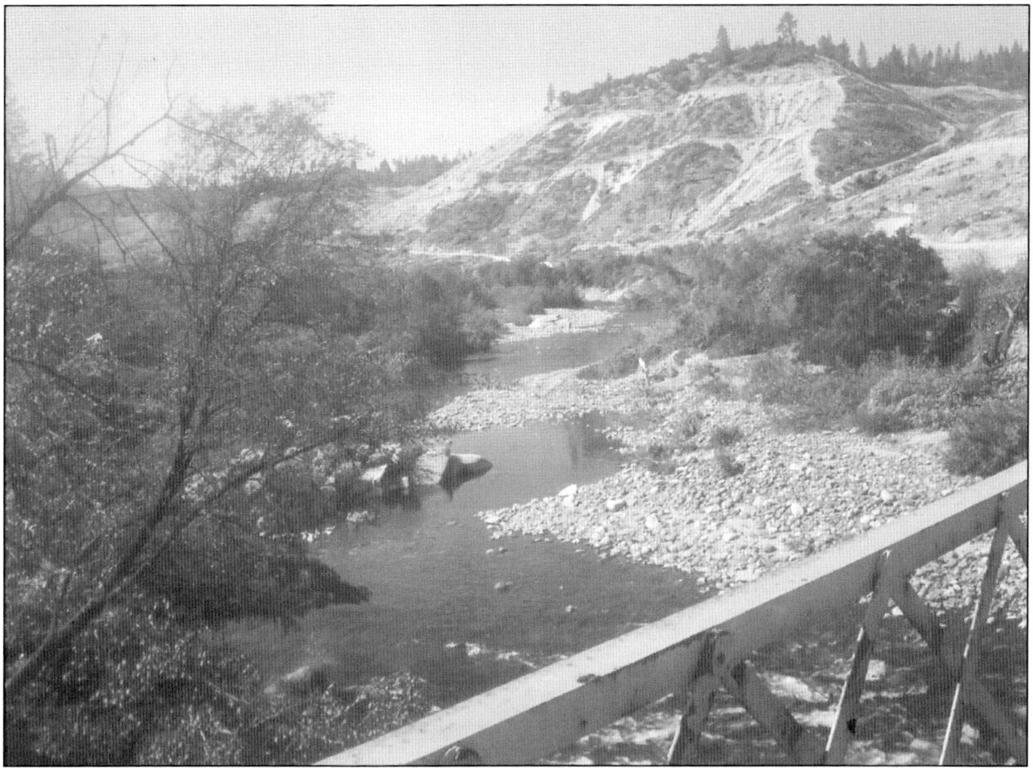

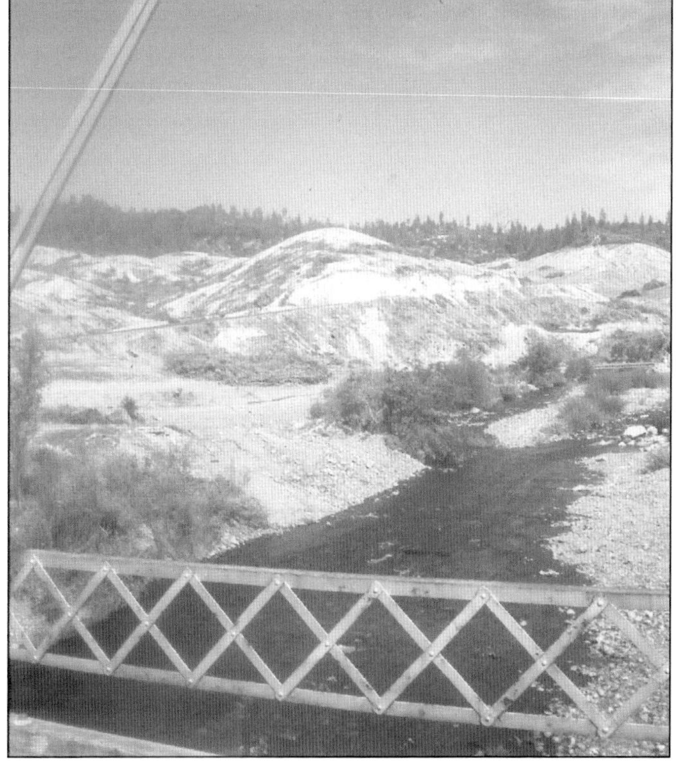

Both of these photographs taken from the Enterprise Bridge probably date to around 1964, as most of the vegetation has been cleared from the canyon. Above is a view looking west, or downstream. At right is the opposite view, looking upstream, where the old log truck bridge and Lumpkin Road, heading up the left side, can clearly be seen. As early as 1947, a survey recommended replacement of the bridge due to its narrowness and fragility. School bus drivers from Feather Falls Village were not allowed to cross the bridge with students aboard. The students were unloaded from the bus and had to walk across the bridge to reboard the bus after it had been driven to the other side. (Both, courtesy of BCHS.)

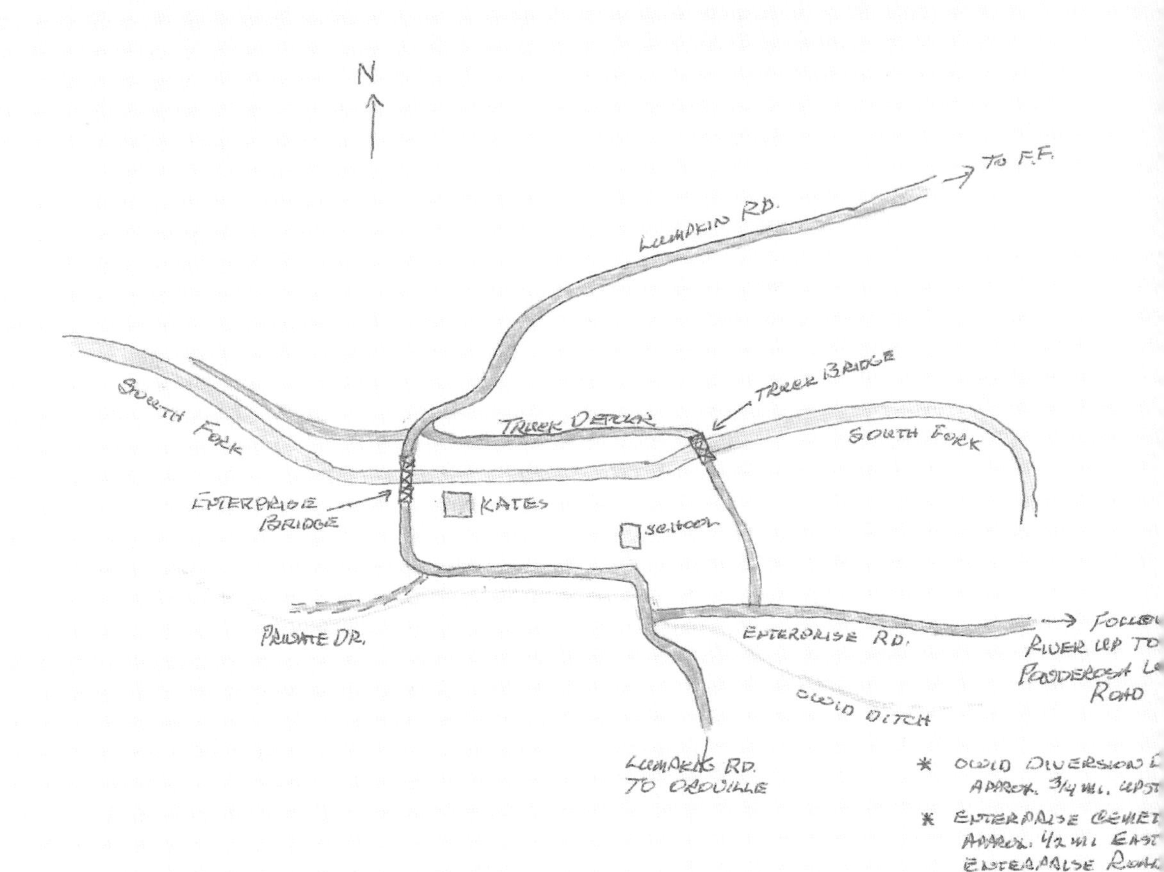

This hand-drawn map gives a clear perspective of various sites at Enterprise. Lumpkin Road comes in from the south, crosses the Enterprise Bridge, and makes its way north toward Feather Falls Village. The locations of Big Kate's Bar and the Mountain Springs School are indicated, along with the logging truck bridge and detour. The Palermo/OWID ditch, or canal, is shown crossing under both the Enterprise and Lumpkin Roads. (Courtesy of Ron Wheeler.)

Four

MOORETOWN AND FEATHER FALLS VILLAGE

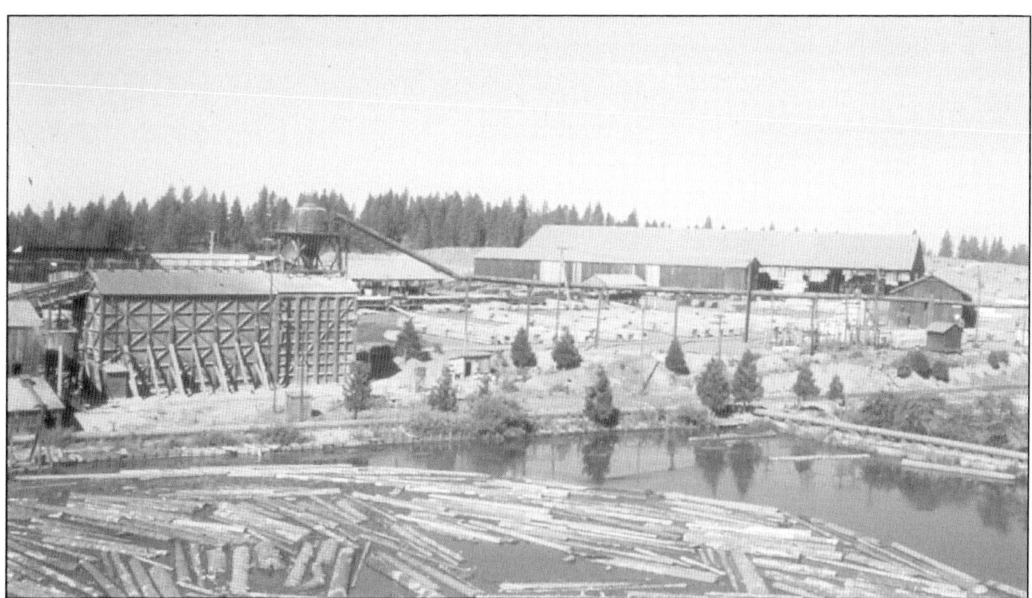

This chapter includes the area around Mooretown and Feather Falls Village, located 25 miles northeast of Oroville. This is a photograph of the Feather River Pine Mills in 1965. It employed approximately 450 workers. The mill was the lifeblood of Feather Falls Village. Without it, the village declined. Unlike with the other communities in this book, there were no rising lake waters to inundate Feather Falls Village. It was a change in circumstances that caused it to fade away. (Courtesy of YFM.)

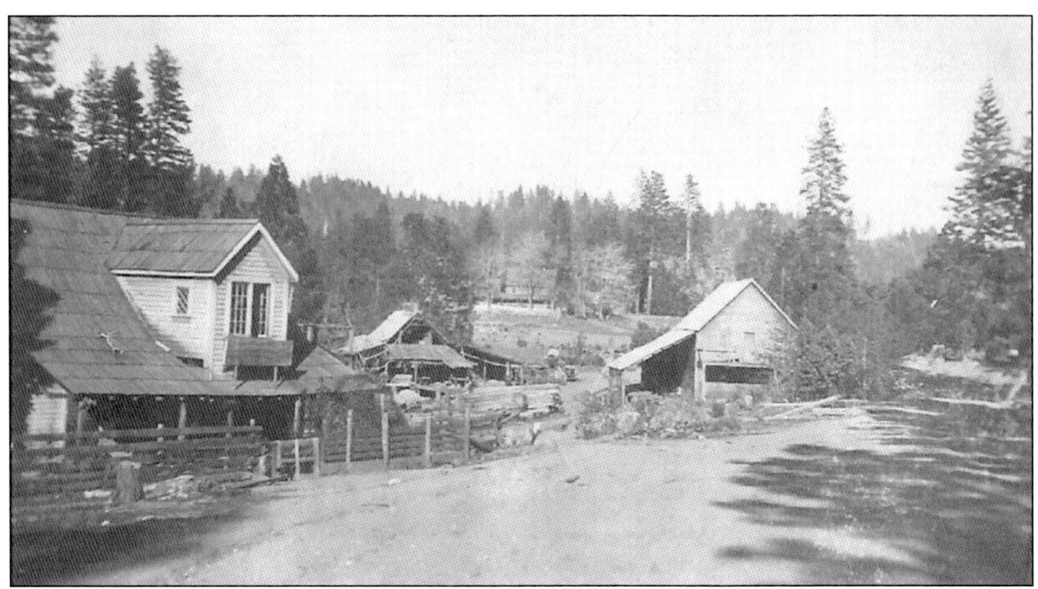

When John Moore established a hotel in the area in the early 1850s, it marked the beginning of what would eventually evolve into Feather Falls Village. The hotel was located near the present-day intersection of Bryant Ravine and Lumpkin Roads, about one mile west of the Feather Falls School. Mooretown eventually formed around the hotel, and by 1867, the town had become a thriving mining and logging center. It consisted of a hotel, dance hall, logging mill, post office, small school, and various other businesses. In 1938, the Feather River Pine Mills built a large mill three-quarters of a mile to the east and the name of the town was changed to Feather Falls. The town hall is seen on the left in the photograph above from 1918. The Mooretown hotel is the large building in the photograph below. (Both, courtesy of WFC.)

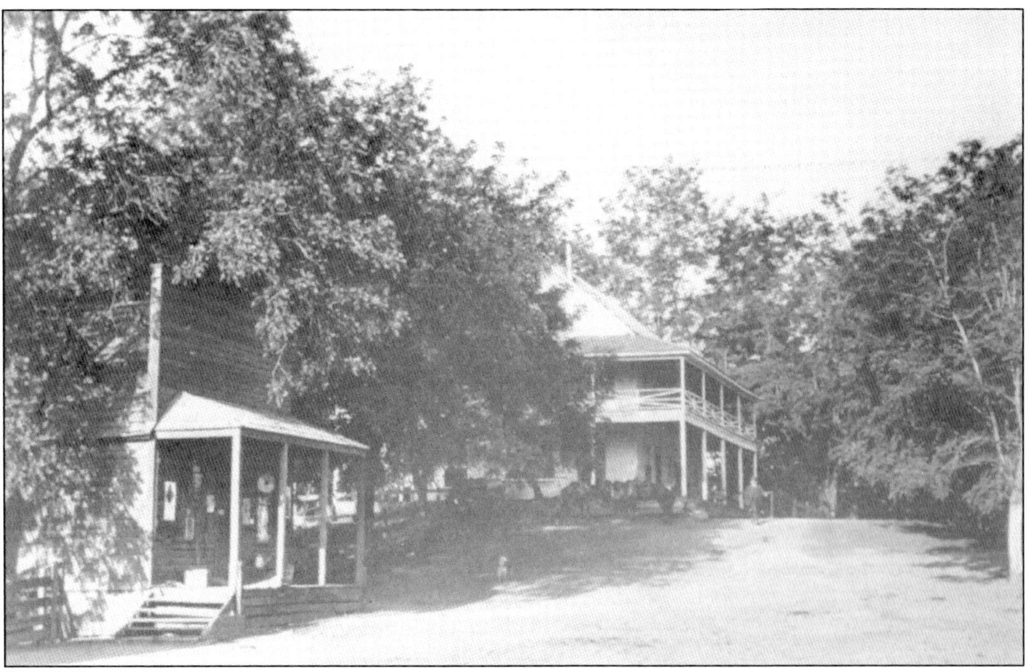

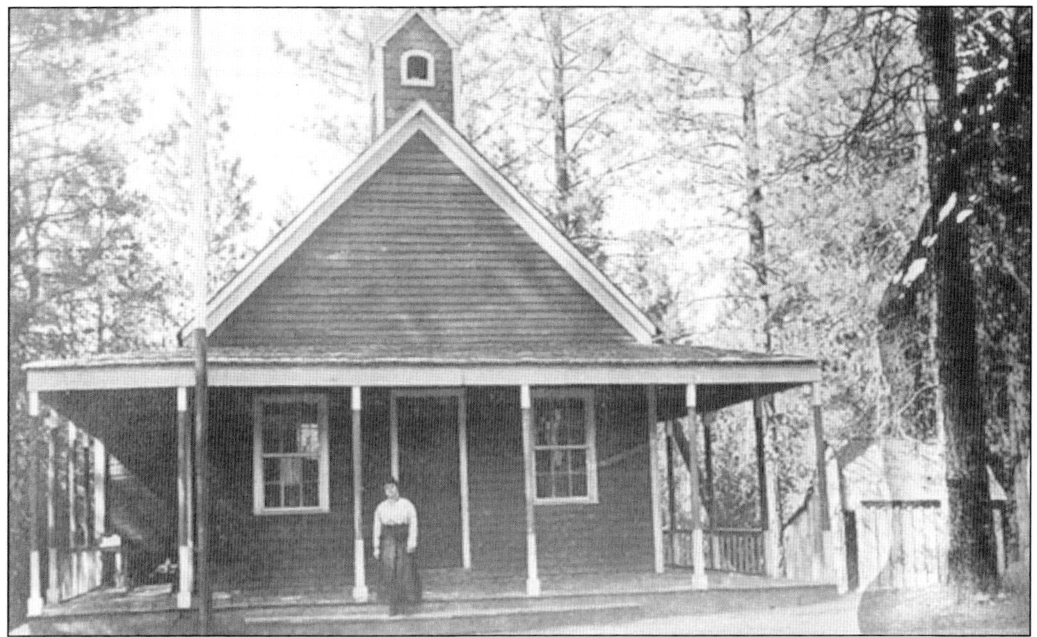

This is the original school at Mooretown in 1910. It is believed to have been located in the area of the present-day Feather Falls Cemetery. That area is on the south side of Lumpkin Road, almost directly across from the intersection with Bryant Ravine Road. The school district was established in 1864. (Courtesy of BCHS.)

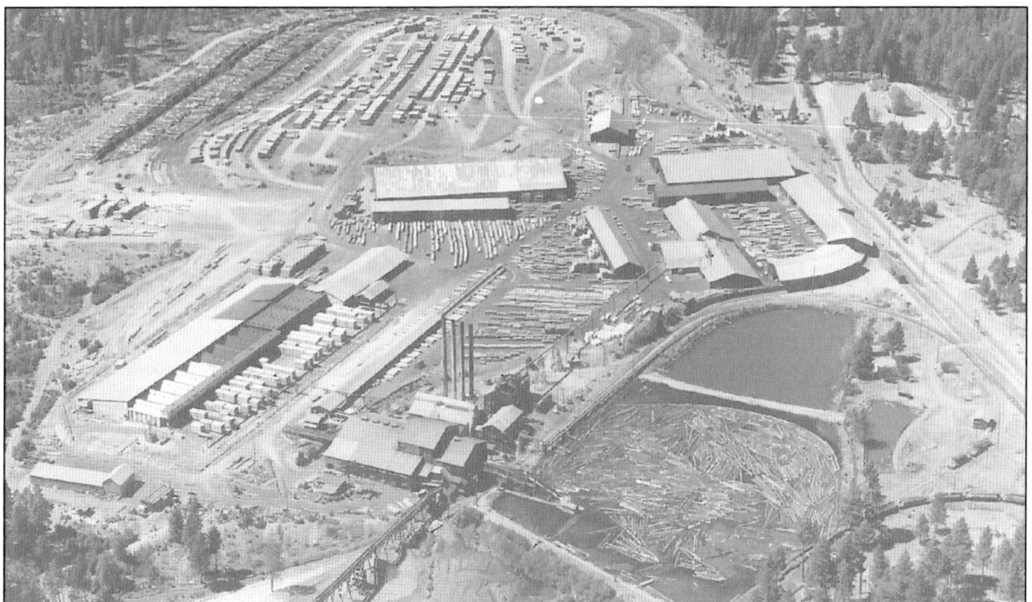

This is a photograph of the Feather River Pine Mills. Looking west, this mid-1940s view shows most of the mill and Lumpkin Road on the right. In the upper right corner is the second Feather Falls School, which was built at the same time as the mill, between 1938 and 1940. This school still stands. The small building just west of the newer school is the original Feather Falls School that was built around 1904. In the 1950s, the old school served as the school library. In the early 1960s, the county condemned the building and it was torn down. (Courtesy of WFC.)

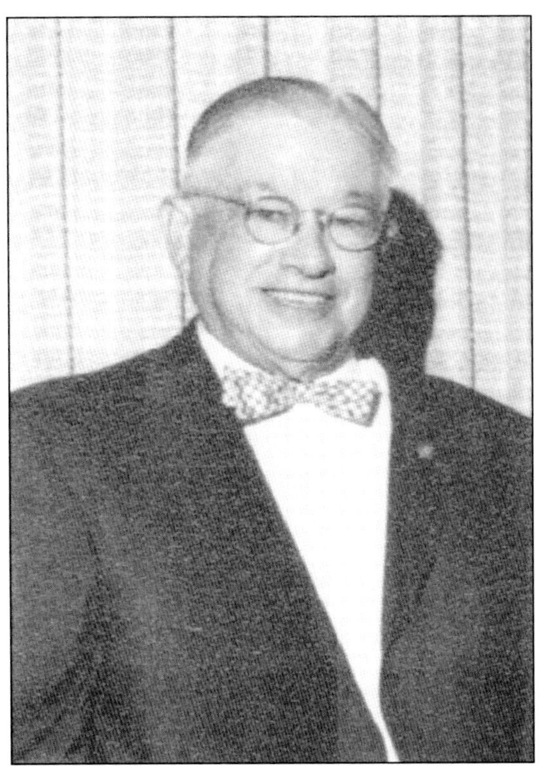

Andrew Hunter Land was the man who established Feather Falls Village. Land obtained a federal loan in 1938 and built the Feather River Pine Mills. He also built the village to house his workers. Several of Land's eight children assisted him in running the mill. Land passed away in 1953. In 1955, the business and the village were sold to Georgia-Pacific Corporation for $7.5 million. The deal also included Georgia-Pacific's purchase of the Feather River Pine Mills manufacturing mill at Bidwell Bar. When the mill closed in 1970–1971, Louisiana-Pacific Corporation split off from Georgia-Pacific and continued to own the village. The village was destroyed in 1994, and Louisiana-Pacific sold the land to Sierra Pacific Corporation in 1996. (Courtesy of WFC.)

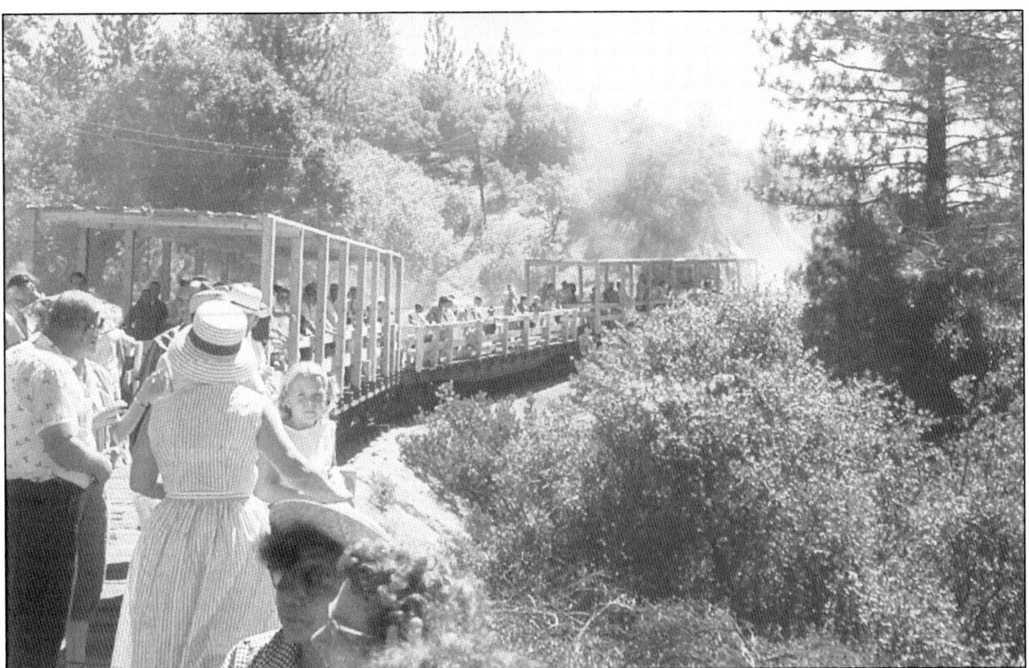

Over the years, Georgia-Pacific Corporation sponsored several train excursions during the summer so that its employees could enjoy a day of picnicking and swimming at the Curry-Bidwell Bar State Park. This 1962 photograph shows employees aboard the train on their way to Bidwell Bar. It took the train several hours to arrive at its destination. (Courtesy of WFC.)

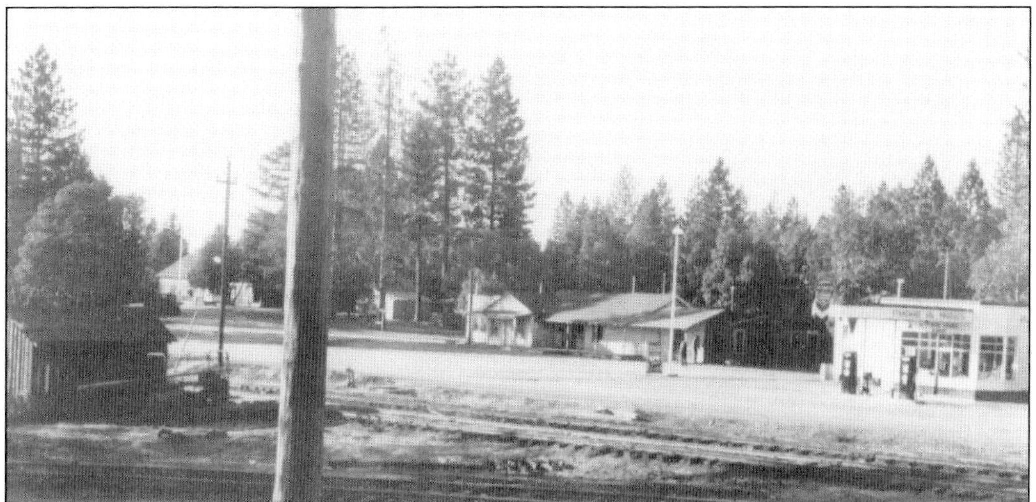

This October 1944 photograph shows, from left to right, the Feather River Pine Mills office, the grocery store and barbershop, and the gas station. At the time, the gas station was owned and operated by Robert F. Hines. The grocery store and barbershop were later moved to the area behind the café. The tracks in the foreground were used to transport lumber to the mill. (Courtesy of WFC.)

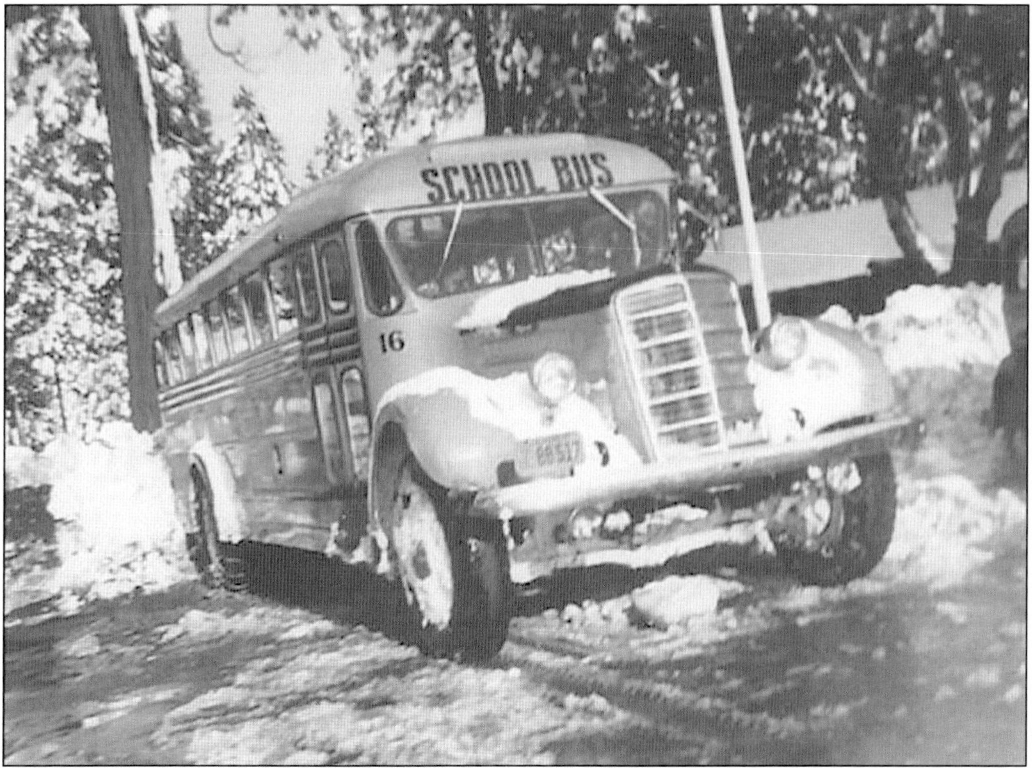

This is a school bus at Feather Falls in 1952. Every weekday, bus drivers would transport high school students down Lumpkin Road, through Enterprise, and on to the high school in Oroville. The road was, and some of it still is, very winding and steep. In the winters, the roads could be treacherous and sometimes impassable. One such incident happened in 1961 when deep snow caused two lumber trucks to jackknife, and the bus could not get to school that day. (Courtesy of WFC.)

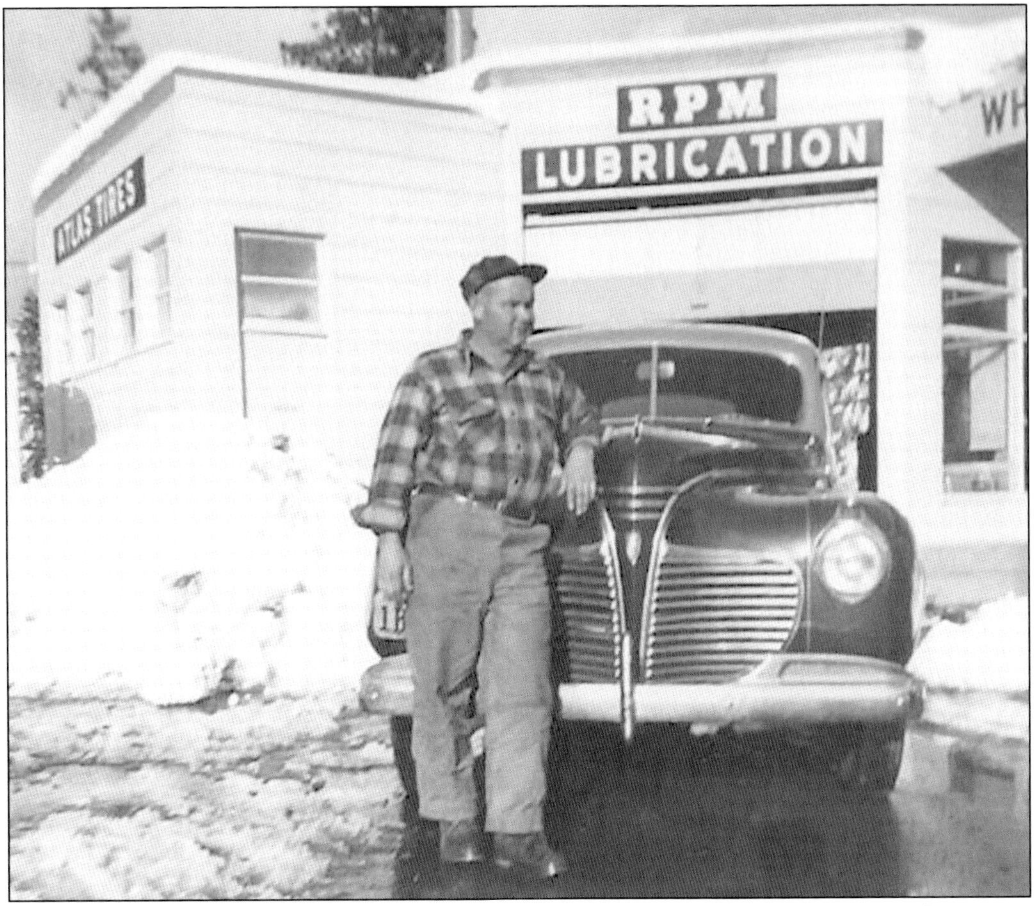

These photographs from 1949 show the new owner of the Feather Falls gas station. Above, new owner Joe W. Wheeler Sr. is pictured with his 1941 Plymouth on a winter day. Below, Joe W. Wheeler Jr. stands in front of the gas pumps. The Wheeler family ran the gas station from 1948 to 1964, when the business was sold to Lloyd and Thelma Mattlick. The Mattlicks also owned the local grocery store. The gas station was later sold to Ed Swain. (Both, courtesy of WFC.)

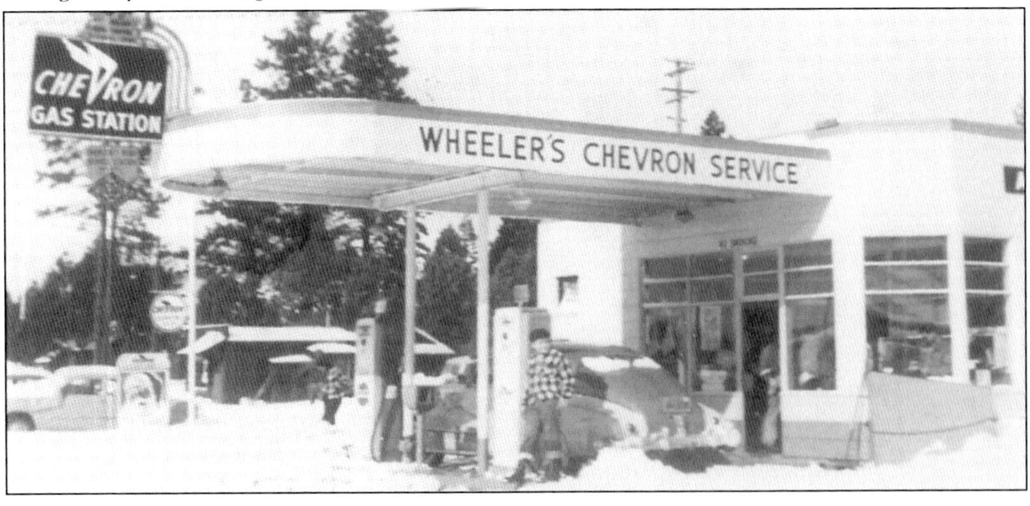

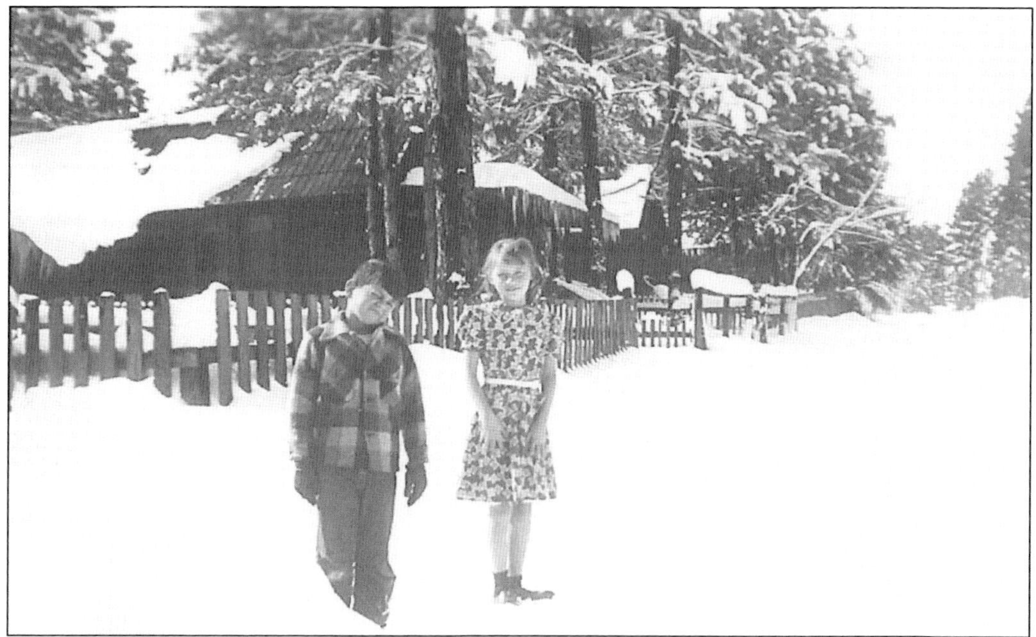

More winter views are pictured here. Above, Ron Wheeler and his cousin Janice Hamilton stand in front of Ron's house at 7 Ponderosa Way in 1952. Janice must have been really proud of her dress for her to stand out in the freezing cold without a coat. Winters at Feather Falls could be tough. The elevation was 2,982 feet, and it snowed almost every year. Snow depths were usually two to three feet. However, during the winter of 1951–1952, the snow accumulated to more than five feet deep. The photograph below was taken about the same time. It depicts the residence at the corner of Madrone Circle and Lumpkin Road. At the time, Charles and Lucille Everett lived there. He was a purchasing agent for Feather River Pine Mills, and she was a daughter of mill owner A.H. Land. (Both, courtesy of WFC.)

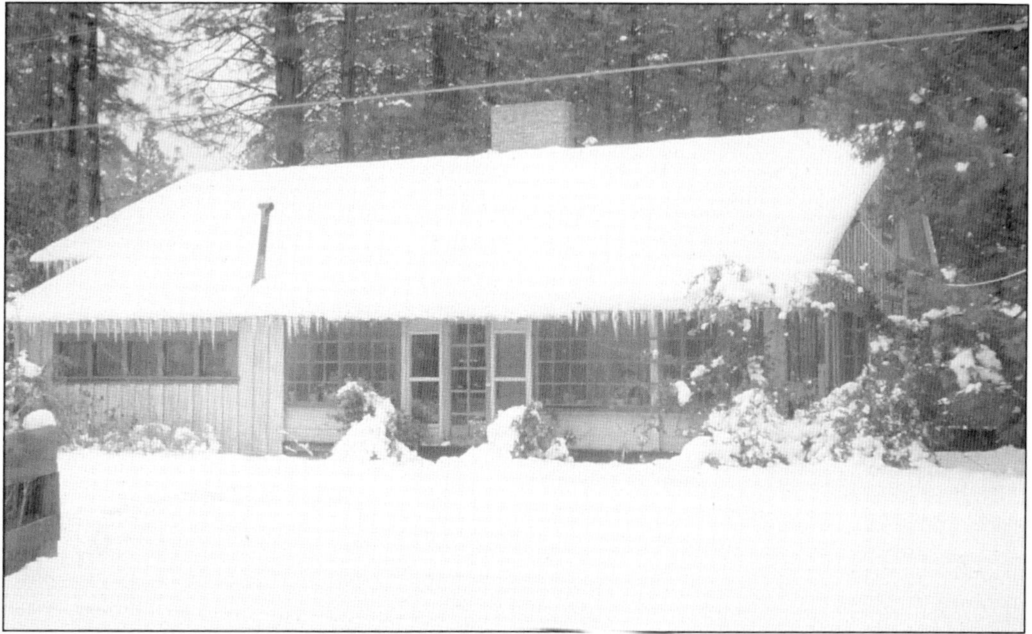

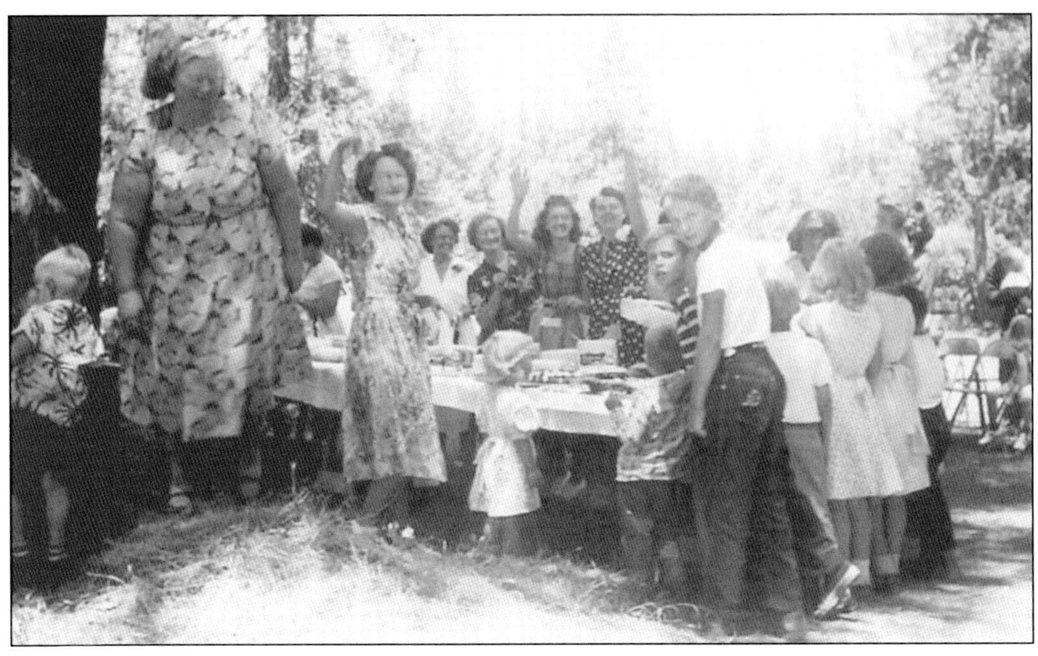

Picnics and potlucks were popular occasions at Feather Falls Village. Above is a potluck at the Little Brown Church in 1947. Below is a similar scene from 1953 at the Jones family house. Attending the potluck are, from left to right, Oren Jones, Vernon Jones, unidentified child, J.W. Rodgers, unidentified woman, unidentified child, unidentified woman, Vickie Jones, Beverly Jones, Verlue Jones, Braxton Jones, Ed Swain, Sylvia Swain, Diane Jones, Margaret Jones, Leota Rodgers, Marcella Rodgers, Margaret Ann Jones, Cheryl Swain, and unidentified boy. (Both, courtesy of MH.)

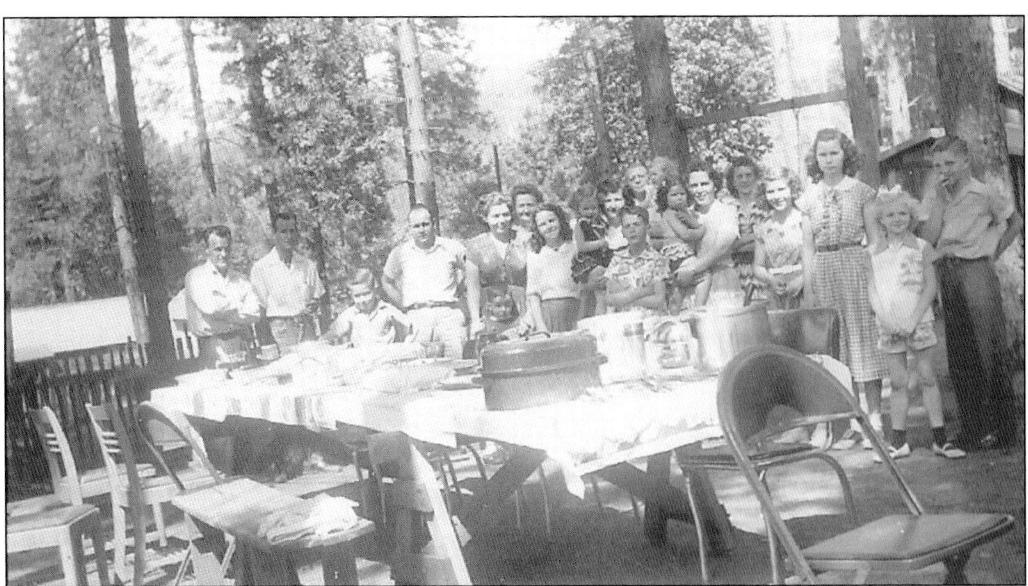

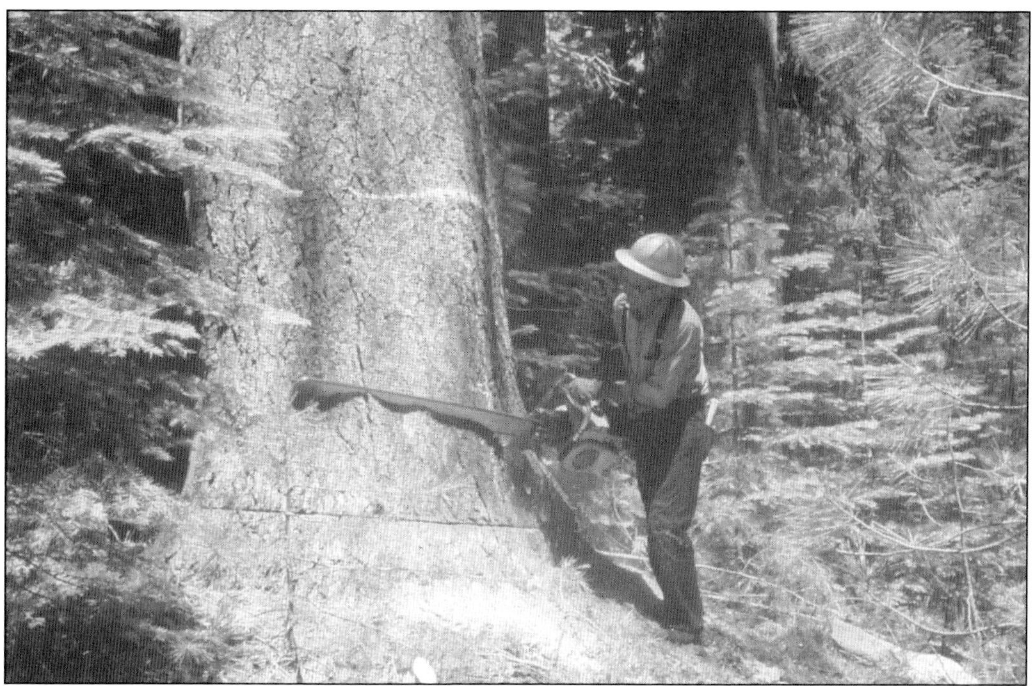

Here are two photographs from the 1960s that represent logging operations in the areas of Cascade and Fall River. The mill at Feather Falls processed lumber from these and other areas. Above, a logger begins to fell a tree with a chain saw. Chain saws of this type weighed approximately 30 pounds. Below, a diesel loader fills trucks at a landing. Trees processed at the mill were sugar pine, ponderosa pine, Douglas fir, white fir, and cedar. (Both, courtesy of WFC.)

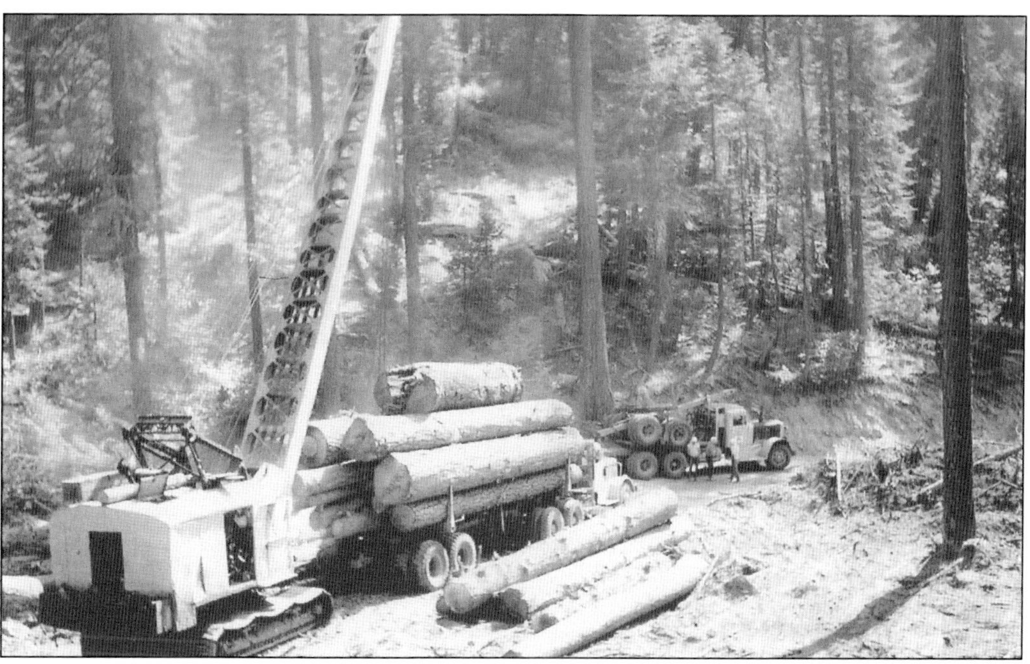

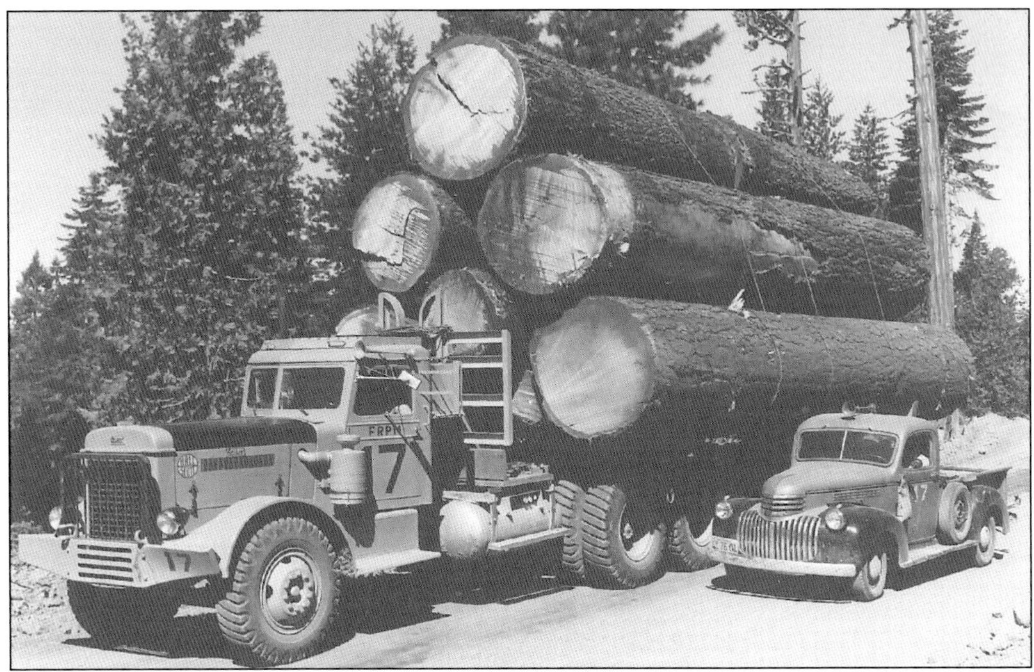

This 1953 photograph documents the largest load of logs ever hauled to the Feather River Pine Mills. This Peterbilt truck carries 40,000 board feet of logs and dwarfs the pickup truck next to it. The lumber trucks ran on butane with Hall-Scott engines. This image was taken near the cat shop at the mill. (Courtesy of WFC.)

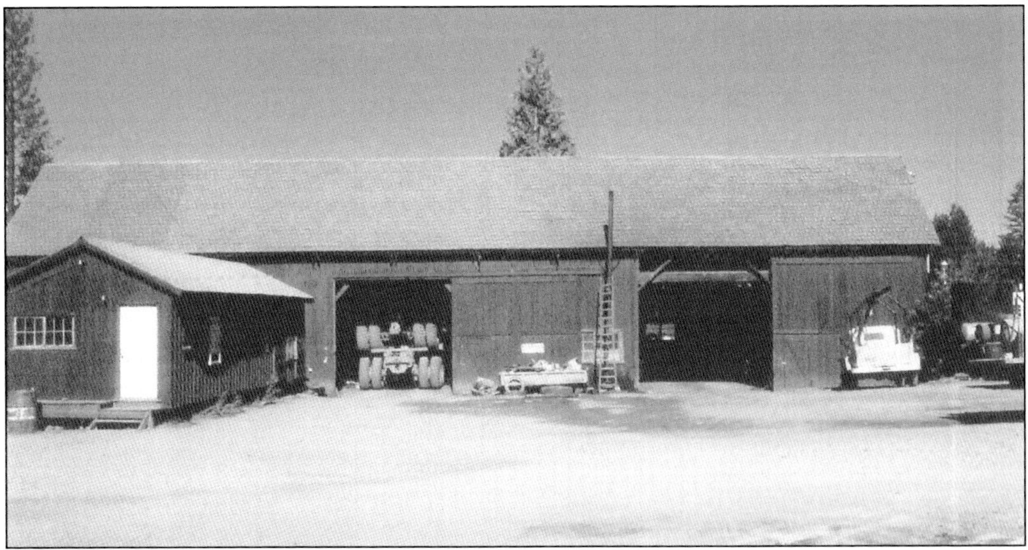

This 1960s photograph shows the cat shop, where maintenance and repair for crummys was performed. Crummys were vans or small buses that the loggers used to drive to the logging sites. Maintenance for logging cats and related equipment, such as loaders, arches, winches, and rigging, was done there. The logging truck fleet was maintained there for low beds, loaders, grease trucks, and fuel trucks. The shop had an overhead trolley crane inside for lifting heavy parts like engines, tracks, and undercarriages. The cat shop is the only building of Feather Falls Village that is still standing. (Courtesy of WFC.)

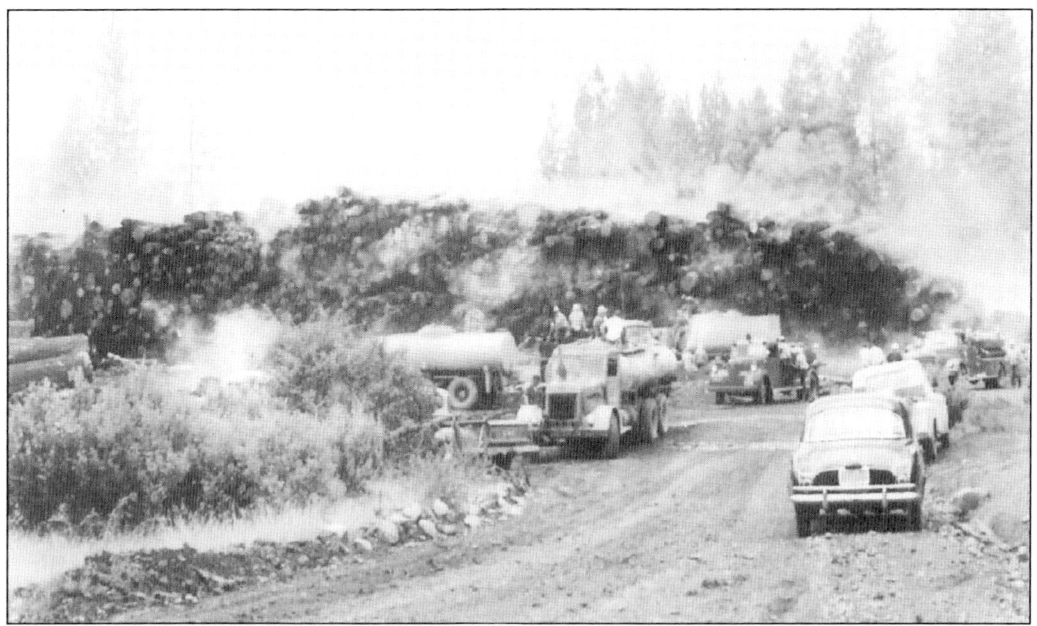

Fire was always a major concern for those living in the mountains. One of the most spectacular fires occurred on September 2, 1960, when a bolt of lightning struck the log deck of the mill. The mill's steam whistle announced the emergency, and fire teams came to fight and contain the blaze. Above, the fire teams are seen right after their arrival. Below, a fire team attempts to fight part of the blaze that has engulfed an enormous stack of logs. For a time, evacuation of the village was considered due to the possibility of a wind shift. The fire burned for at least two weeks, destroying six million board feet of lumber. (Both, courtesy of WFC.)

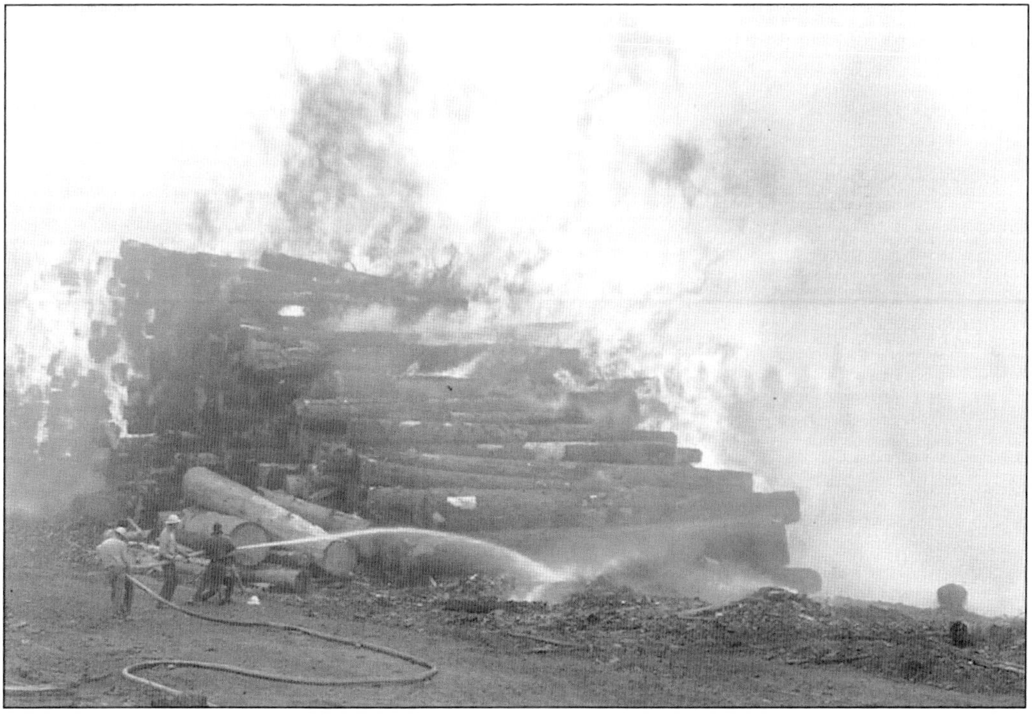

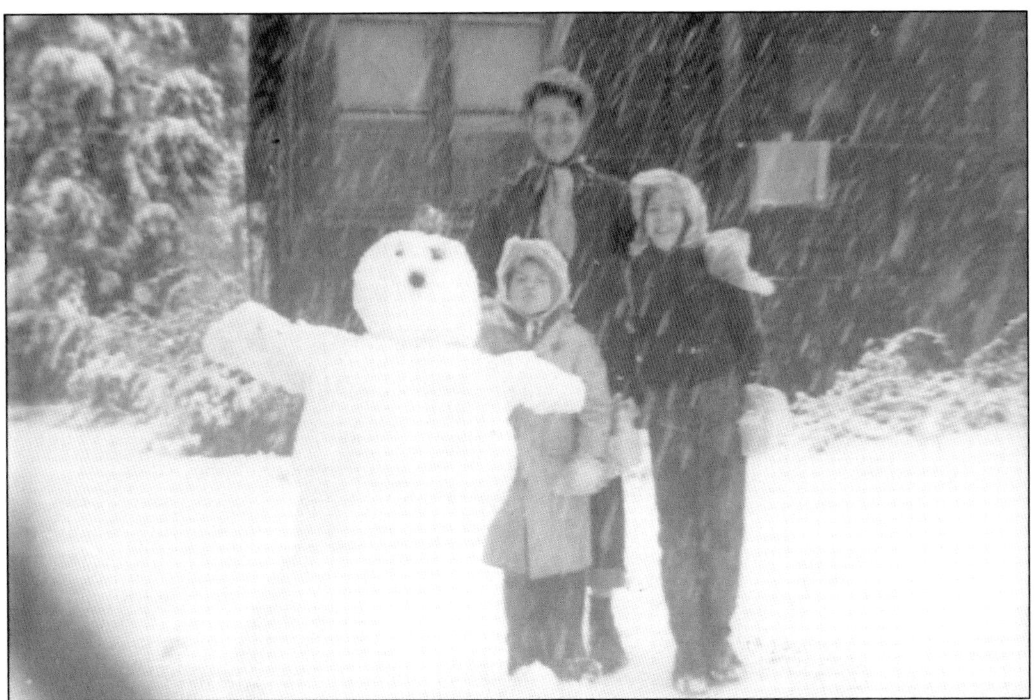

Bob Jackson took this photograph of his family in front of their house during the winter of 1962. His son Garrett stands next to the snowman, along with his wife, Bobbi, and daughter Jodi. Jackson was the principal of Feather Falls School from 1960 to 1962 and later taught at Las Plumas High School for many years. The same house is pictured below in the 1970s. This home was reserved for whoever held the position of principal at the school. It was located on the north side of Lumpkin Road, just east of the gas station and across from the cat shop. (Above, courtesy of Bob Jackson; below, courtesy of MW.)

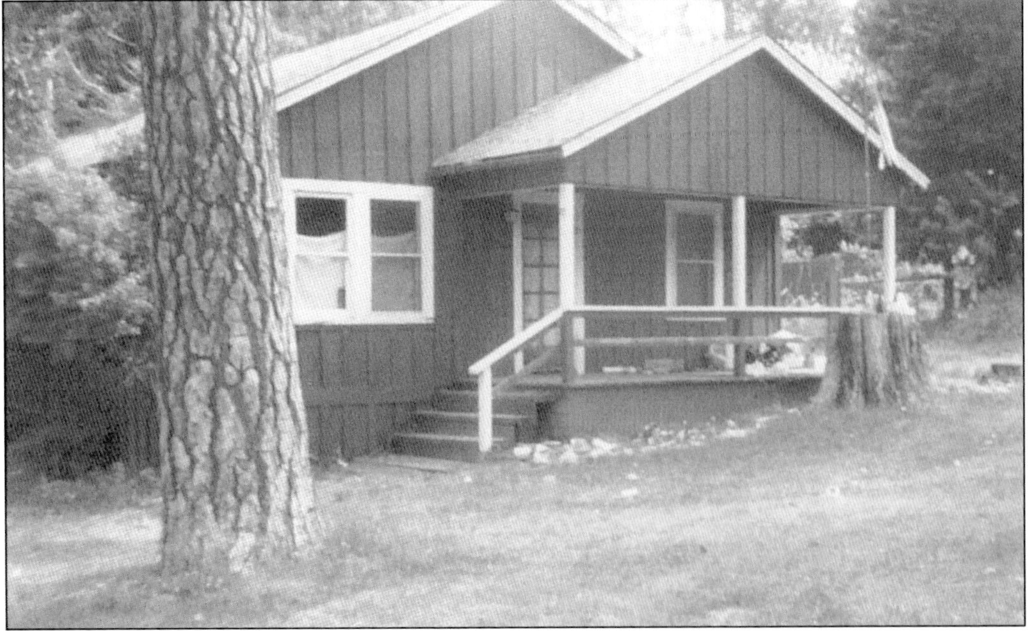

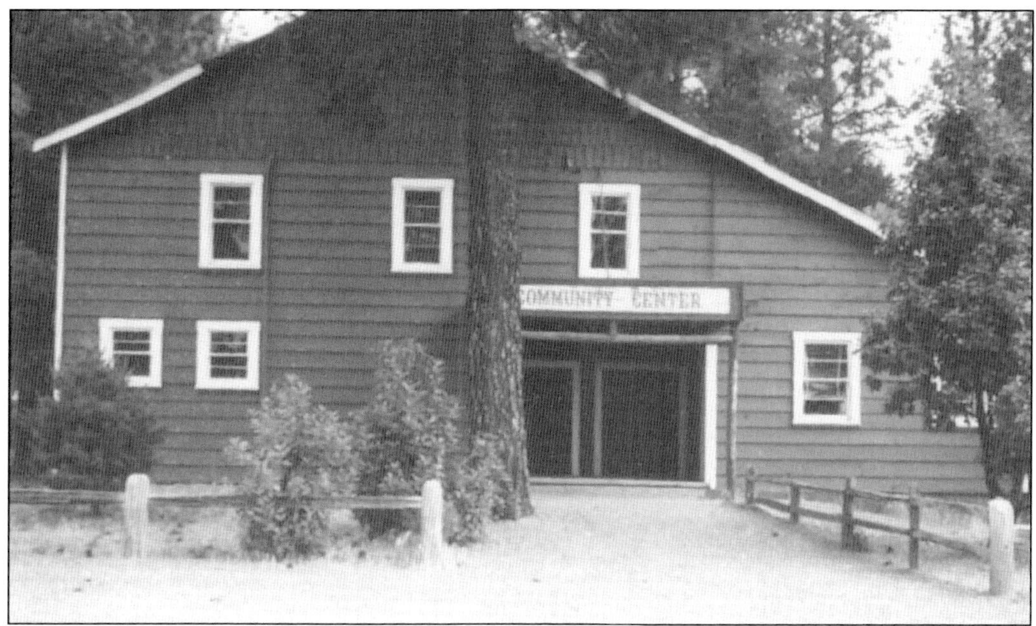

The Feather Falls Community Center is pictured above in the 1980s. It was the social center of the village. The community library was located on the right side of the ground floor. The upstairs contained the projection room where movies were shown. It is believed that a dance floor existed on the upper level at one time. The building burned down around 1990. After the fire, the village needed a new location for the library. A new addition was made to the main office building at Louisiana-Pacific. The new library addition is pictured below in the 1990s. (Both, courtesy of WFC.)

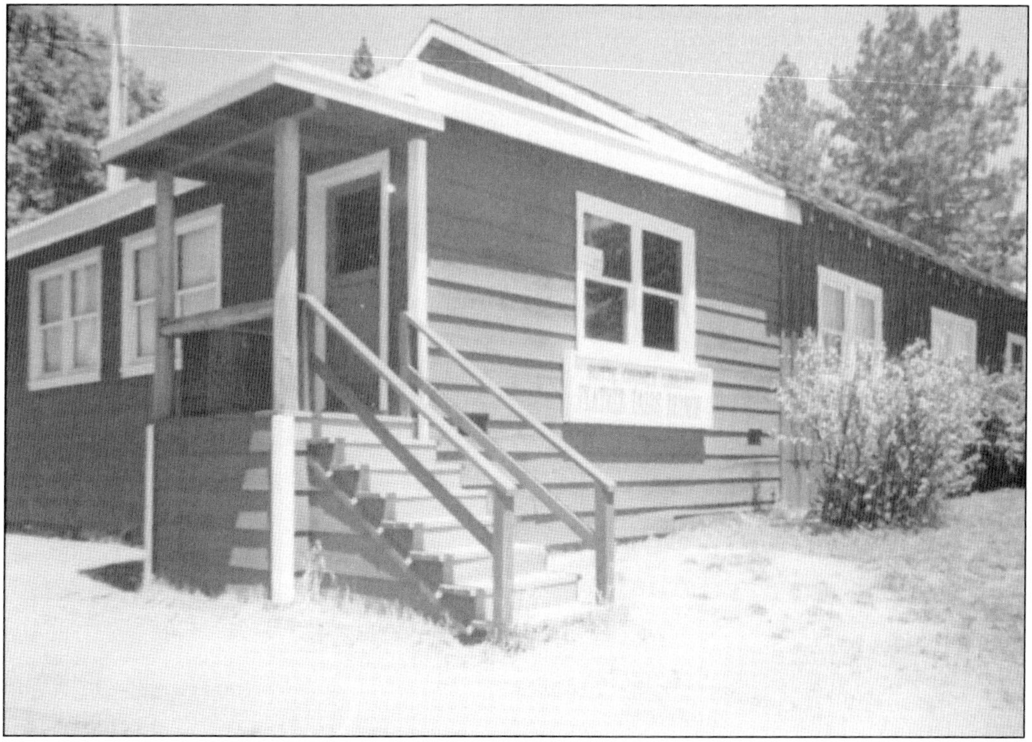

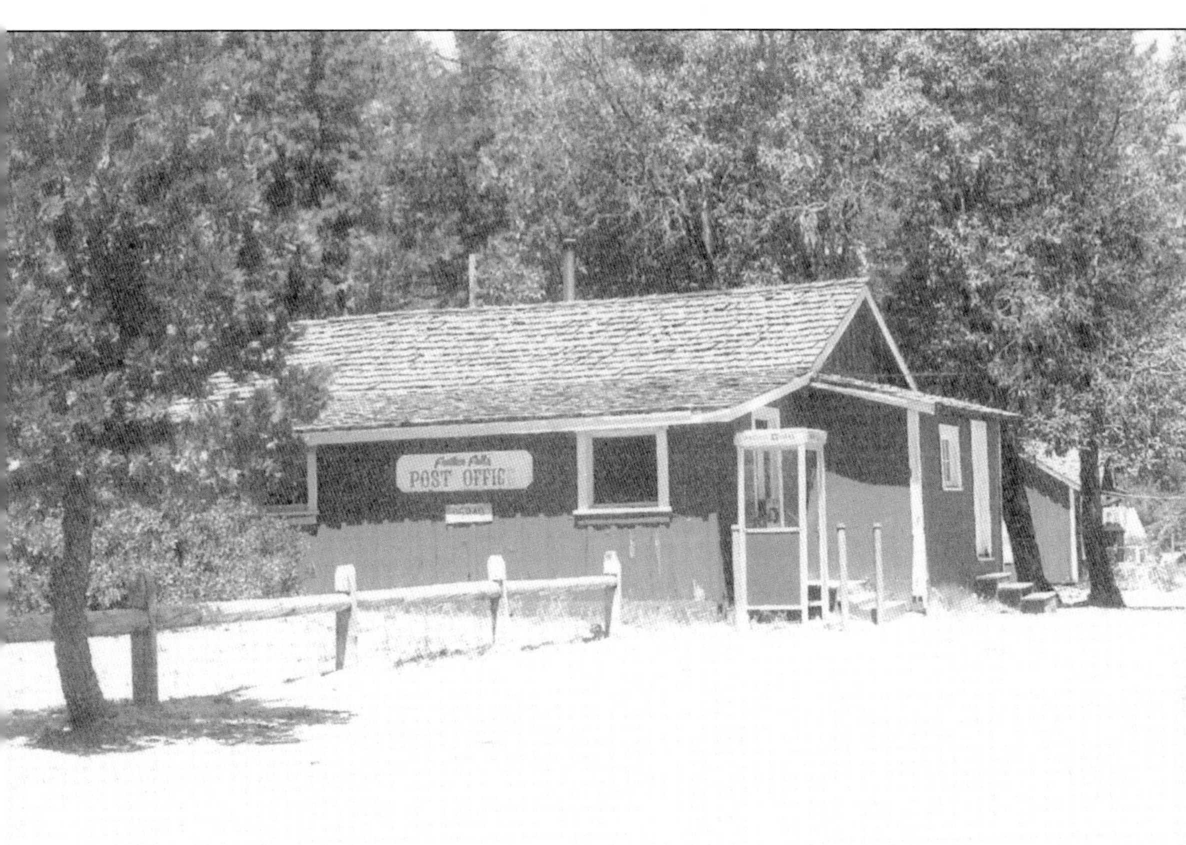

The Feather Falls Village Post Office is seen in this photograph from the late 1980s. This was not the first post office to be named for Feather Falls. When the area was still called Mooretown, the Feather Falls Post Office was located to the east at Camp One. When the new mill was being built in 1938, the post office was moved to this location and Mooretown was renamed Feather Falls. When the town was leveled in 1994, the post office was moved four miles west down Lumpkin Road to the Gold Flake Club. It exists there to this day. (Courtesy of MW.)

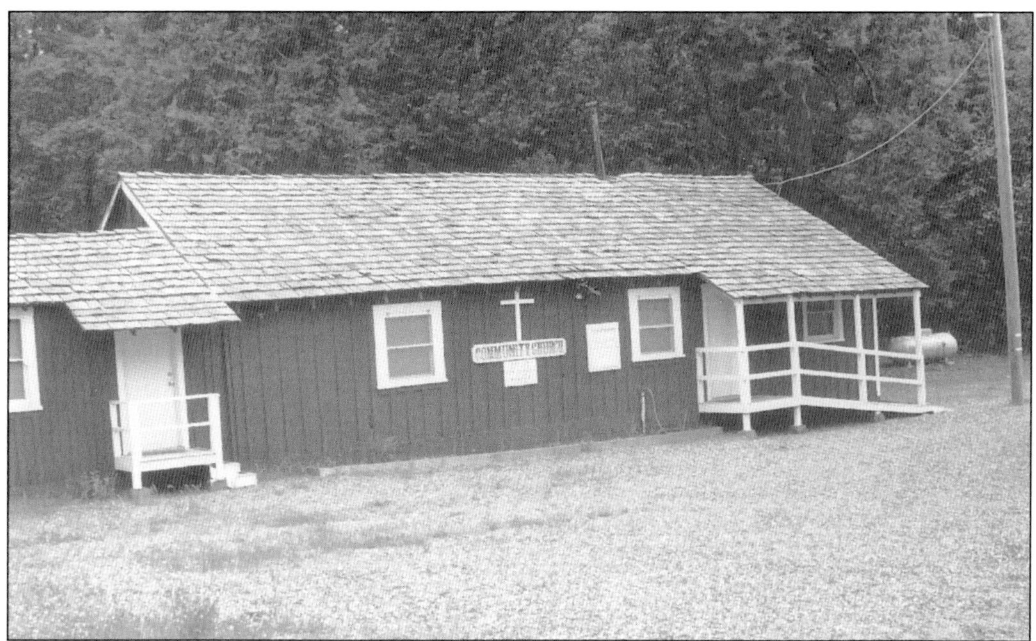

Feather Falls Village had one church, and it was called the Little Brown Church. It was located right across Lumpkin Road from the Feather Falls School. As can be assumed, it was originally brown, but by the time this photograph was taken in the late 1980s, it had been painted red with white trim just like all the other village buildings. (Courtesy of MW.)

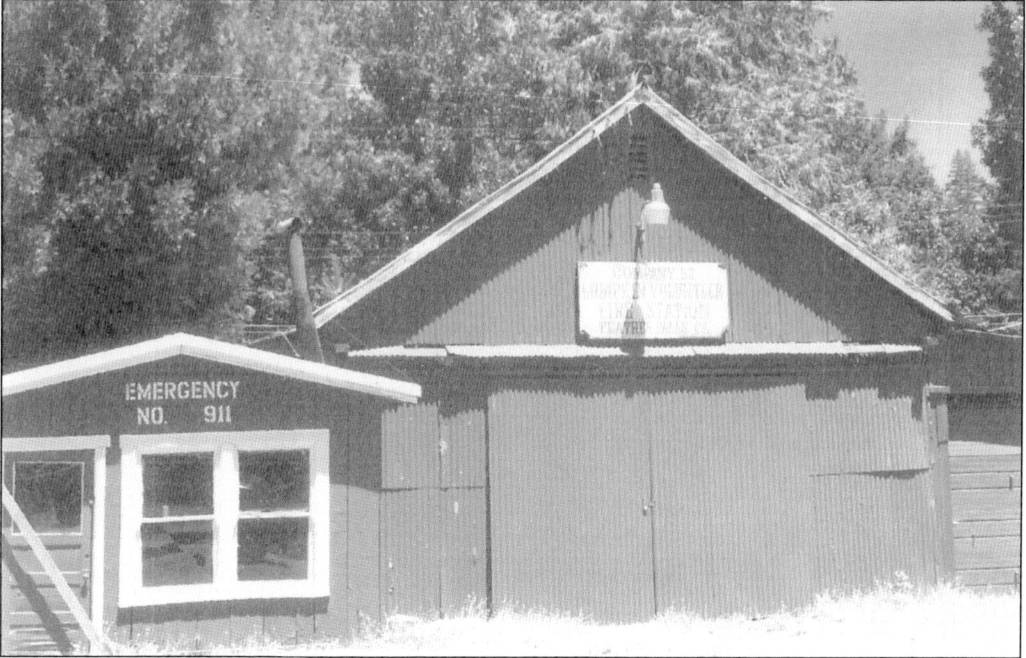

This view shows the Boy Scout hall and the fire truck garage in the 1970s. Scouting was popular in the area from the 1950s to the 1970s. There were usually 20 to 25 boys enrolled at any given time. The volunteer fire department also consisted of about 25 members. The fire truck was kept in this garage at night, then moved to the mill during the daytime. (Courtesy of MW.)

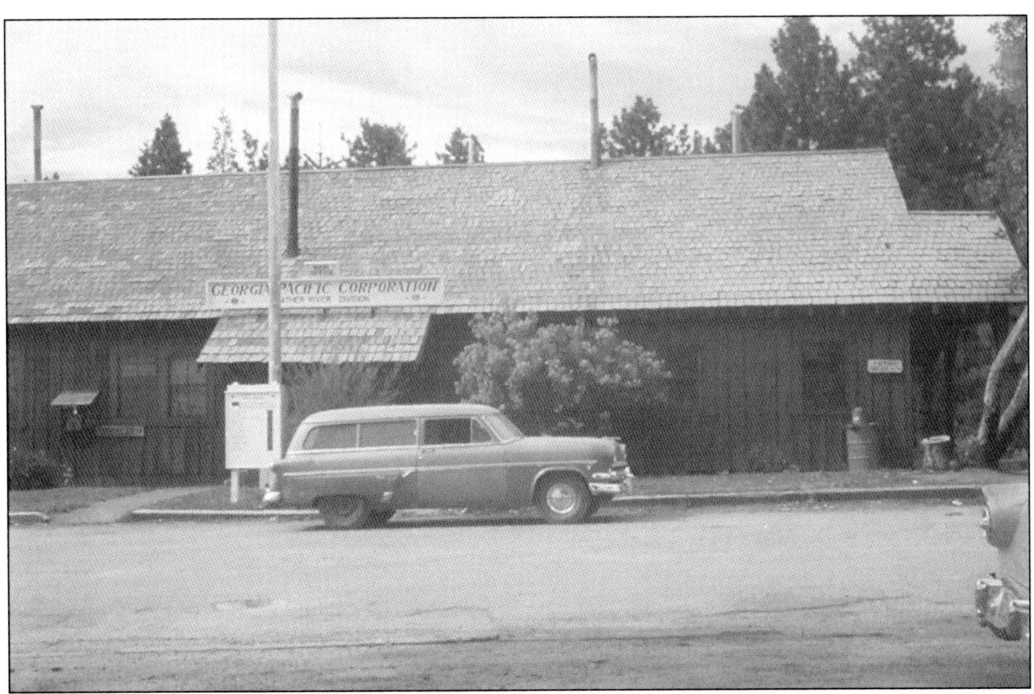

Due to changing circumstances over the years, some of the community buildings took on different looks and uses. Above is the Georgia-Pacific Corporation office in 1963. The station wagon sitting in front of the building had operated as the Feather Falls Ambulance from 1954 to 1960. During that time, at least three children were born within the confines of that vehicle. By the time this photograph was taken, a Georgia-Pacific employee had bought it to serve as a private vehicle. Below is the same building in the mid-1980s. After the Louisiana-Pacific Corporation took over, the building was renamed the Feather Falls Town Hall. (Above, courtesy of WFC; below, courtesy of MW.)

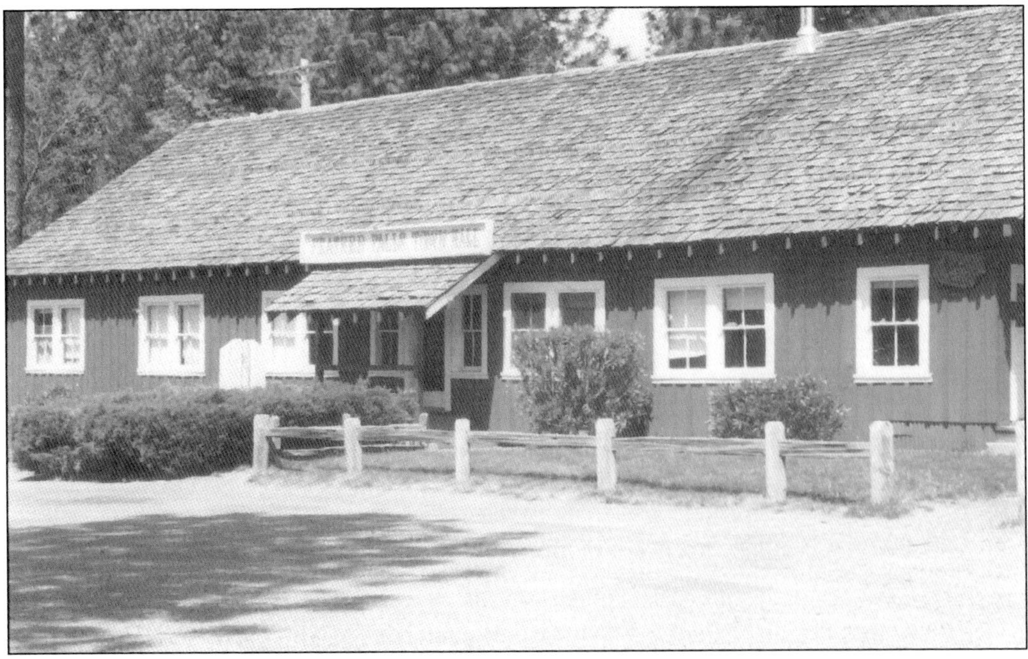

Here is another example of a building whose appearance was changed for a different use or a different business name. At right, the structure is seen in the 1960s as the U-Drop In that advertised itself as a grocery, café, and bar. Below, the same building has now become the Feather Falls Eating and Drinking Establishment in the 1970s. The parking lot looks pretty busy that day. It is not known why the Paradise Union School District bus was there. Perhaps it was to ferry students to Feather Falls for a sporting event or for a hike to the falls. (Right, courtesy of MW; below, courtesy of BCHS.)

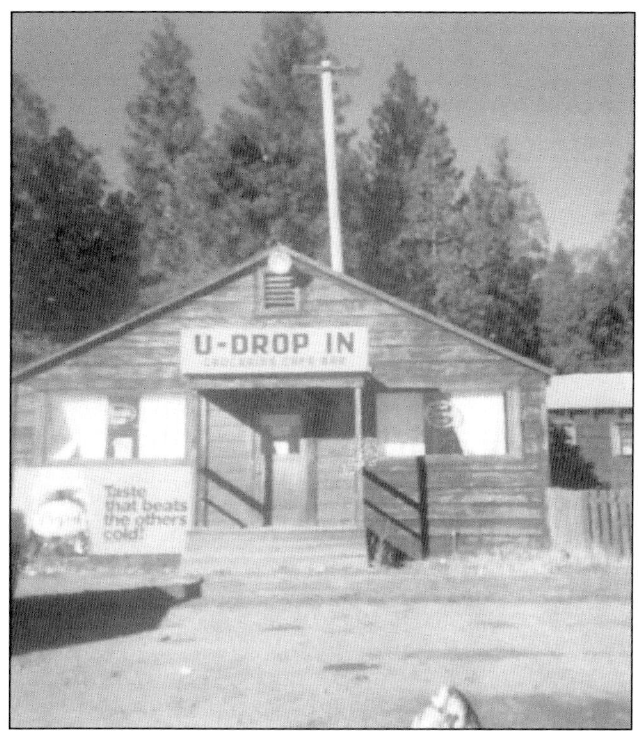

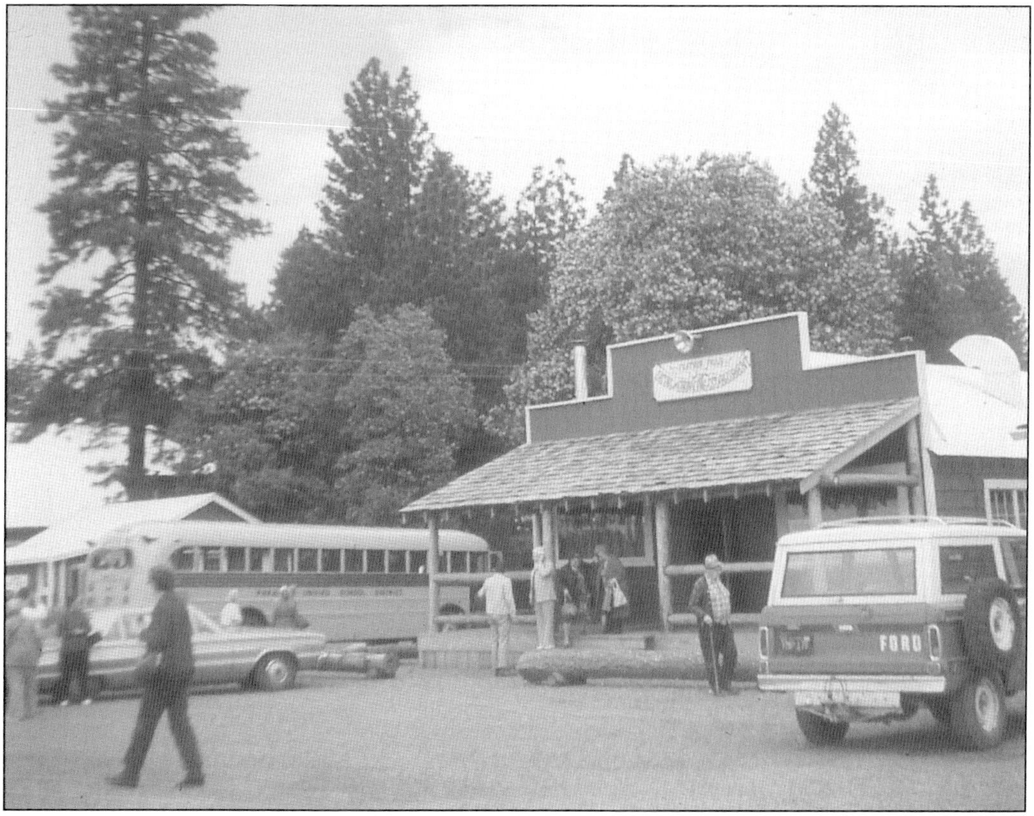

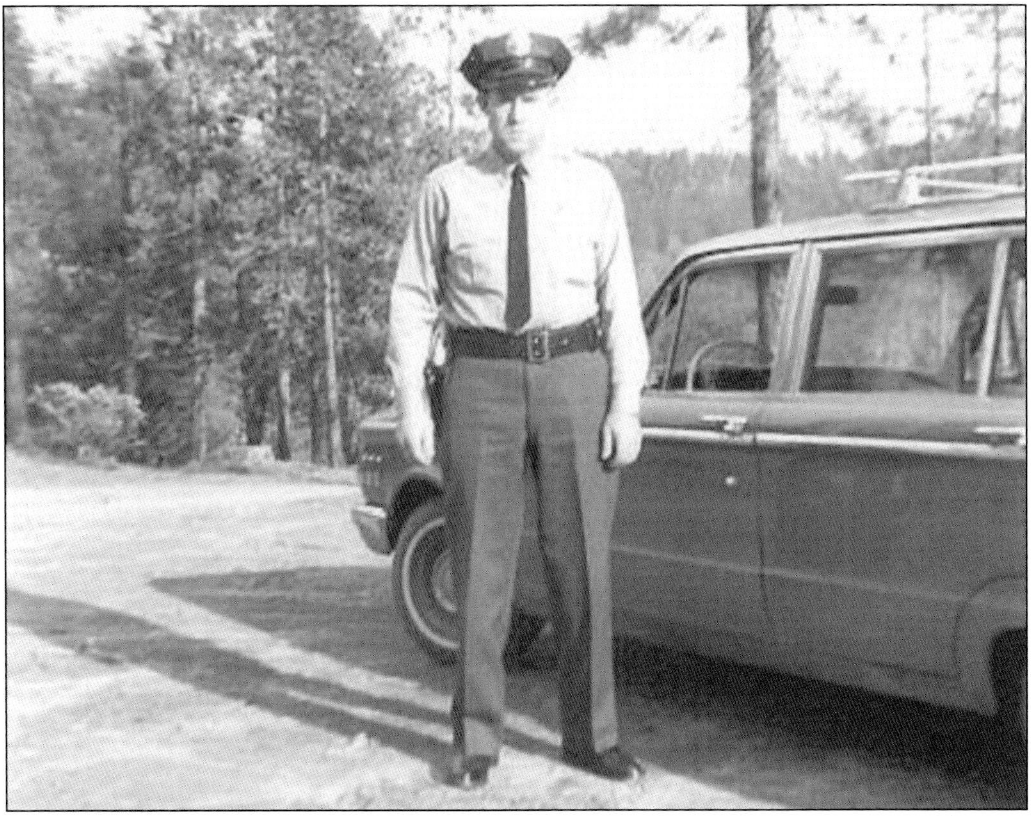

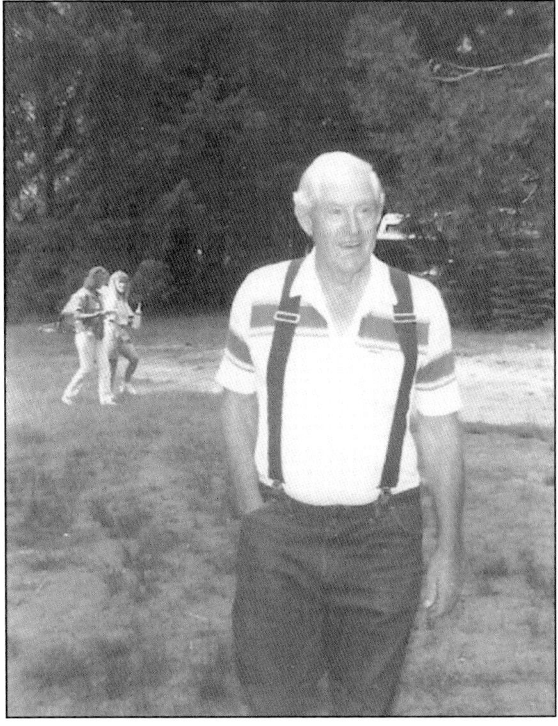

Jessie "Rookie" Davis was one of the best-known and most respected members of the Feather Falls family. He served as the part-time deputy sheriff for the area for 28 years, from 1948 to 1976. As part of his duties, Davis would patrol the road from Feather Falls to Enterprise each night. He is remembered as a tough but fair law enforcement officer. The photograph above shows him in his Butte County Sheriff's Office uniform in 1962. The photograph at left was taken at a 1983 Feather Falls reunion at Fall River Crossing. In addition to serving in the US Army during World War II, Davis worked for the Civilian Conservation Corps, Feather River Pine Mills, and Louisiana-Pacific. He passed away at age 96 on January 2, 2015. (Above, courtesy of Davis family; left, courtesy of Mollie Fitzsimmons.)

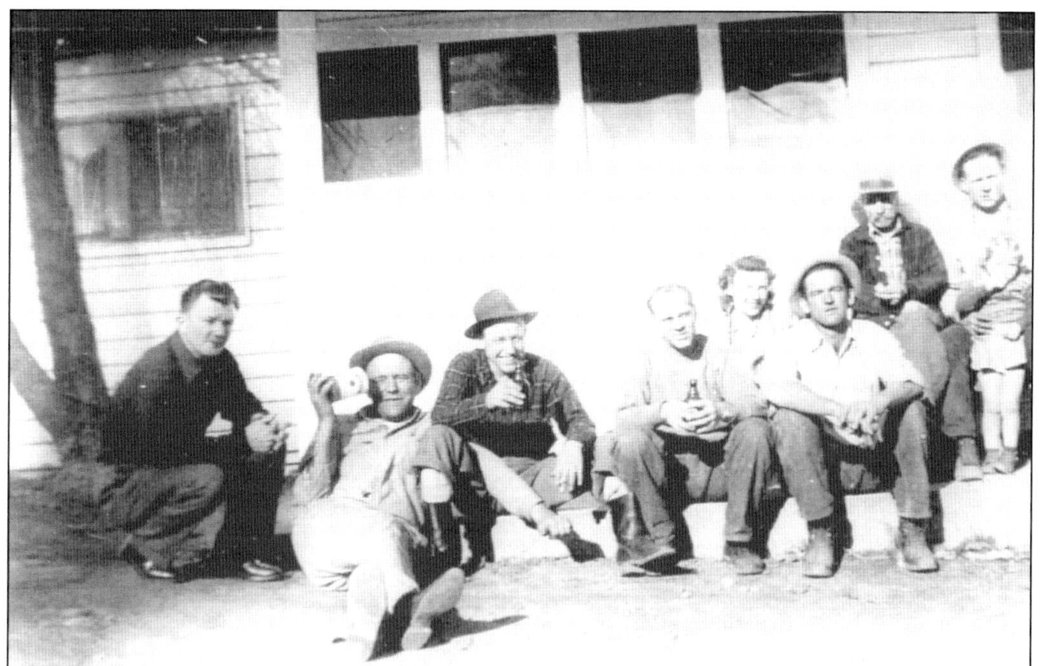

The 76 Bar and gas station was located on Lumpkin Road, about two miles west of Feather Falls Village. A few of the locals are pictured above in 1944. From left to right are Roy Hale, "Ole Jake" (aka "Kilowatt"), Tom Bigelow, Skee Burdick, Juanita Edwards, Si Edwards, Tom Boney, Norman Whittier, and the child, Viola "Cookie" Edwards. Roy Alston, owner of the 76 Bar and gas station, is shown in a photograph taken on August 1, 1948. Today, it is hard to tell that any building ever stood at this location. (Both, courtesy of MW.)

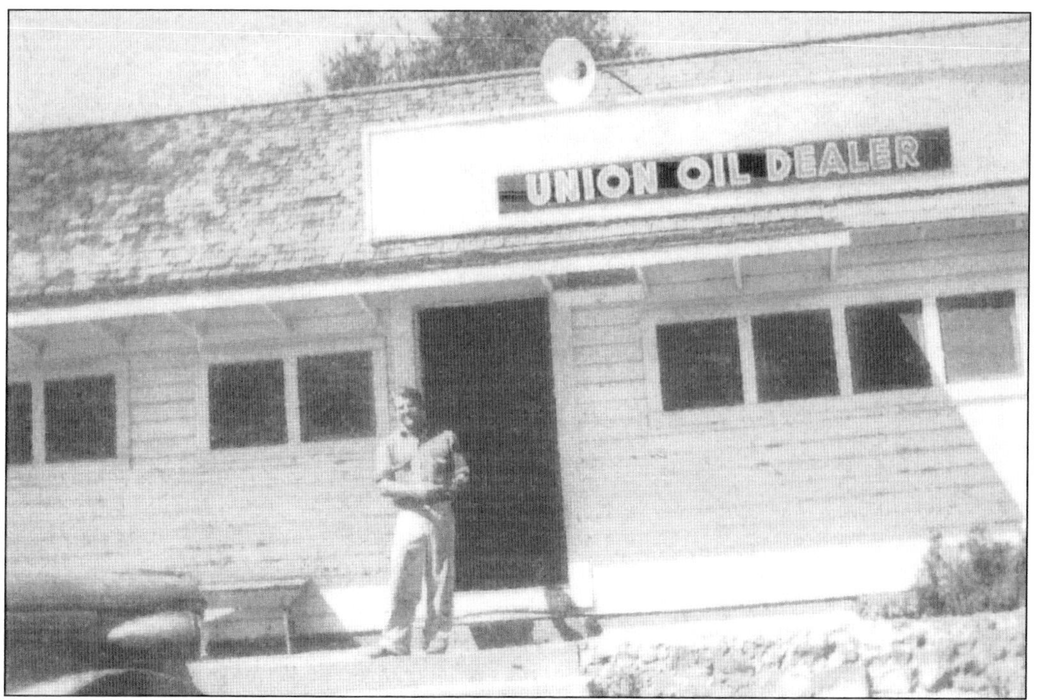

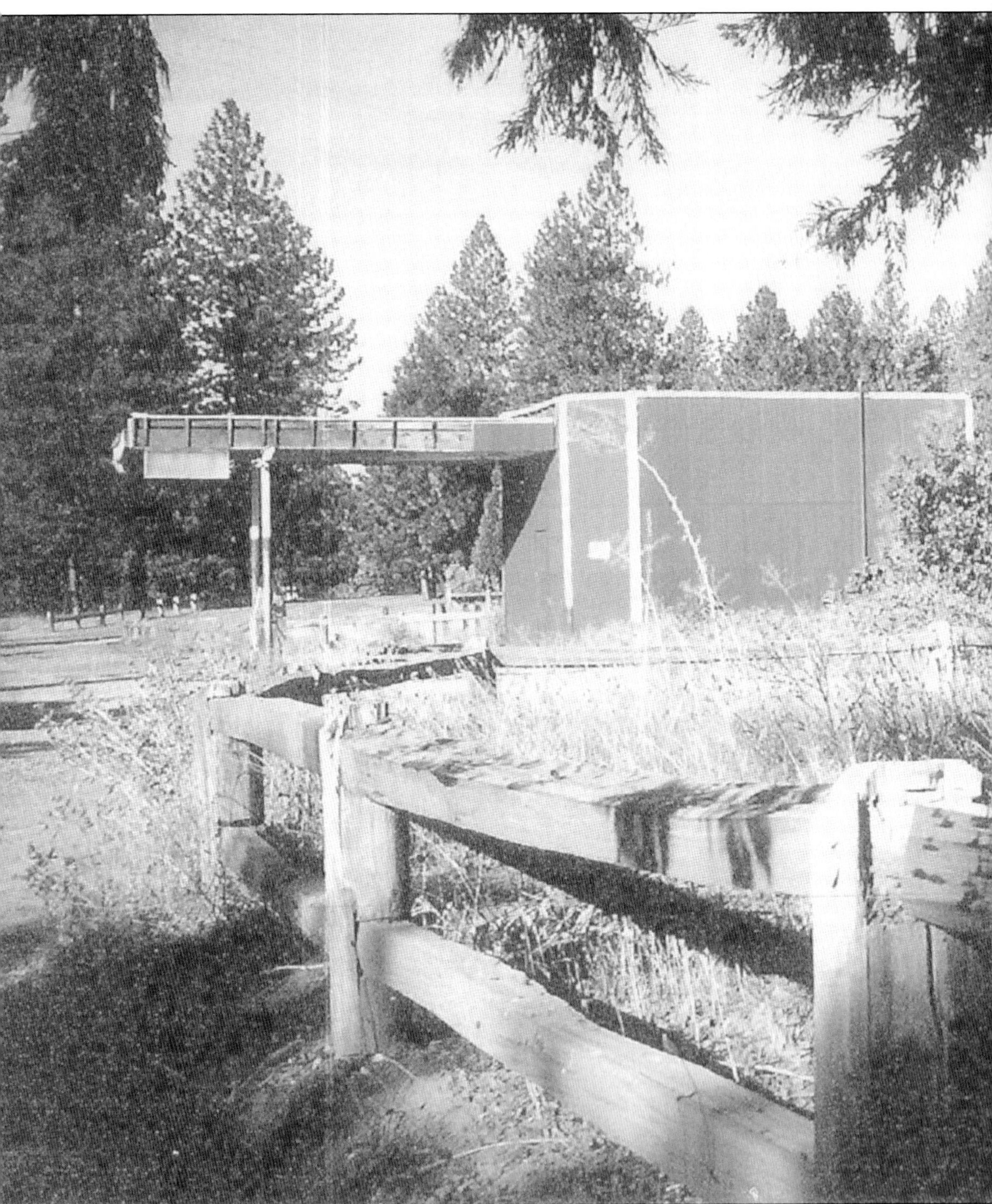

April 1, 1994, was a memorable day for the residents of Feather Falls Village. On that day, they received a certified letter advising them that they had 75 days to vacate their rented cottages. At that time, 25 families were living in the village and paying about $40 per month in rent. Many residents had spent most of their lives there. The Louisiana-Pacific Corporation had decided to get out of

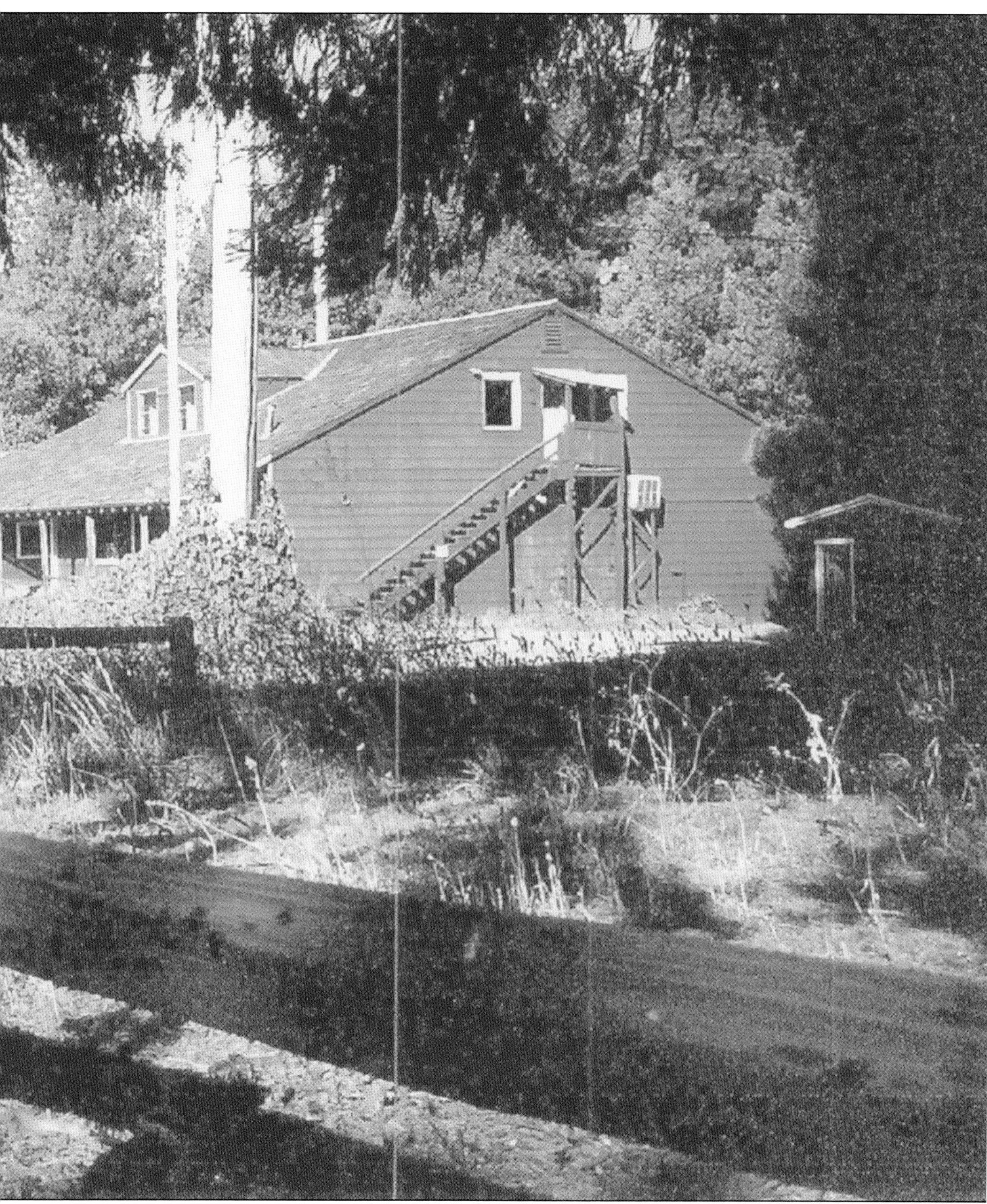

the landlord business, level the 60-acre community, and revert the area back to timber-growing lands. This photograph shows the gas station and store just a few days prior to their destruction. (Courtesy of WFC.)

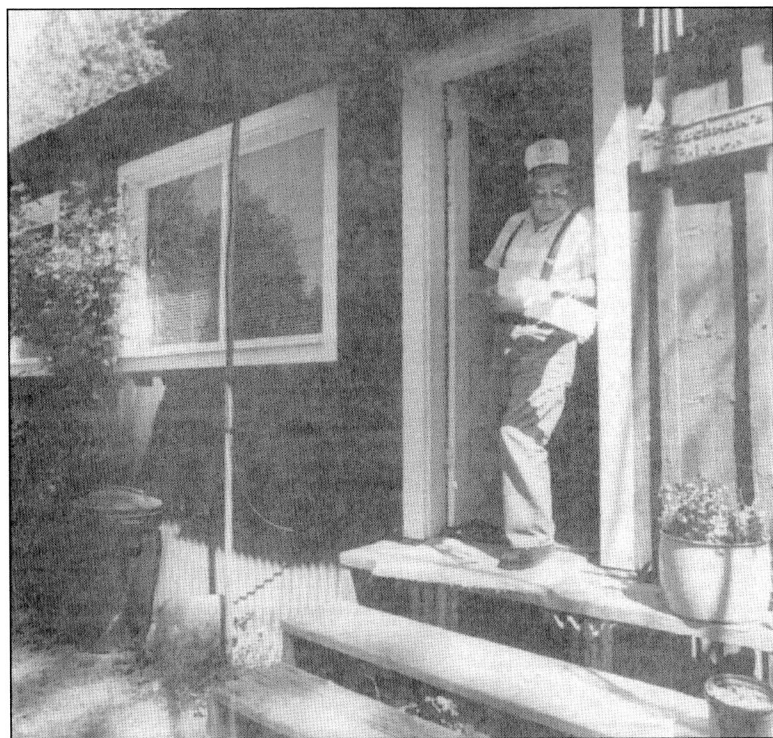

Walter H. Buschman stands on the front porch of his home in early April 1994. He is reading the certified letter that he just received notifying him to vacate his cottage home by June 15, 1994. Some residents were on a fixed income, and the prospect of having to move was daunting. (Courtesy of ER.)

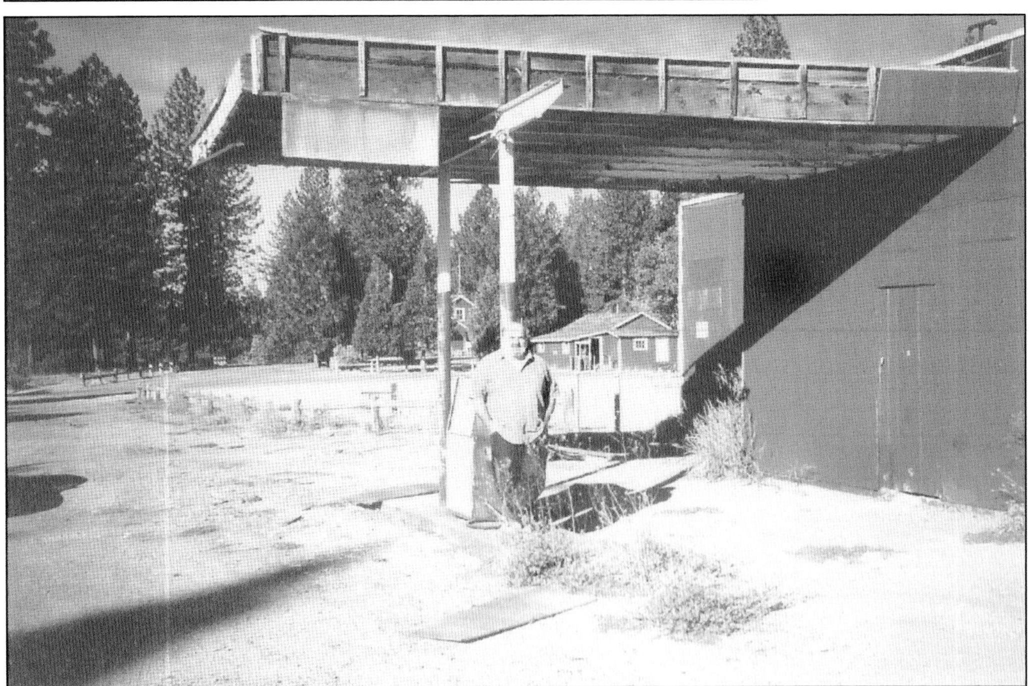

A few days prior to the destruction of the main town buildings, Ken Wheeler stands at the very spot where his brother Joe stands in a photograph from 1949, when his family owned and managed the gas station (see page 84). The post office and community center are visible behind him. The family ran the station for 16 years. (Courtesy of WFC.)

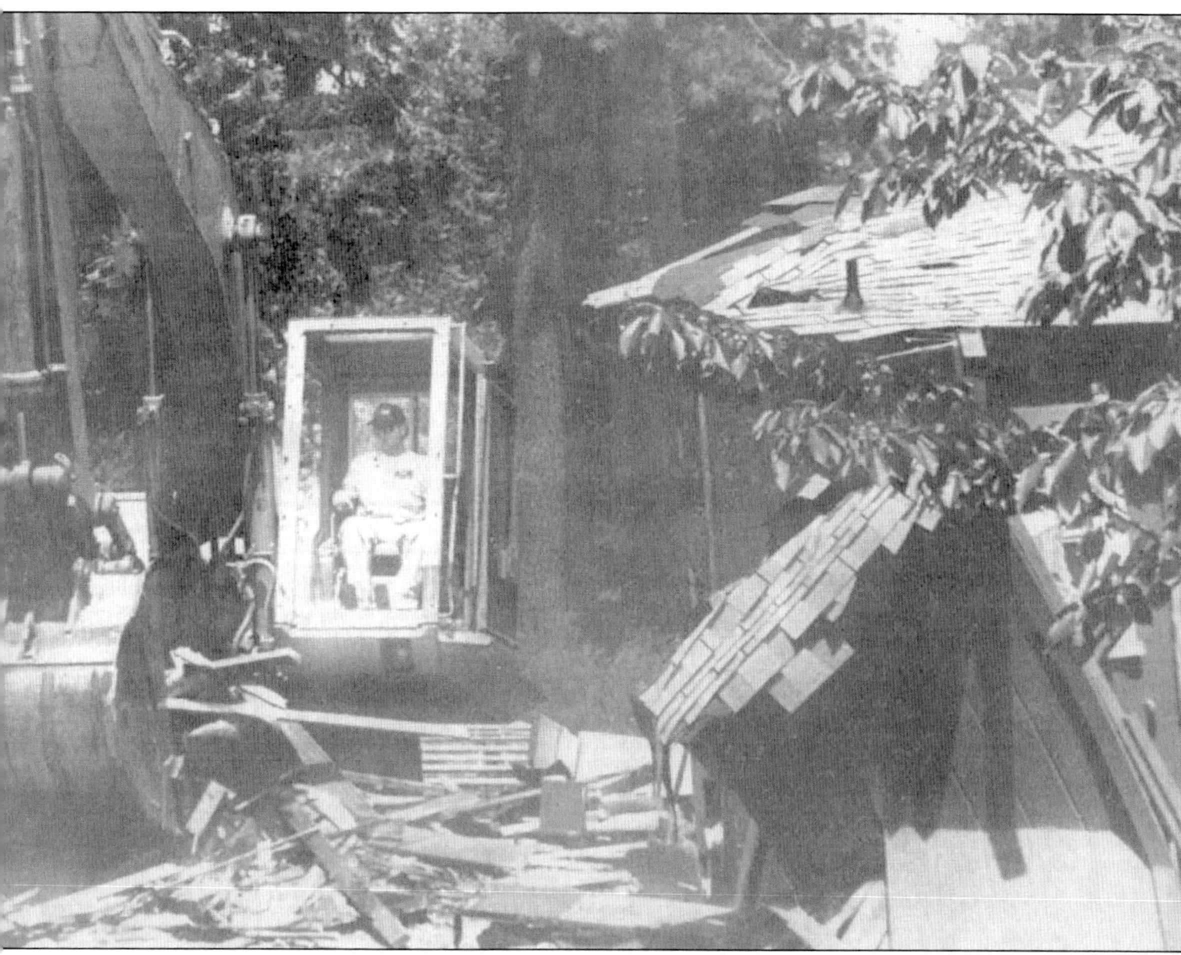

It was the beginning of the end when destruction came to a Feather Falls cottage on May 23, 1994. A bulldozer shreds a building down to the ground. Over the next several months, more than 50 wood-frame homes would be leveled, along with the church, gas station, store and café building, post office, main office, and utility buildings. Soon, the only building standing would be the old barnlike cat shop across the road from the village. The cat shop, the concrete slab for the gas station, and the concrete vault for the main office can still be found today. (Courtesy of ER.)

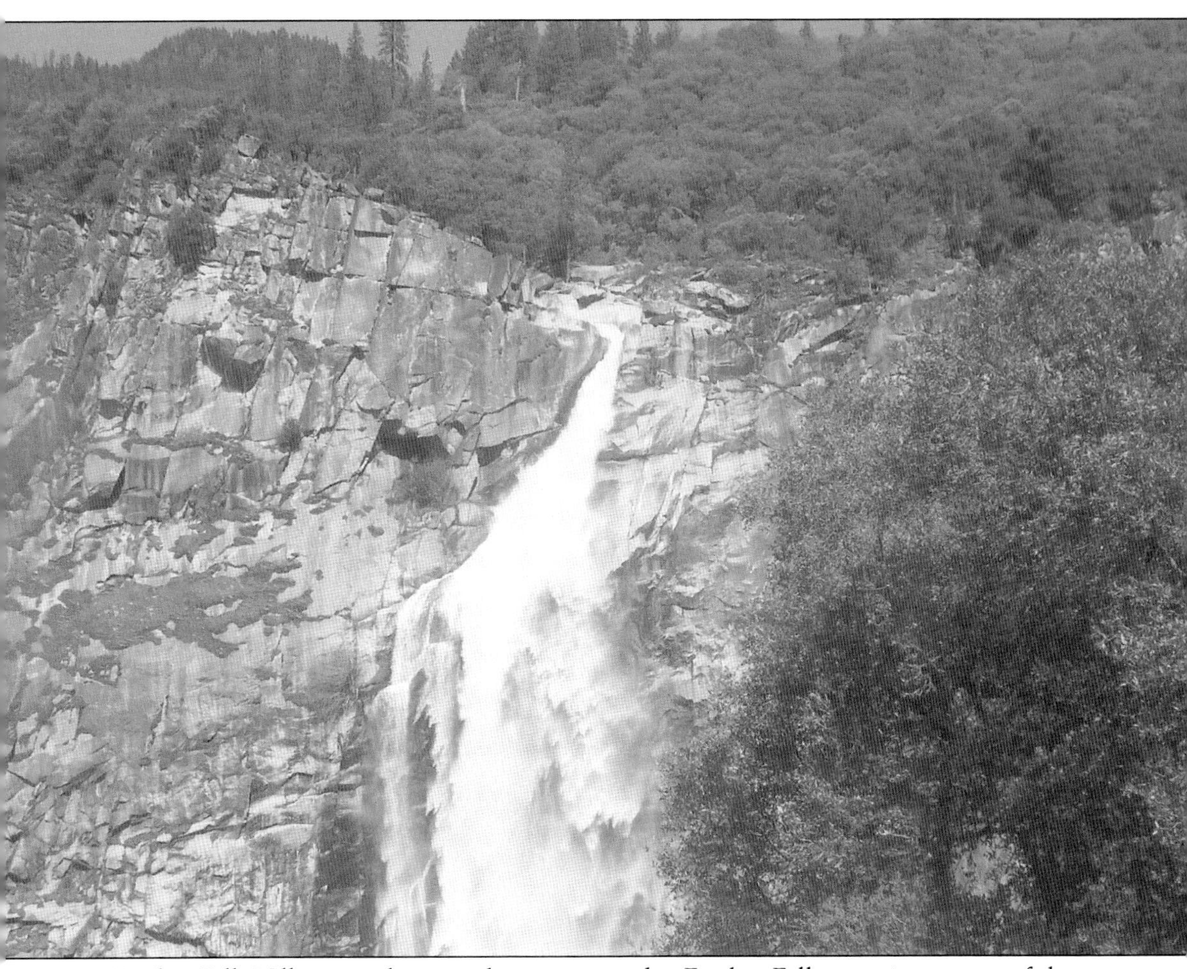

Feather Falls Village may be gone, but its namesake, Feather Falls, remains as one of the most beautiful and majestic natural gems in California. The Fall River feeds the falls, which are shaped like a feather. For many years, it had been estimated that the falls were 640 feet tall. Measurements made by waterfall photographer Leon Turnbull in 2008 seem to confirm its height at 410 feet. He used a laser range finder and clinometer to measure the height of the falls. Regardless of its height, the waterfall is gorgeous, and the eight-mile round-trip hike through lush vegetation is a once-in-a-lifetime experience. (Authors' collection.)

Five

Saving Historic Icons

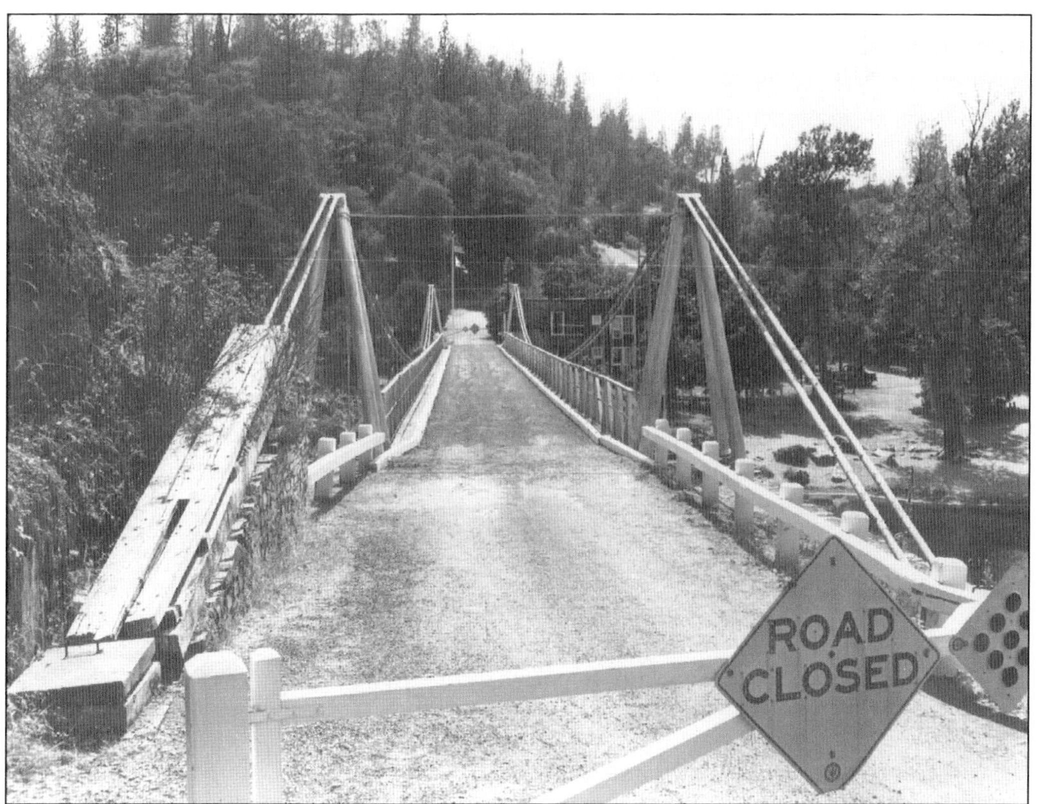

In July 1964, time was running short for the Bidwell Bar suspension bridge, the old tollhouse, and the Mother Orange Tree. That summer would mark an effort resulting in the removal and preservation of all three of the historic icons at Bidwell Bar. This photograph shows one last look at the old suspension bridge before its dismantling. (Courtesy of BCPW.)

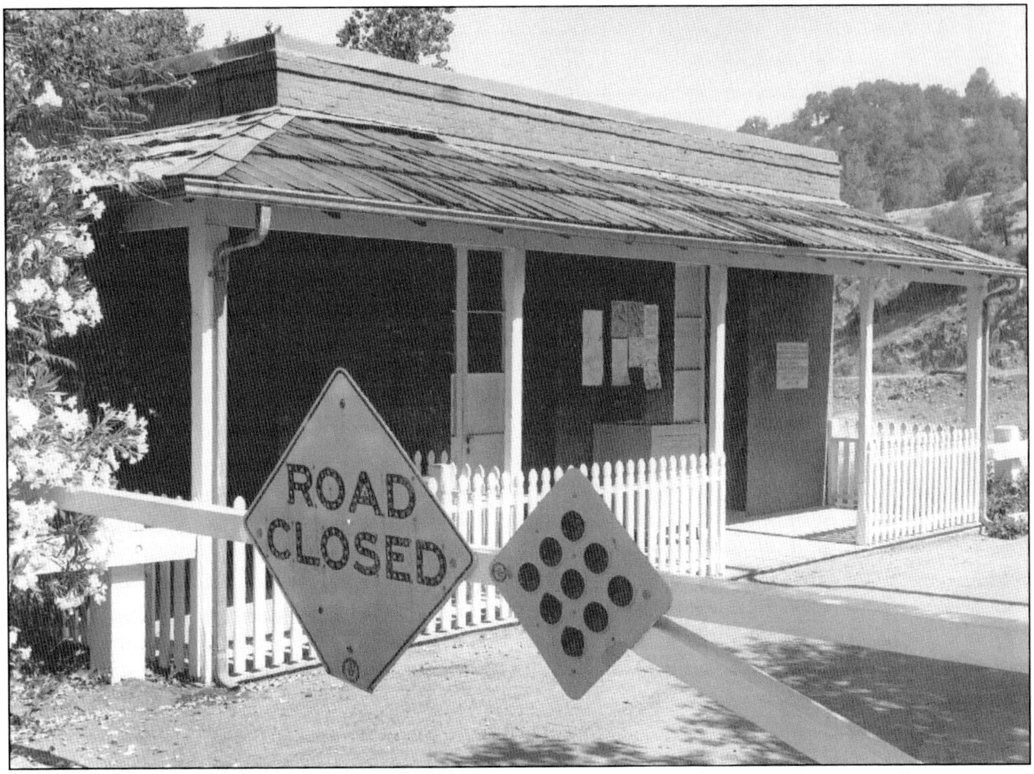

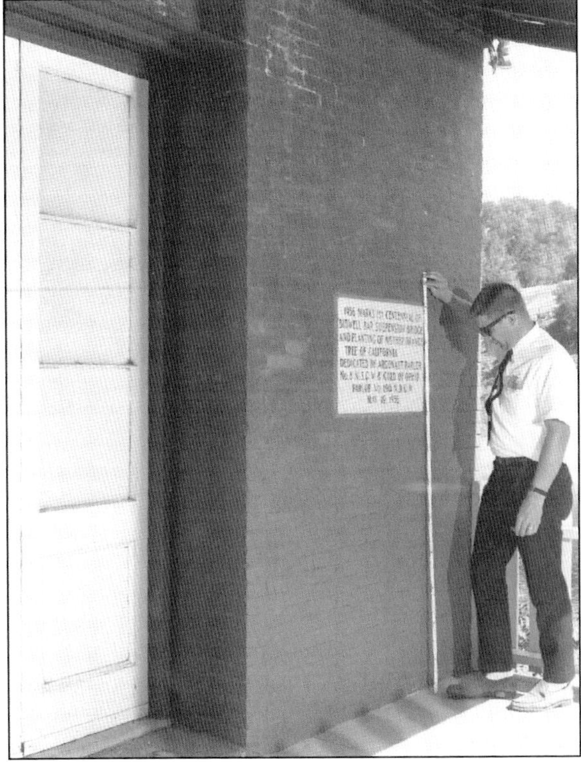

These photographs were taken on July 6, 1964. Above, the front of the Bidwell Bar Bridge Tollhouse is seen. The tollhouse, along with the suspension bridge, had been in service at that location since 1856. At left, an unidentified man is shown measuring a portion of the outside of the tollhouse. The plaque next to him commemorates the 100th anniversary of the suspension bridge and the original planting of the orange tree. The ceremony had taken place on May 19, 1956. (Both, courtesy of BCPW.)

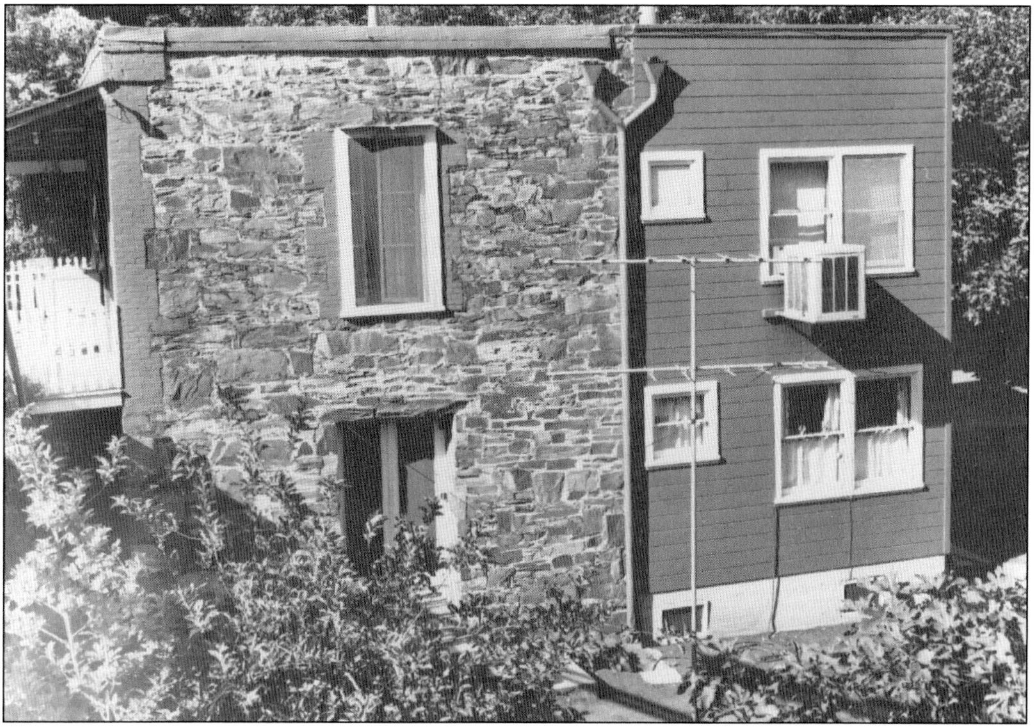

Here are two more views of the tollhouse from July 6, 1964. Above, the north side of the old tollhouse can be seen. Below, the back, or west side, of the building is shown. The tollhouse was a two-story building that measured approximately 25 feet by 30 feet. The tollhouse was necessary to collect the fee for crossing the bridge from 1856 to 1883. There was a charge of 10¢ per pedestrian and 25¢ for a horse and rider. Teams and wagons were charged according to the size of the load. (Both, courtesy of BCPW.)

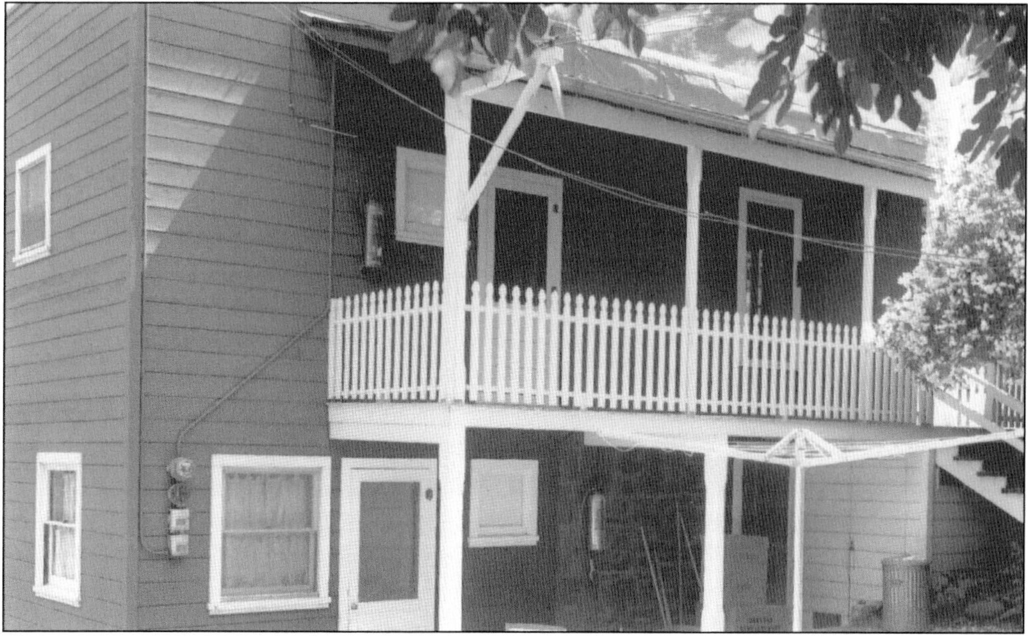

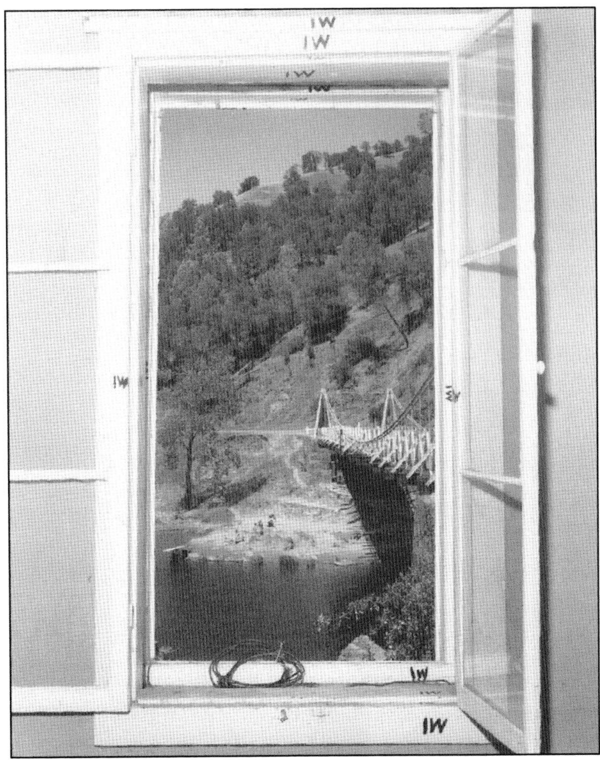

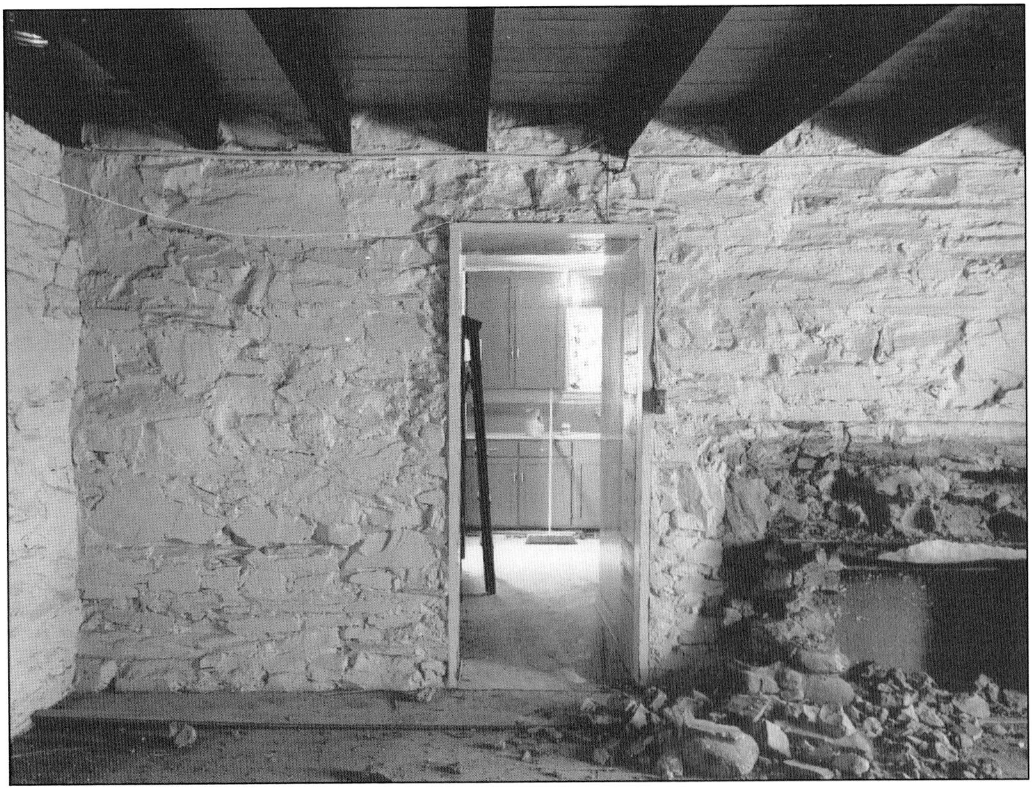

These interior views of the Bidwell Bar Tollhouse are from July 8, 1964. Every piece of the tollhouse was marked with numbers and catalogued for future reassembly of the building. At left is a view showing some of those identification numbers, as well as a look at the old suspension bridge out the window to the north. Even during that time when the tollhouse and bridge were being prepared for removal, people came to enjoy one final summer at the Curry-Bidwell Bar State Park. Below is a rare look into the living room and kitchen area of the tollhouse. The crumbling fireplace can be seen as well. (Both, courtesy of BCPW.)

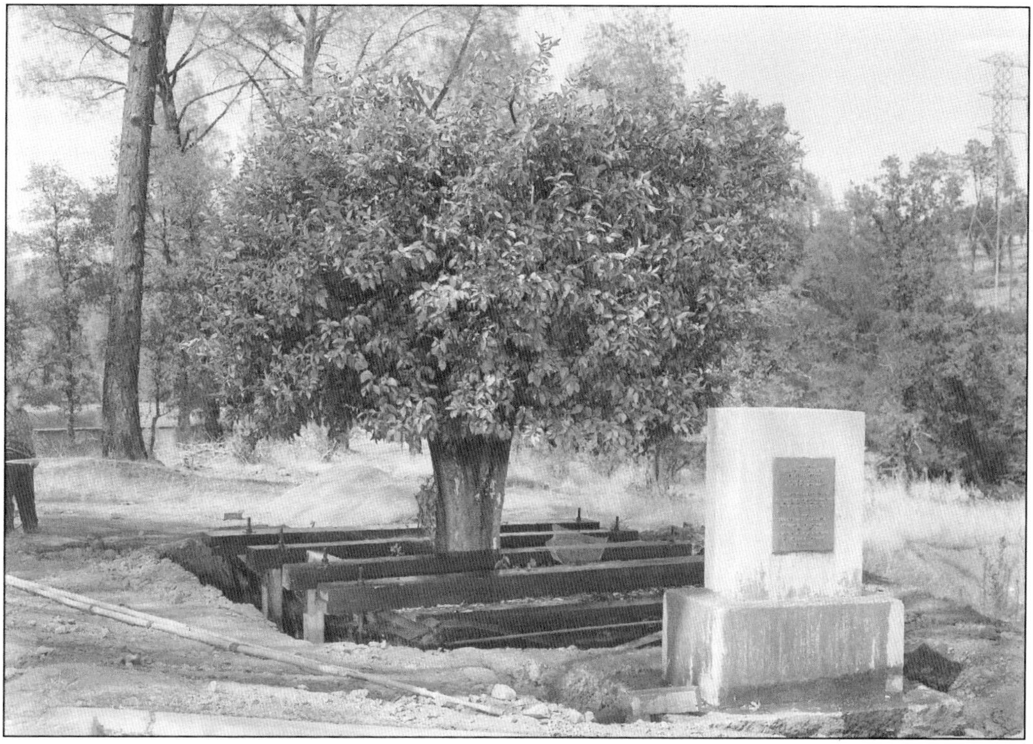

These are two views of the Mother Orange Tree on August 4, 1964, the day it was removed from the canyon. Above, the tree has been prepared for movement. In front of it stands the plaque from the 70th-anniversary ceremony in 1926. Its base was reinforced with timbers so that it could be safely raised from the place in which it had resided and flourished for more than 100 years. At right, the tree is slowly raised out of the ground. Some spectators have gathered to watch the historic event. (Both, courtesy of CDWR.)

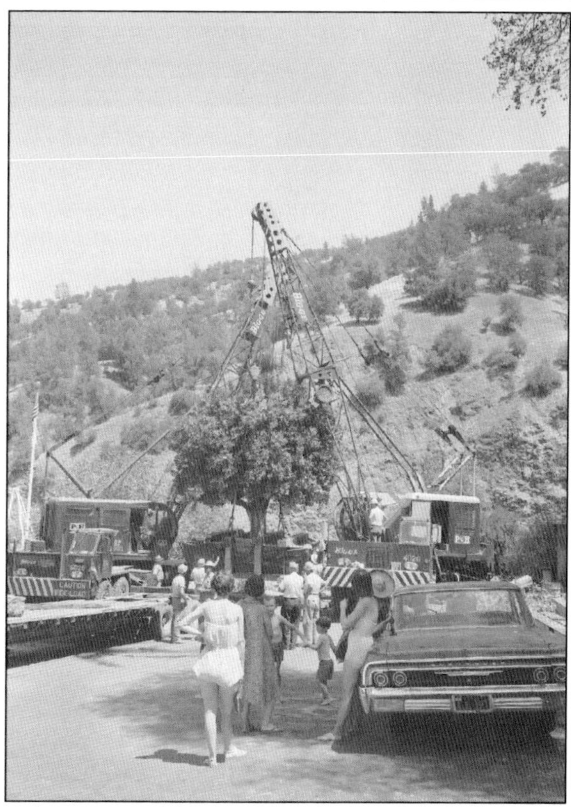

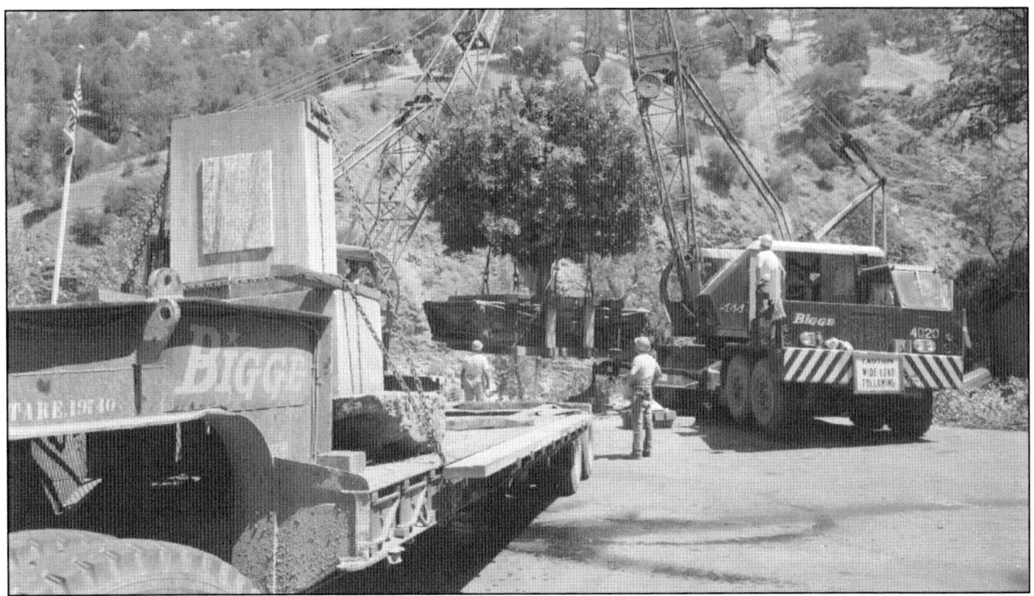

Both of these photographs were taken on August 4, 1964. Above, the Mother Orange Tree is lifted higher and is about to be loaded onto the truck for transportation. Below, the tree has made the six-mile journey from the canyon to 400 Glen Drive and is about to be lowered into its new home. The new facilities of the California Department of Parks and Recreation are seen under construction behind it. The Mother Orange Tree continues to thrive at this site. (Both, courtesy of CDWR.)

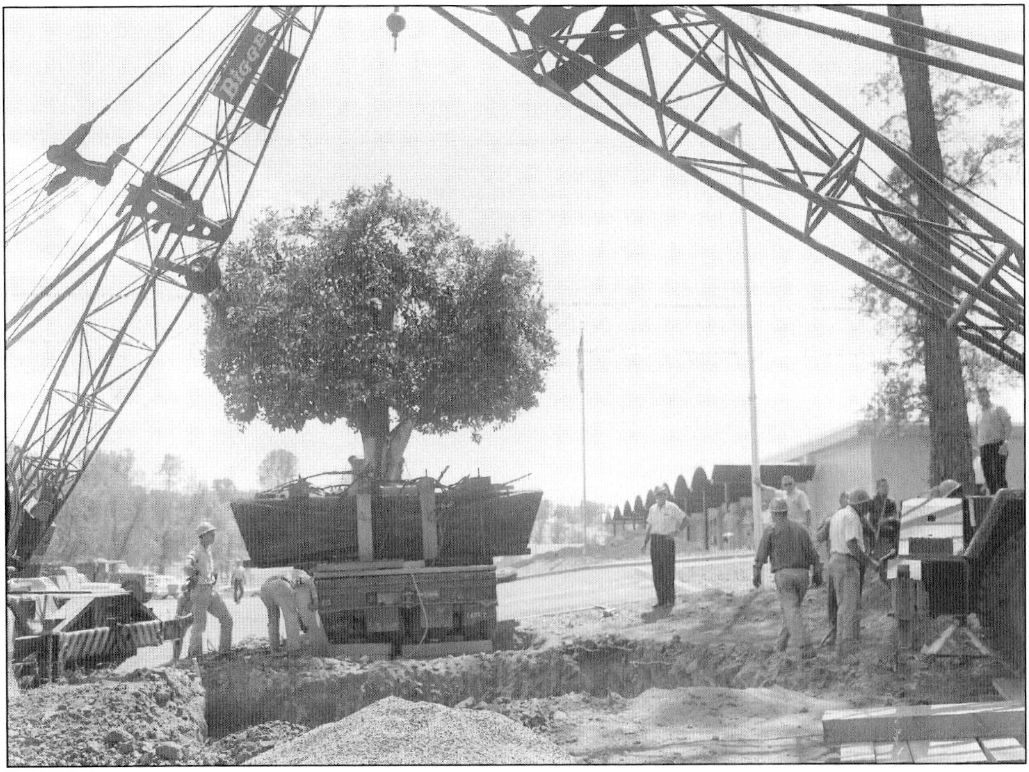

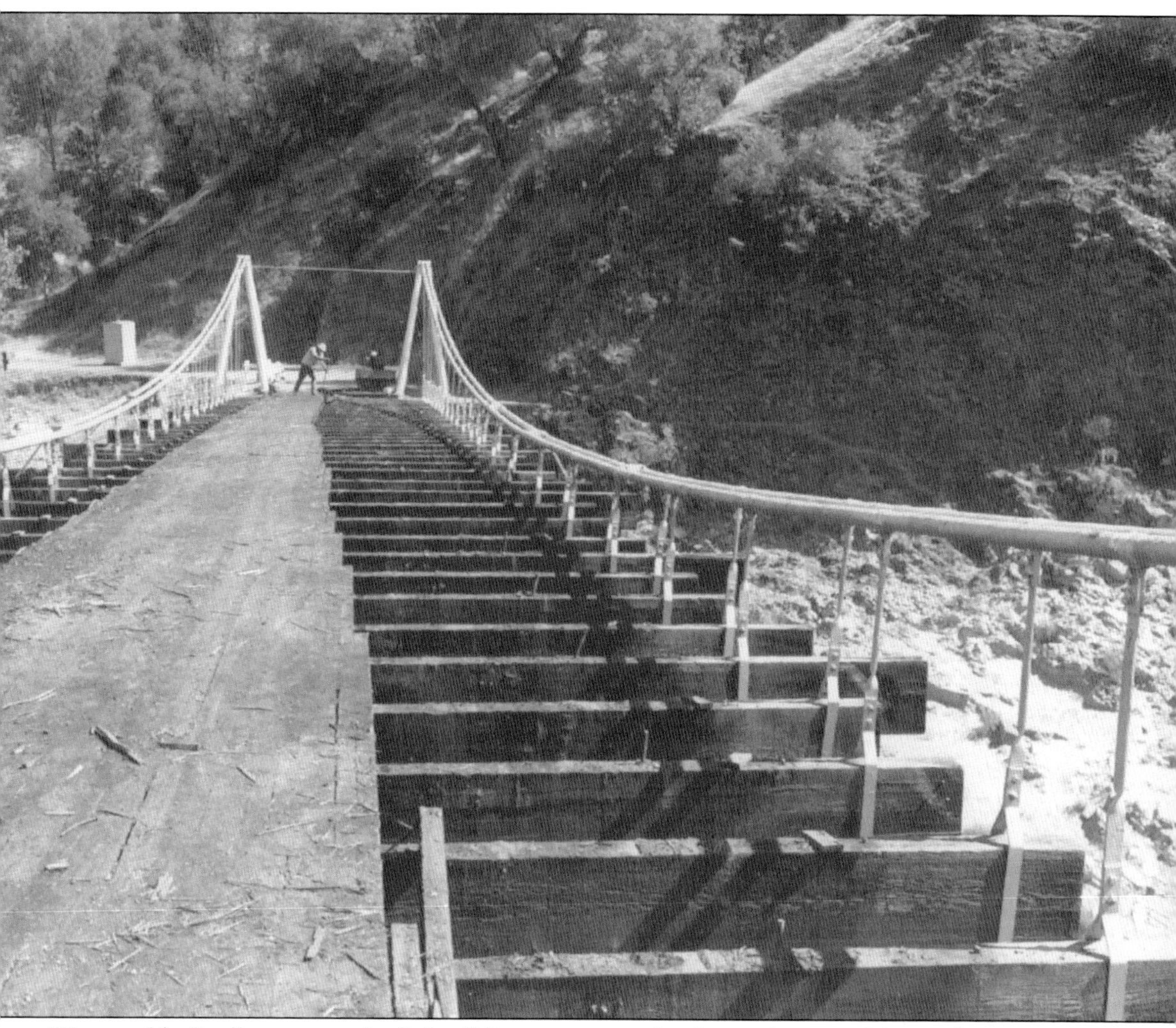

Disassembly finally came to the Bidwell Bar suspension bridge in August 1964. In this view, a worker is shown at the far north end of the bridge removing sections of the 108-year-old wooden roadbed. It looks like about half of the 240-foot roadway has been removed. It was hoped that, after a few years of storage, both the bridge and the tollhouse would be moved to a safe location and reassembled. But it would be a much longer wait than anyone had predicted. (Courtesy of BCPW.)

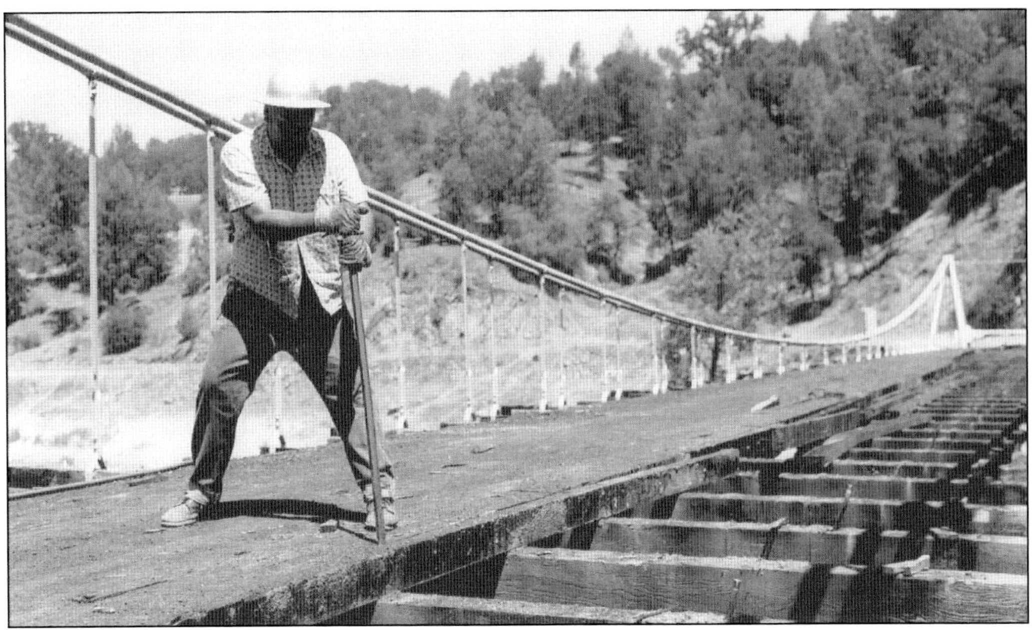

Both of these photographs from August 1964 show views looking toward the north. Above, dismantling of the bridge continues as a worker pries off another piece of the roadway. Below, disassembly has progressed to the point where the roadway has been removed except for the north end of the bridge. That part continues to hang from the bridge's suspension cables. The workers use an overhead crane to remove a piece of the bridge. (Both, courtesy of BCPW.)

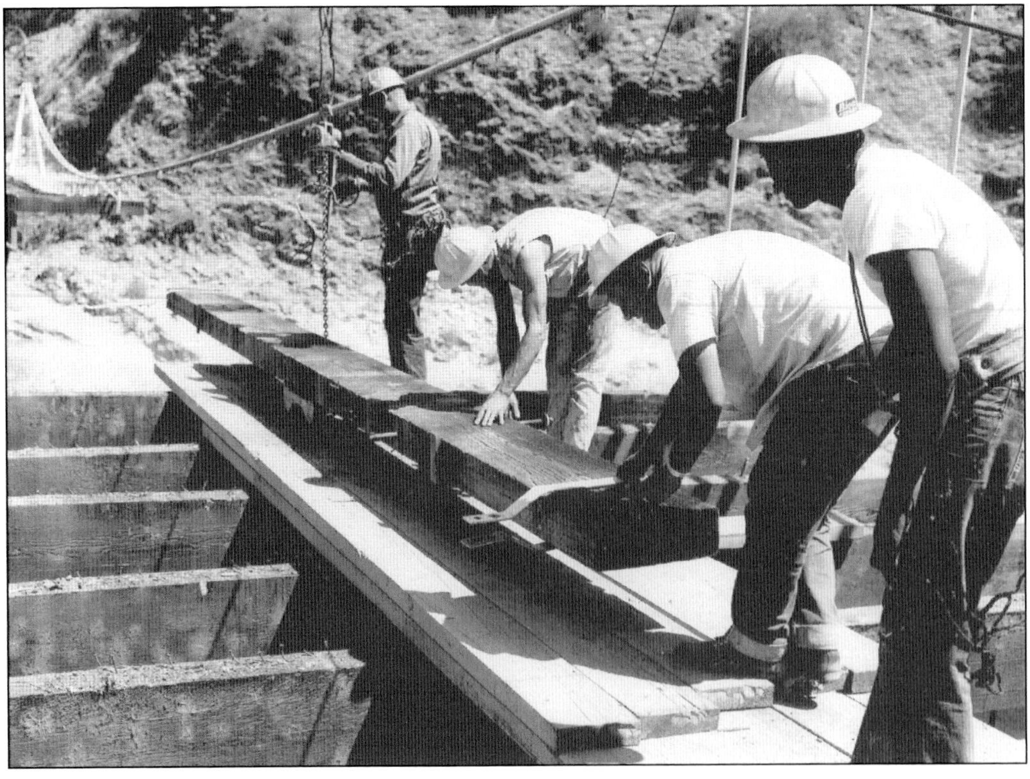

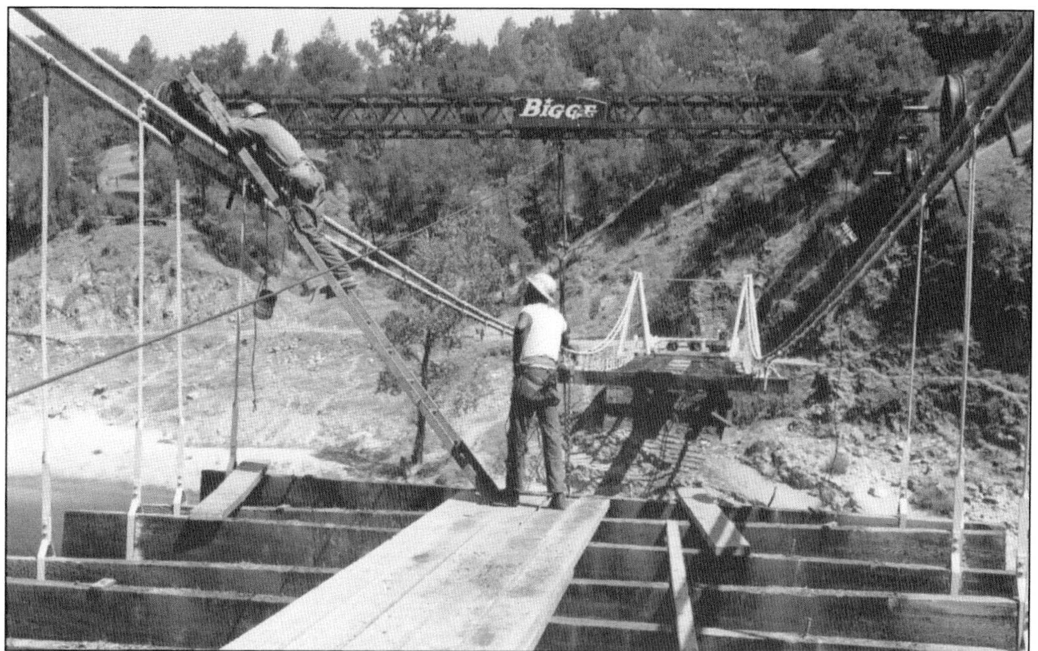

The crane that was used to disassemble the bridge is seen in these two views from August 1964. It ran across the old bridge cables. Above, one worker appears to be in a rather dangerous position on a ladder near where the crane sits on the cables. Below, a worker is operating the crane cable to lift a portion of the bridge at the north end. Judge Joseph Lewis paid most of the $34,922 to construct the bridge, which was made of wood, wrought iron, and cast iron. (Both, courtesy of BCPW.)

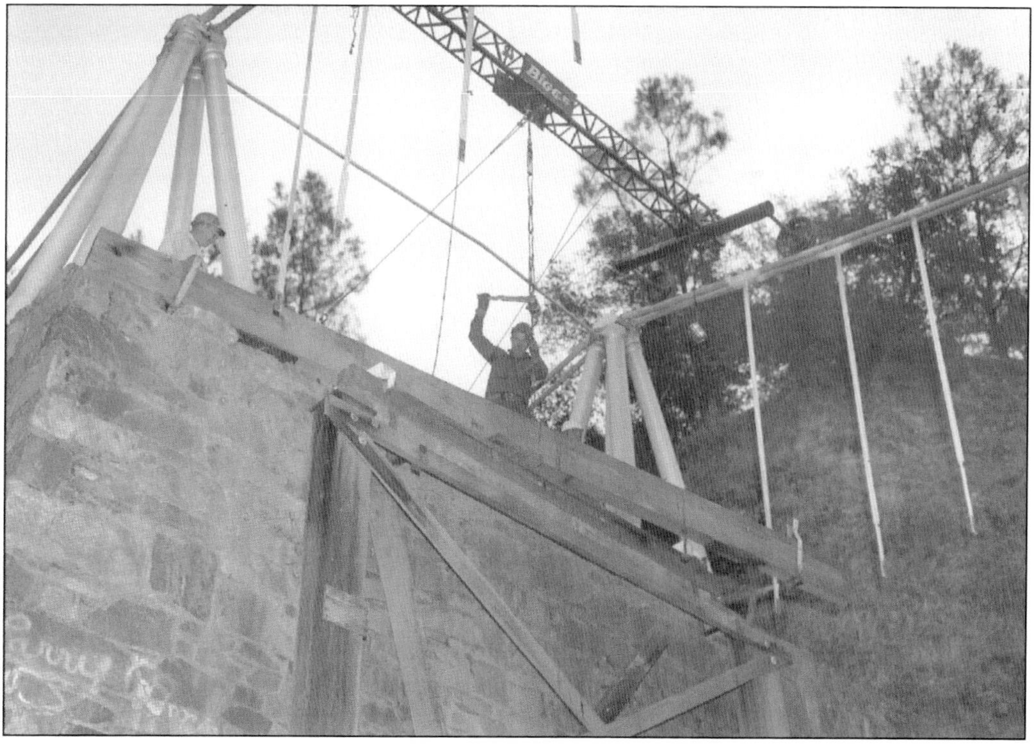

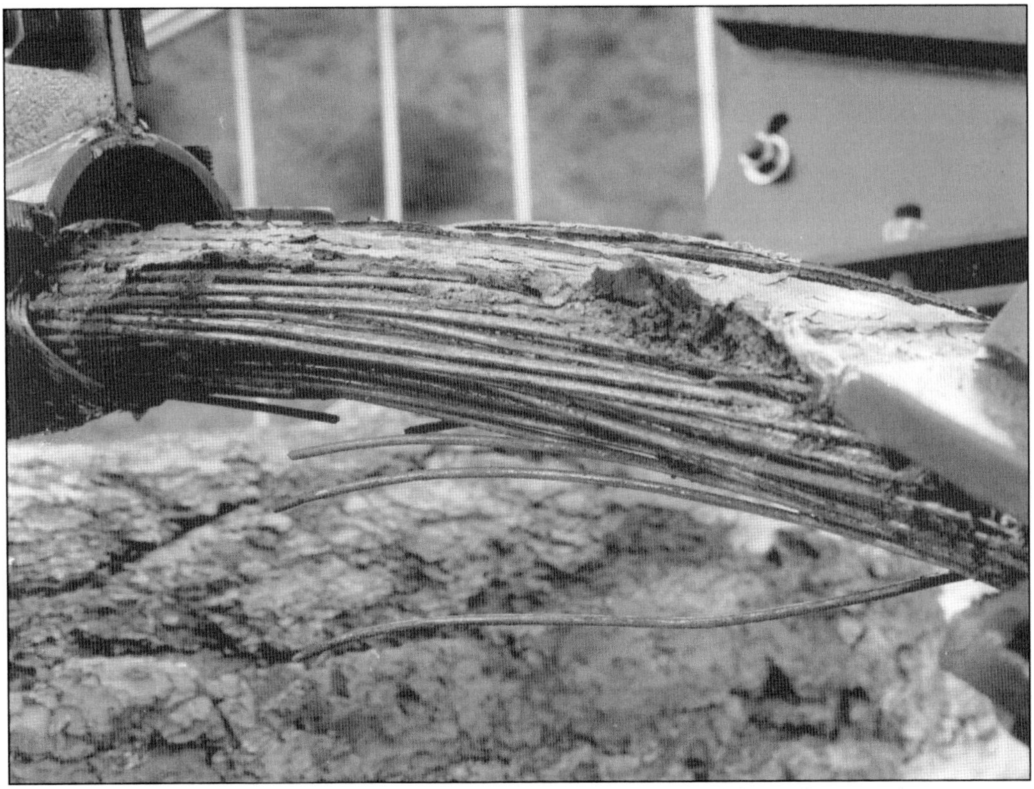

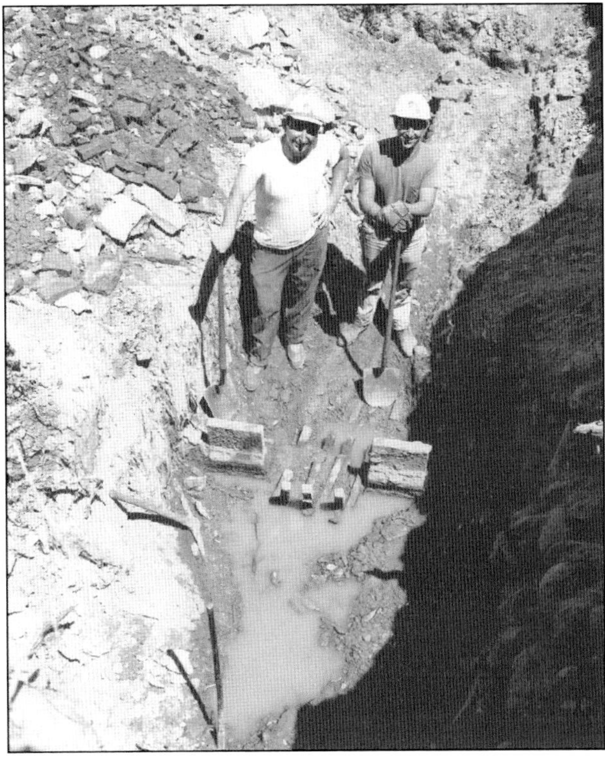

Both of these photographs were taken in August 1964. Above is a close-up view of one of the old bridge cables. At left are two unidentified workers at one of the anchors for the bridge cables. There were four cables on the bridge, with two on each side. Each cable was seven inches in diameter and made up of about 300 No. 10 wires wrapped in wrought iron wire and painted. The cables were anchored to bronze bent bars. The Jones and Murray Company of Sacramento assembled the bridge, the main parts of which were manufactured by Starbucks Iron Works in Troy, New York. They were carried by ship to California around Cape Horn, at the tip of South America. (Both, courtesy of BCPW.)

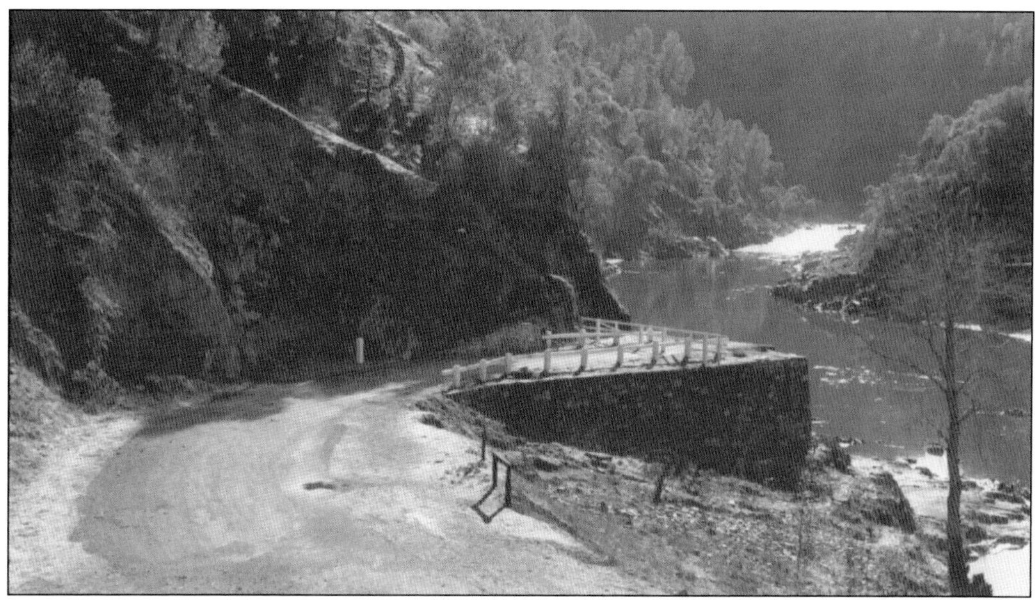

By the end of the summer of 1964, the Mother Orange Tree had been removed from the canyon and replanted. Additionally, the Bidwell Bar suspension bridge and the tollhouse had been disassembled and put into storage. These photographs show the north abutment of the Bidwell Bar Bridge on December 3, 1964. It turned out that the removal of all the historic icons was very timely. That month, massive storms hit the West Coast, lasting from December 18, 1964, to January 7, 1965. Known as the Christmastime or 100-year flood, it caused devastation in Washington, Oregon, and California. It was the worst flood in recorded history on nearly every major stream and river in Northern California. Gov. Edmund G. Brown declared 34 counties in California as disaster areas. If those historic items had still been in the canyon when it flooded, there may not have been anything left to preserve. (Both, courtesy of BCPW.)

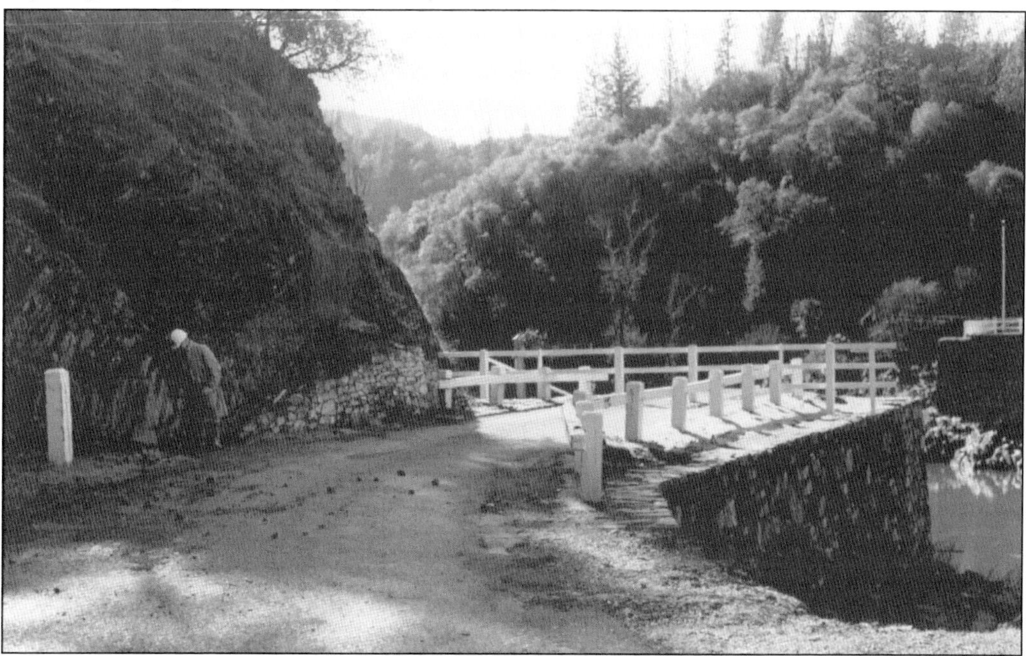

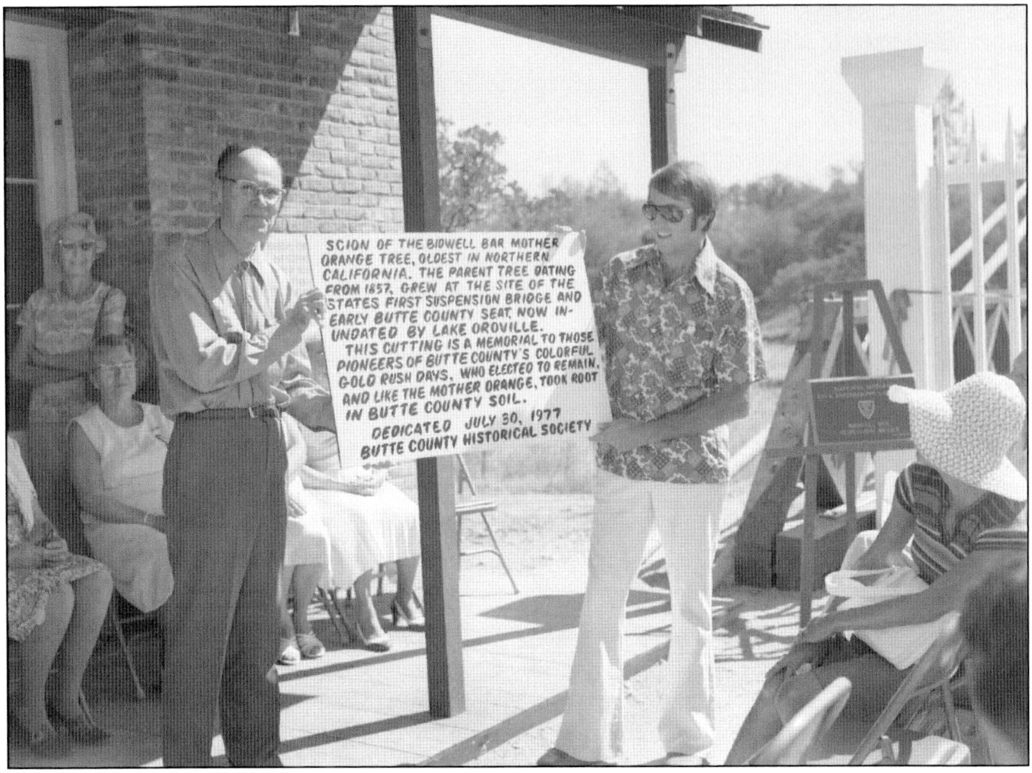

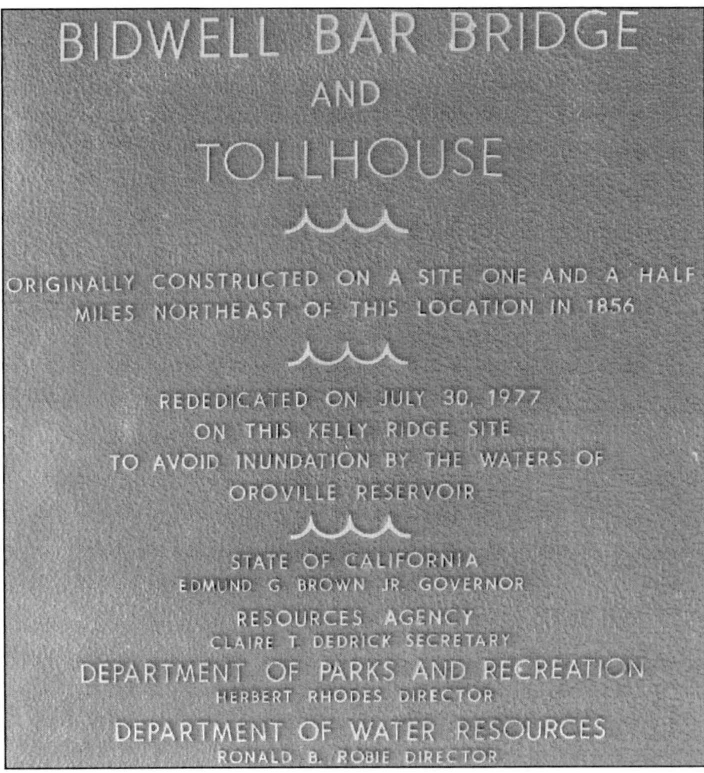

It took 13 years for the Bidwell Bar Bridge and its tollhouse to be relocated and rededicated. That dedication occurred on July 30, 1977. Above are Norris Bleyhl (left), vice president of the Butte County Historical Society, and Robert Van Horn, deputy director of the Department of Parks and Recreation. The sign they are holding indicates that a cutting from the Mother Orange Tree was donated to the site. The plaque pictured was dedicated that day. The relocation and rebuilding of the bridge and tollhouse cost $350,000. (Above, courtesy of CDWR; left, authors' collection.)

Six

Relics

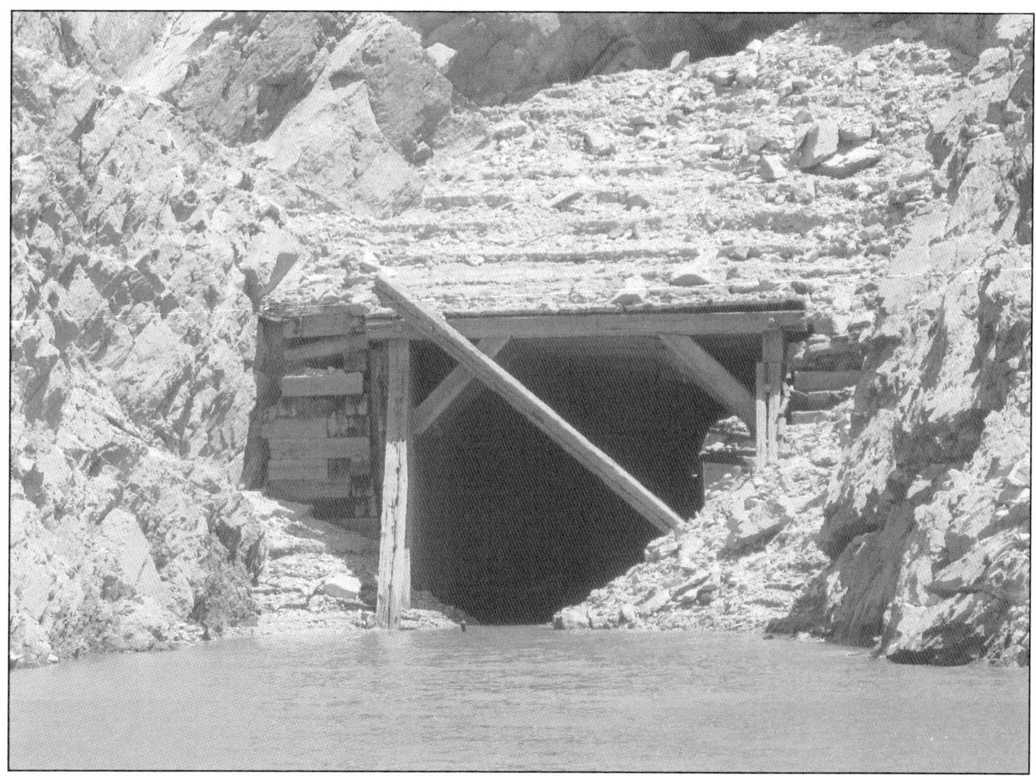

Historic relics from the lost communities can still be located. The drought that radically reduced the level of Lake Oroville in 2014 and 2015 gave historians an opportunity to search those areas, and interesting things have been found. In 2014, this No. 6 railroad tunnel was exposed in the North Fork, near Berry Creek station. The maximum depth of Lake Oroville at this location is around 200 feet. (Courtesy of John Hastie.)

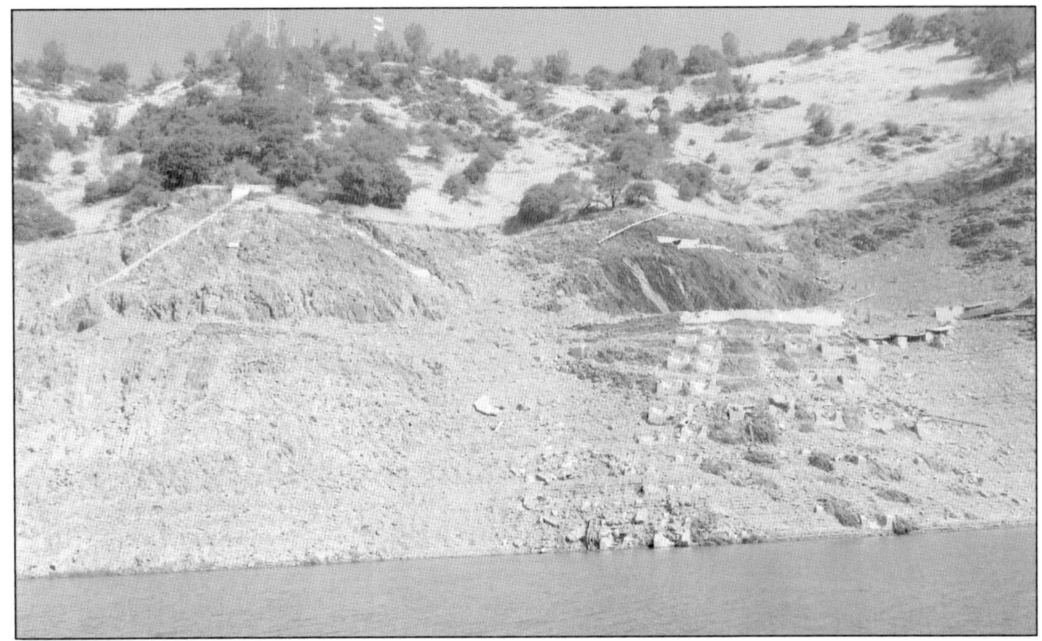

This view, taken on August 6, 2015, shows what is left of the Big Bend Powerhouse. The overflow spillway can still be seen on the left. The spillway is the only part of the structure that always stays above lake level. The concrete foundations for the penstocks and the car bridge are recognizable as well. The lake level on this date was 682.54 feet. (Authors' collection.)

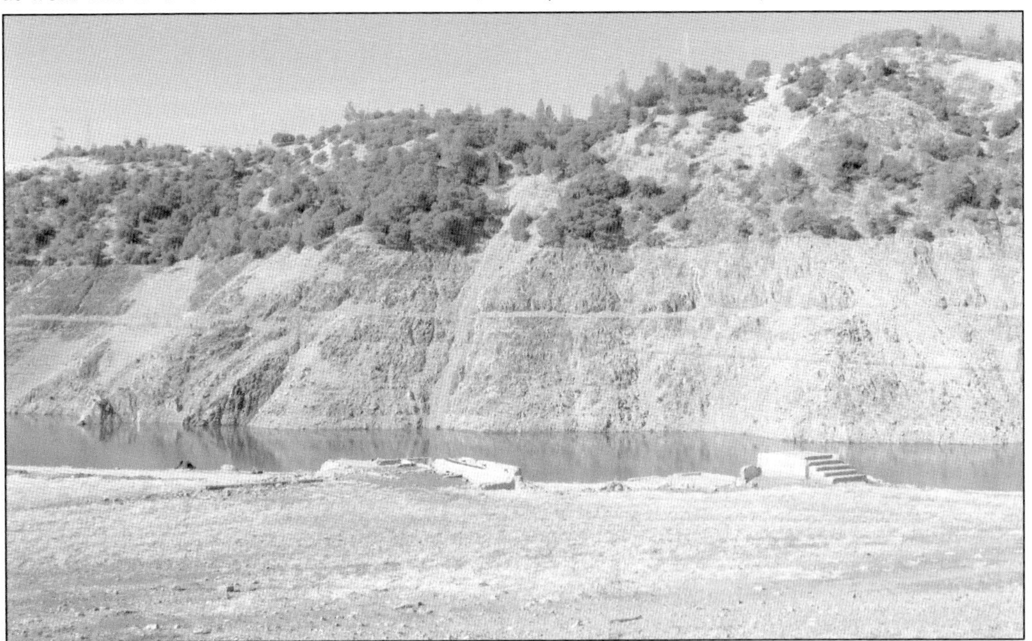

Taken on November 19, 2015, this photograph of the foundation and concrete steps of the Las Plumas School shows what the area looks like almost 50 years after the school was burned down and the area was flooded. Compare this view with the one on page 34, and it shows that the school was located fairly close to the edge of the slope and that the hills shown in the earlier photograph were actually across the river on the north side. (Authors' collection.)

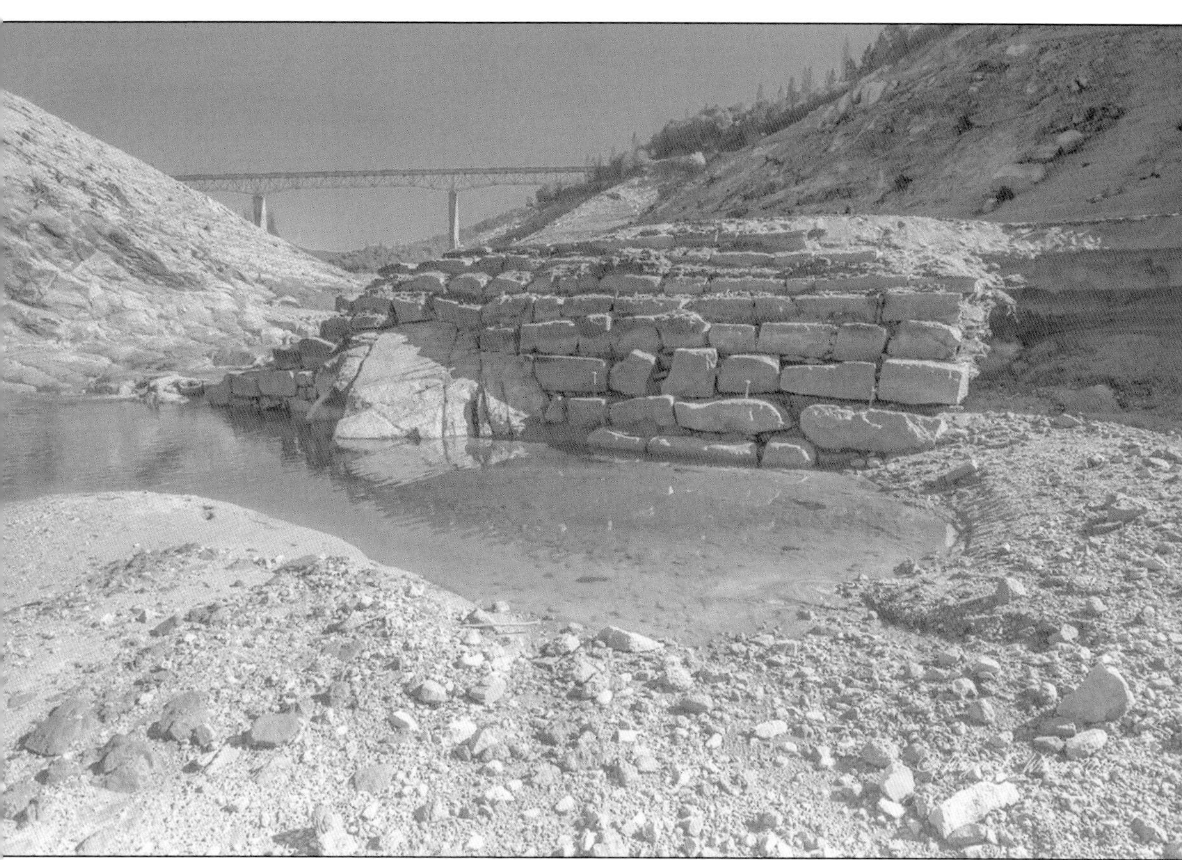

The first dam built upstream from Enterprise was erected in 1849. There were at least three more built at that location because the flooding South Fork kept taking them out each winter. The dams were used to divert the river for the miners' diggings in the area. The 2015 drought revealed these remains of the last older dam. Known by locals as the "Forty-Niner Dam," it was the original starting point for the Palermo Canal. The dam was built from granite rocks that had been blasted from the canyon. The rocks were then cut and shaped by using wedges and lifted into place by water-powered wooden derricks. The 1948 dam was built 100 yards upstream from this dam. This photograph was taken on November 12, 2015. (Courtesy of WW.)

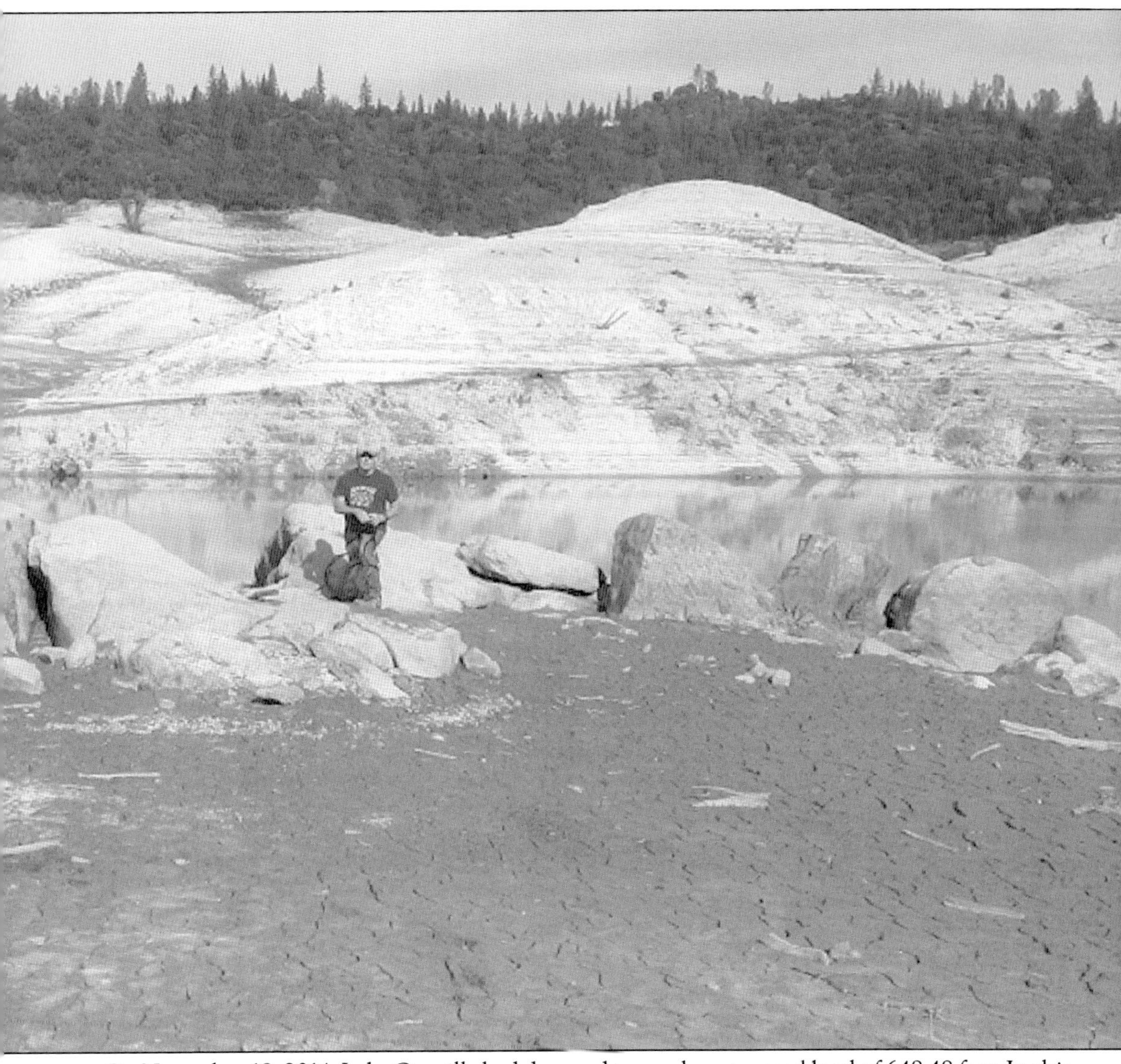

On November 18, 2014, Lake Oroville had dropped to an almost record level of 648.48 feet. In this photograph is the location of the Mountain Springs School at Enterprise. It can be noted that the split boulder on the left is the same rock formation seen in the photograph of the school on page 65. Three days later, the lake hit its lowest level in 2014 at 647.74 feet. The all-time record low was 645 feet on September 7, 1977. (Authors' collection.)

This is the handheld school bell from Las Plumas that teachers had used at the various Big Bend and Las Plumas schools that served the community from about 1930. Before the school was burned down, this bell was saved, and it is now in the care of Robyn (Foster) Payne. (Authors' collection.)

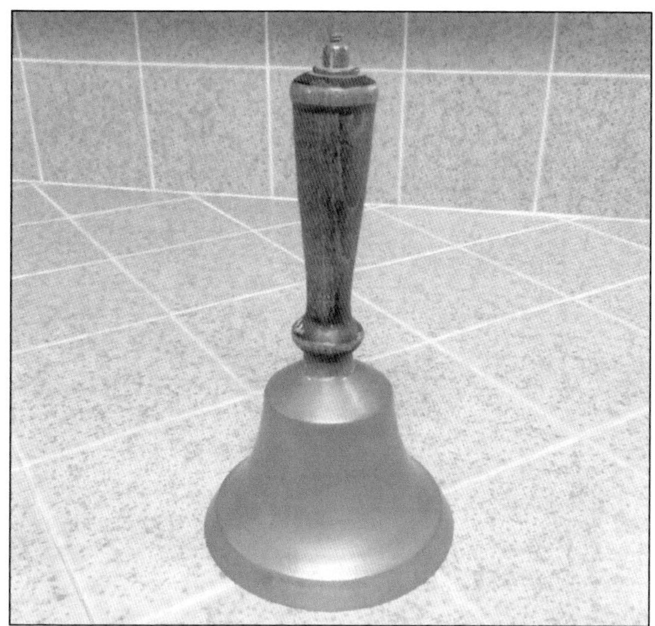

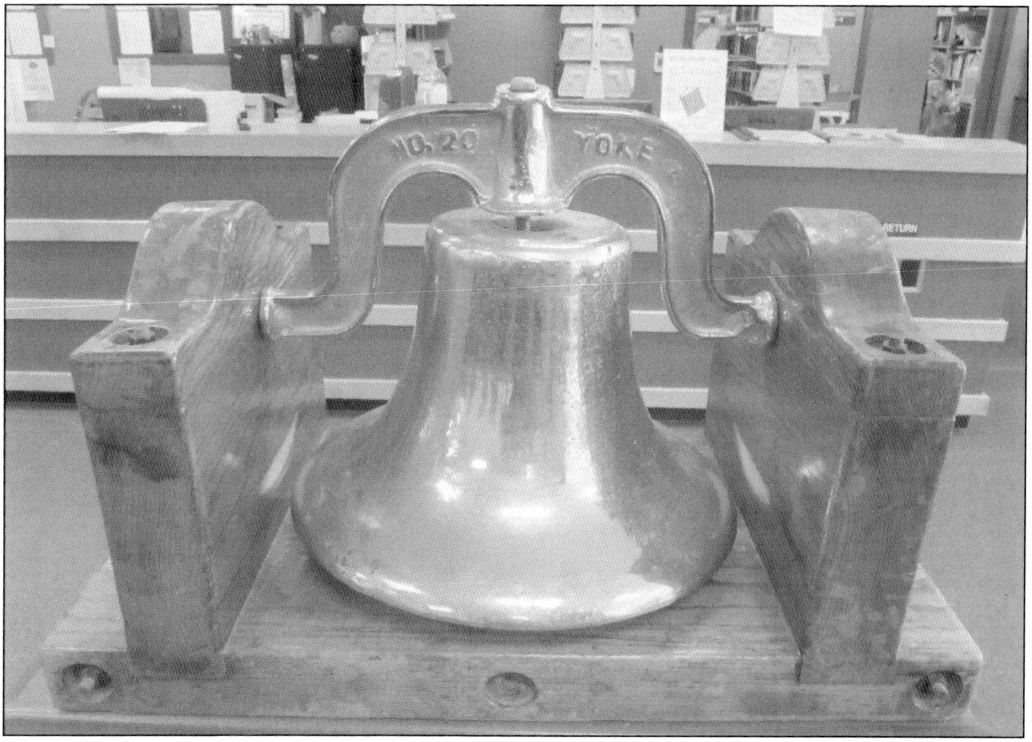

When the original Feather Falls School was torn down in the early 1960s, the school bell was saved. Some local residents may not realize that the bell went on to perform a very famous service. Since that time, the bell has served as the Victory Bell. It is the bell that the varsity football teams of Oroville High School and Las Plumas High School compete for every fall. The first Victory Bell game was played on October 26, 1962. As of 2015, the score has been tallied at 40 wins for Oroville, 12 wins for Las Plumas, and 2 ties. (Authors' collection.)

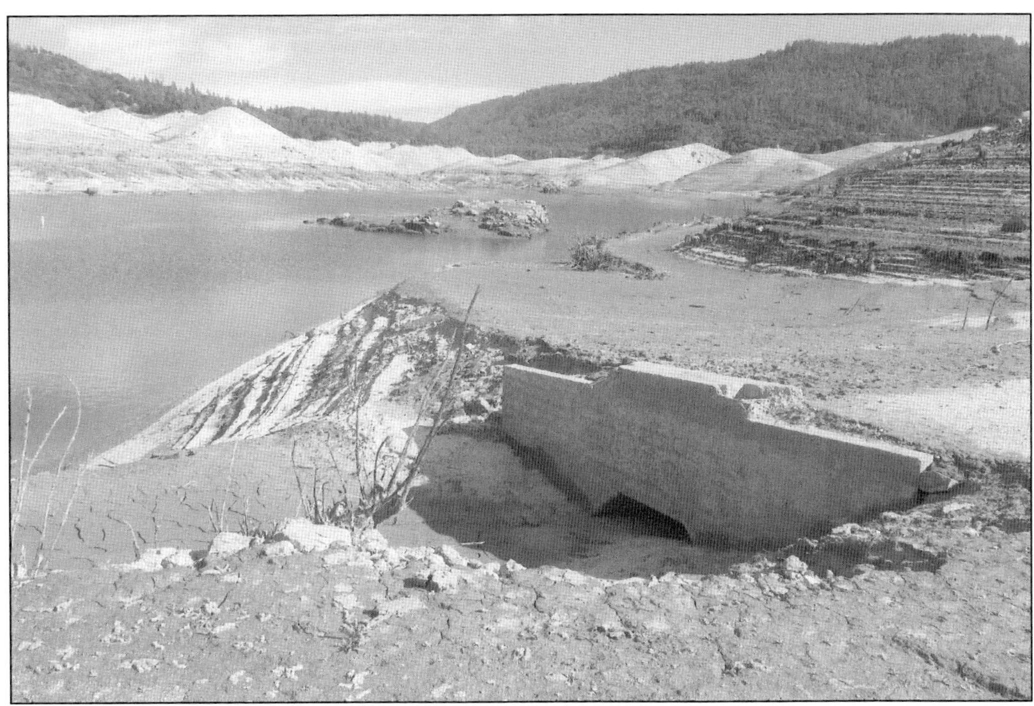

The photograph above was taken on October 29, 2014, and shows the area of Enterprise where the Enterprise Road, Lumpkin Road, and the OWID/Palermo Canal intersect. The canal came around from the left side of the hill, crossed under the road, and came out from under the concrete bulkhead in the foreground. The photograph below was taken on August 26, 2014, and shows the remains of a bridge crossing of the old canal, not far from the site of the old Enterprise Cemetery. (Above, authors' collection; below, courtesy of HP.)

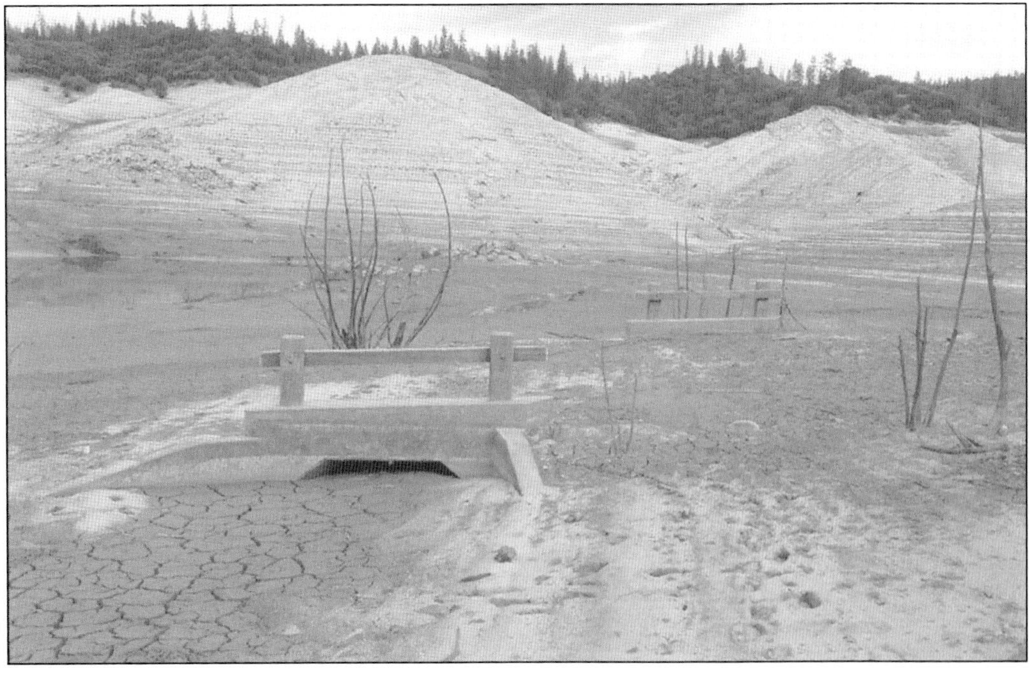

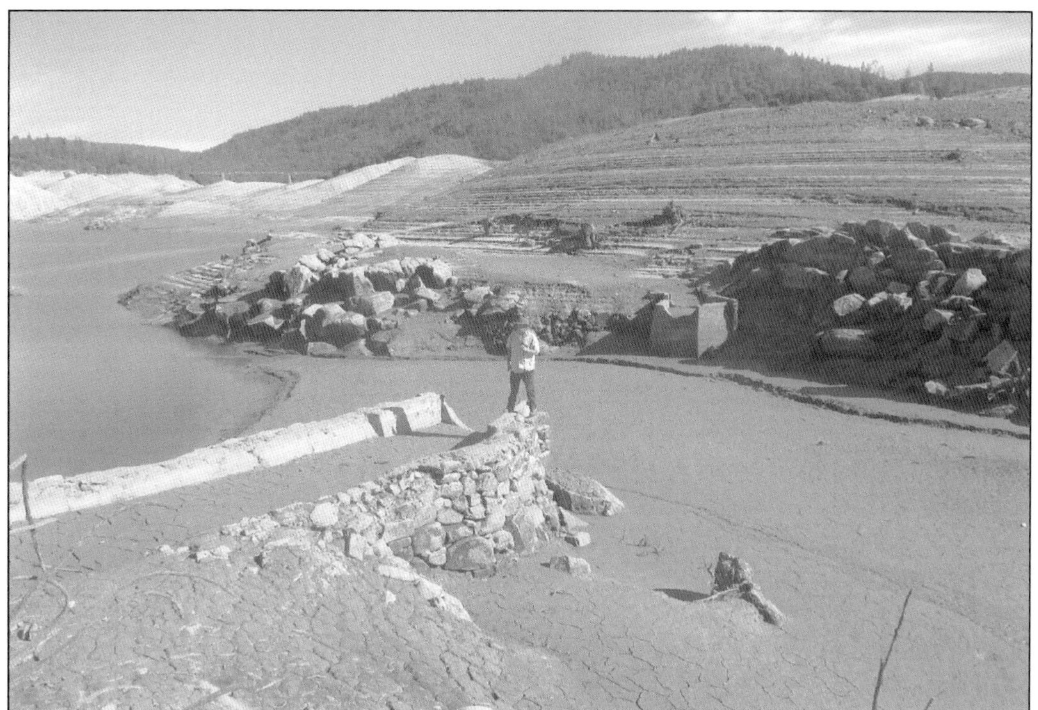

This view looks east across Powell Creek at the old flume. Coauthor Scott Roberts stands on the west abutment, just below the previous location of Spencer's Mill. This is one of several major flumes that brought water from the OWID diversion dam. The Enterprise Bridge is seen in the background. This photograph was taken on October 29, 2014. (Authors' collection.)

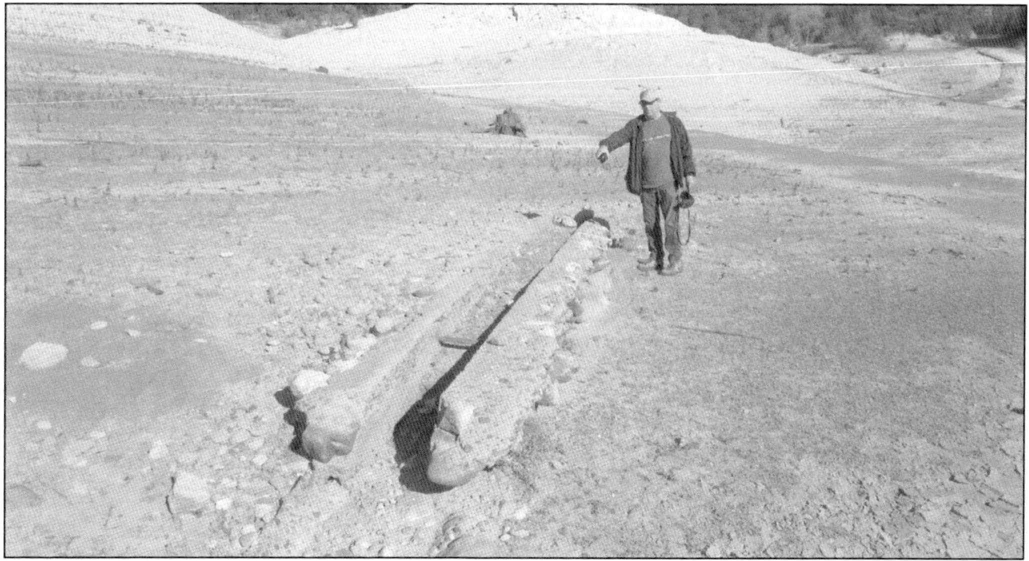

In this January 15, 2014, photograph, coauthor Larry Matthews points to the last remnant from the Sunnyside House Hotel. The lowered water level of Lake Oroville has revealed the foundation of the old concrete watering trough. The hotel was located on the north side of the Feather River in the South Fork. The bottom of the Enterprise boat launch ramp can be seen up the hill in the upper right of the photograph. (Authors' collection.)

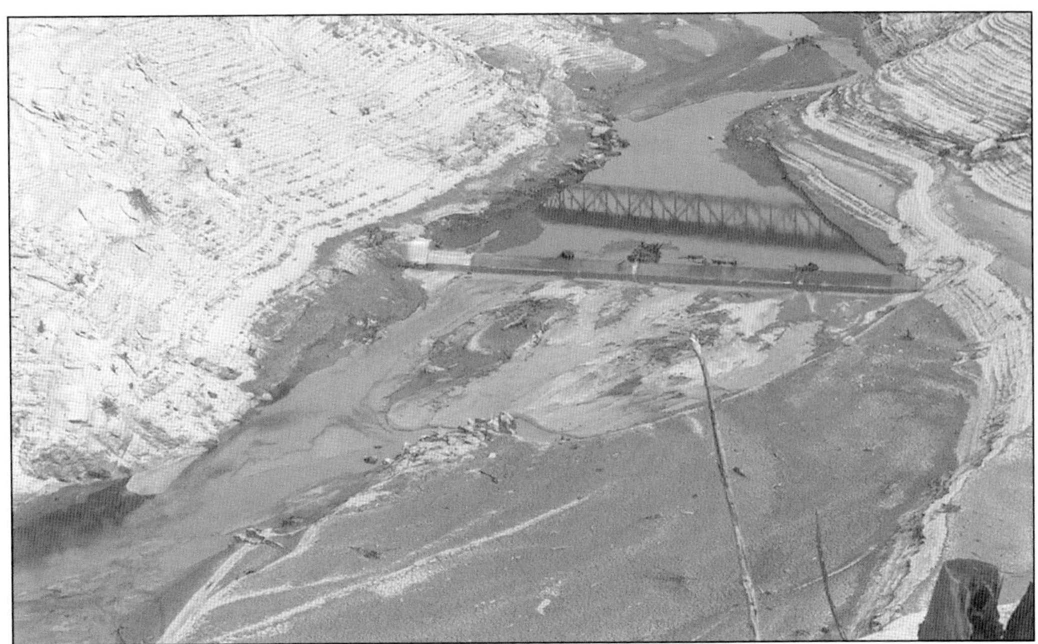

Above, the newly revealed OWID dam is shown on October 22, 2014. The new Enterprise Bridge casts the shadow right above the dam, built in 1948. Photographer Wayne Wilson indicates that, in the 1950s, his family had a cabin in the area where the three lines come together at the bottom of the photograph. Below, the OWID dam is seen in a close-up view from November 8, 2014, with the Enterprise Bridge behind it. (Above, courtesy of WW; below, courtesy of HP.)

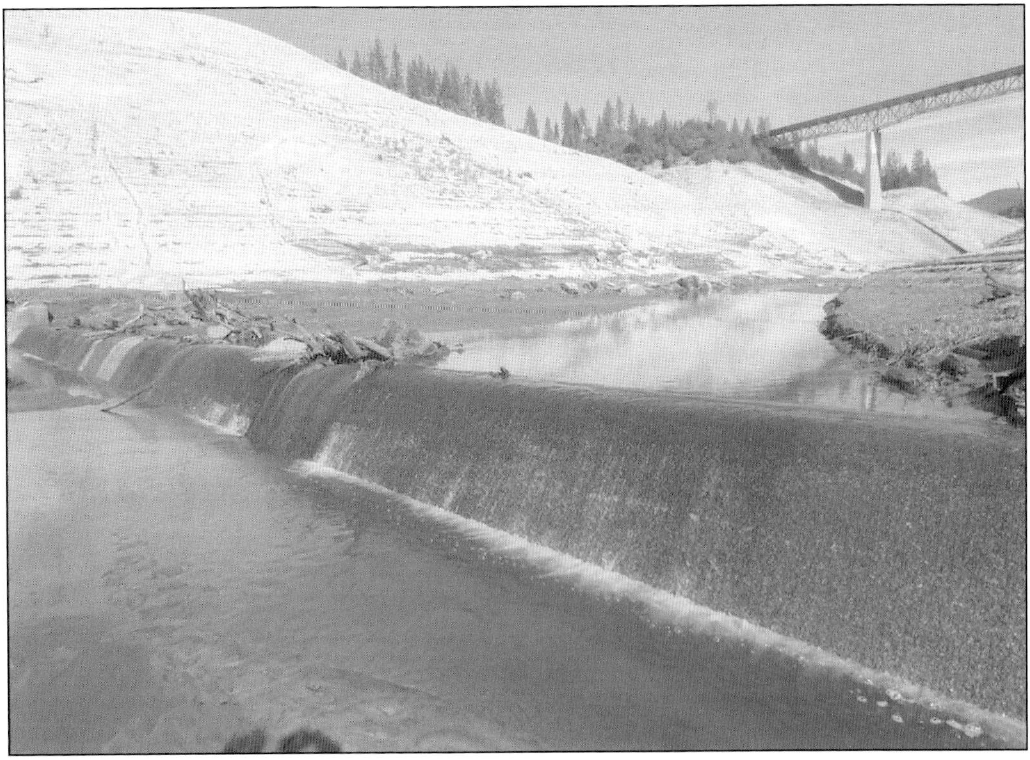

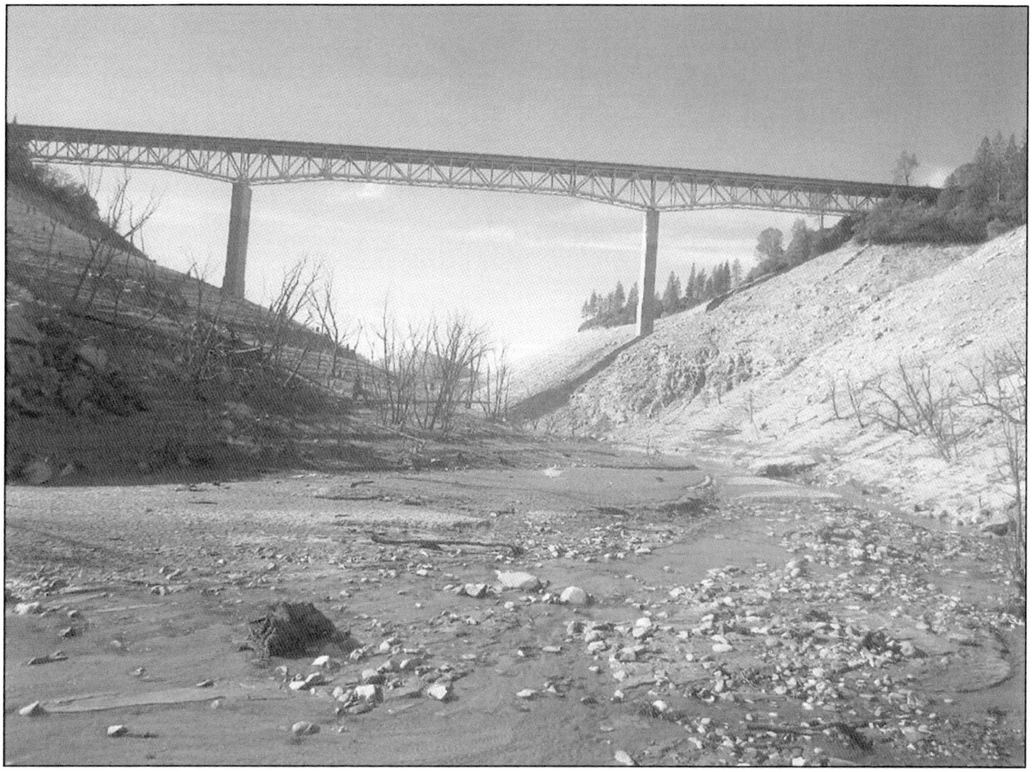

This view was taken upstream from the Enterprise Bridge on November 8, 2014. This bridge became the symbol of the drought in print, online, and on television by representing just how bad conditions had gotten in 2014. Two aerial views of it were shown, one with plenty of water beneath it and one with the river back within its original banks. This photograph shows the reality of what the South Fork had developed into during this drought. (Courtesy of HP.)

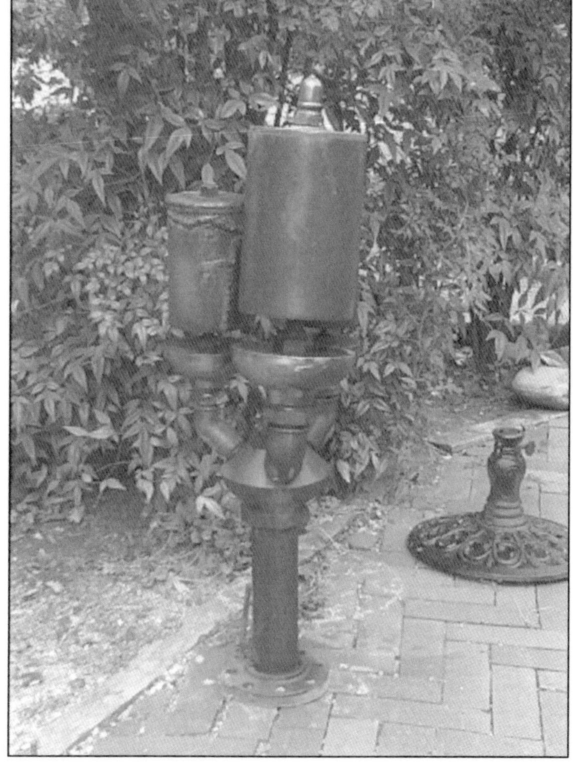

The old steam whistle from the Feather River Pines Mills in Feather Falls Village is pictured here in 2013. At that time, it served as a backyard decoration in Paradise, California. The four-foot whistle was used at the mill at least during the 1960s and possibly much earlier than that. (Courtesy of Bonnie Baron.)

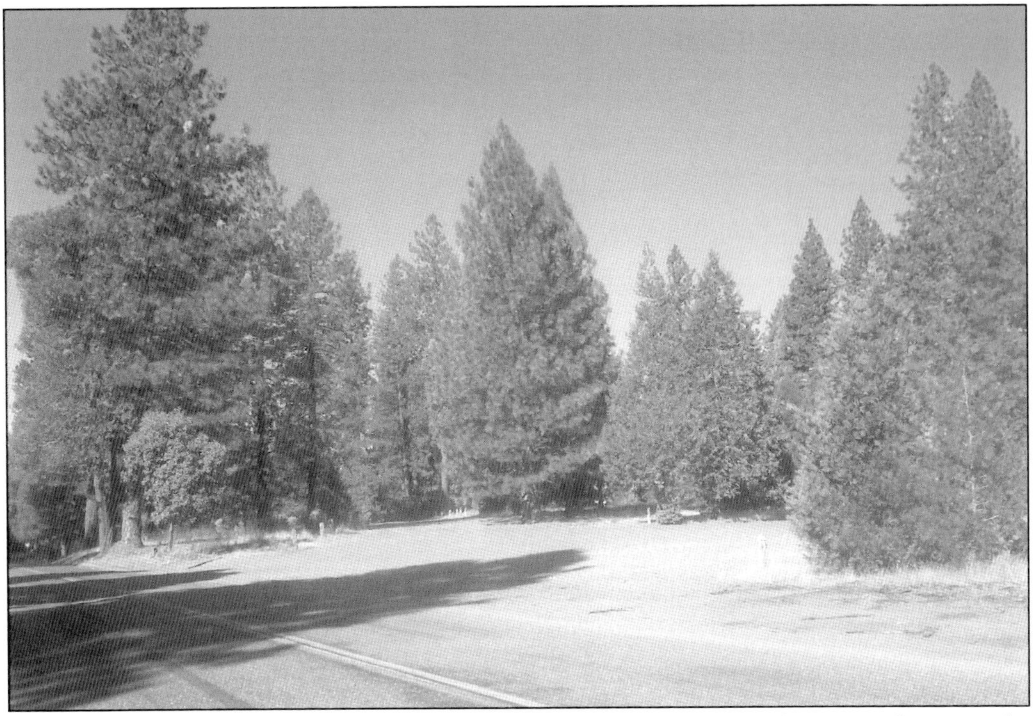

These photographs from 2010 show that Feather Falls Village is now mostly just a wide spot in the road. Prior to the leveling of the village, the Georgia-Pacific office, town hall, library, post office, restaurant, and store would have been seen in the above view. In the photograph below, the view looks in the opposite direction, toward Lumpkin Road. A pickup truck sits right behind the location of the old gas station. (Both, authors' collection.)

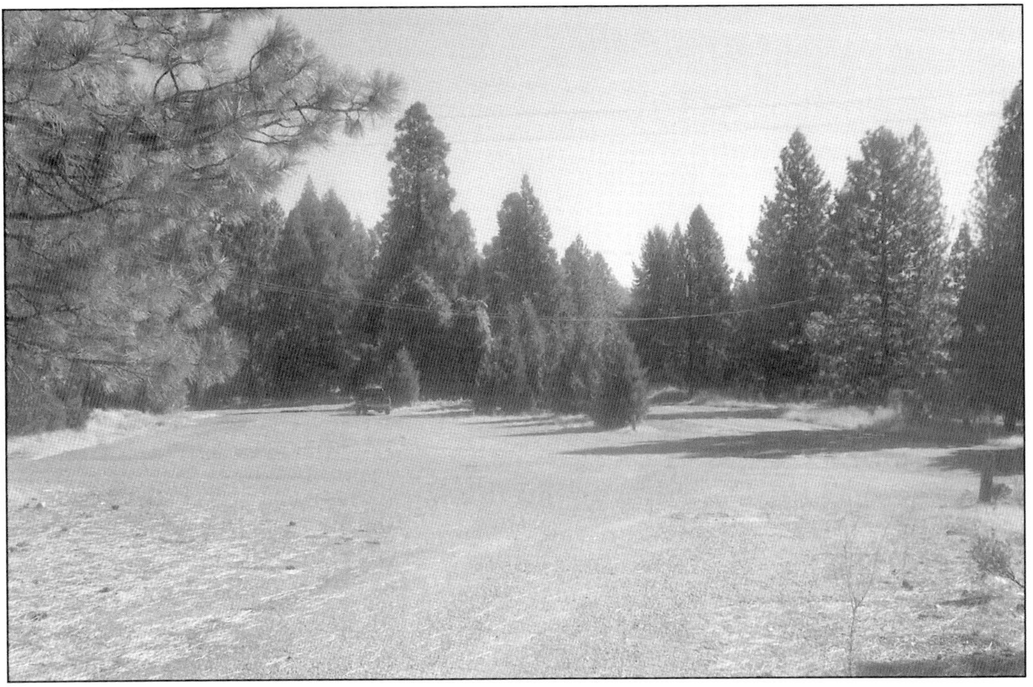

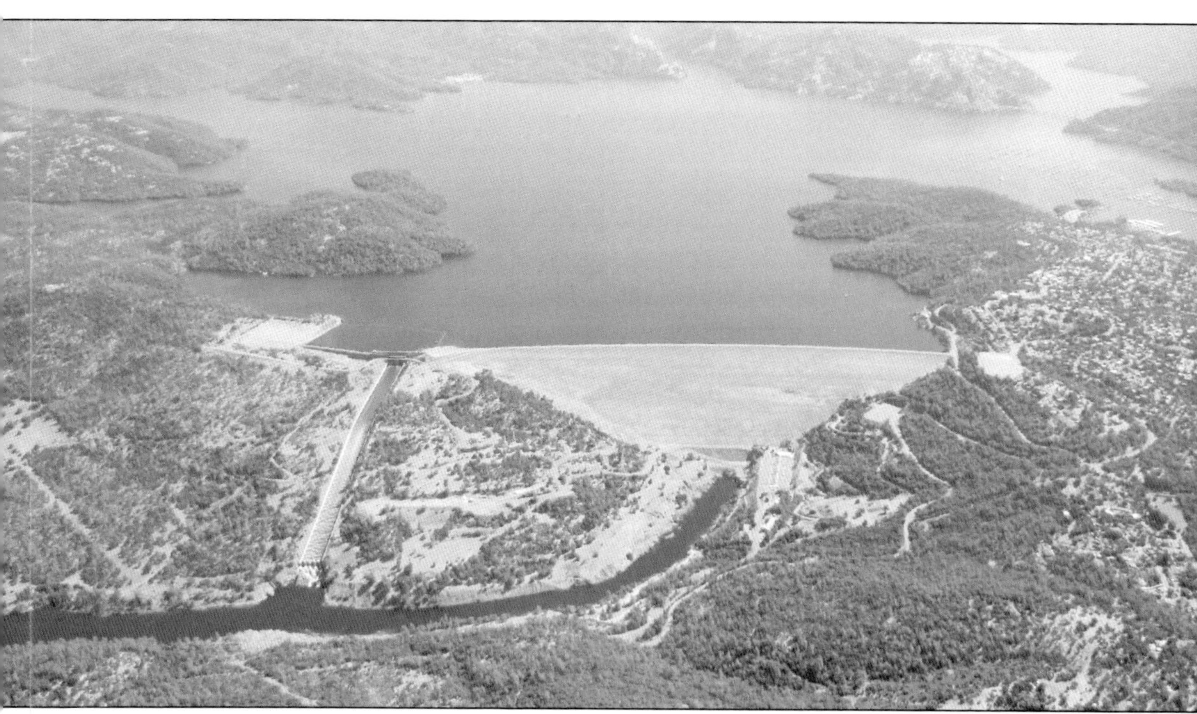

The lake is full in this aerial photograph of Lake Oroville and Oroville Dam from 2012, prior to the drought. Part of the North Fork of the lake appears on the left. The Middle Fork can be seen under the new Bidwell Bar Bridge on the right. The South Fork branches off from the Middle Fork on the other side of the bridge. The location of Bidwell Bar lies just to the left of the bridge, around 600 feet below the surface. The spring of 2016 brought heavy rains to Northern California, along with the renewed hope that the drought would end. In April 2016, the lake level had risen to within just a few feet of its maximum level. (Courtesy of Gonzalo Peewee Curiel.)

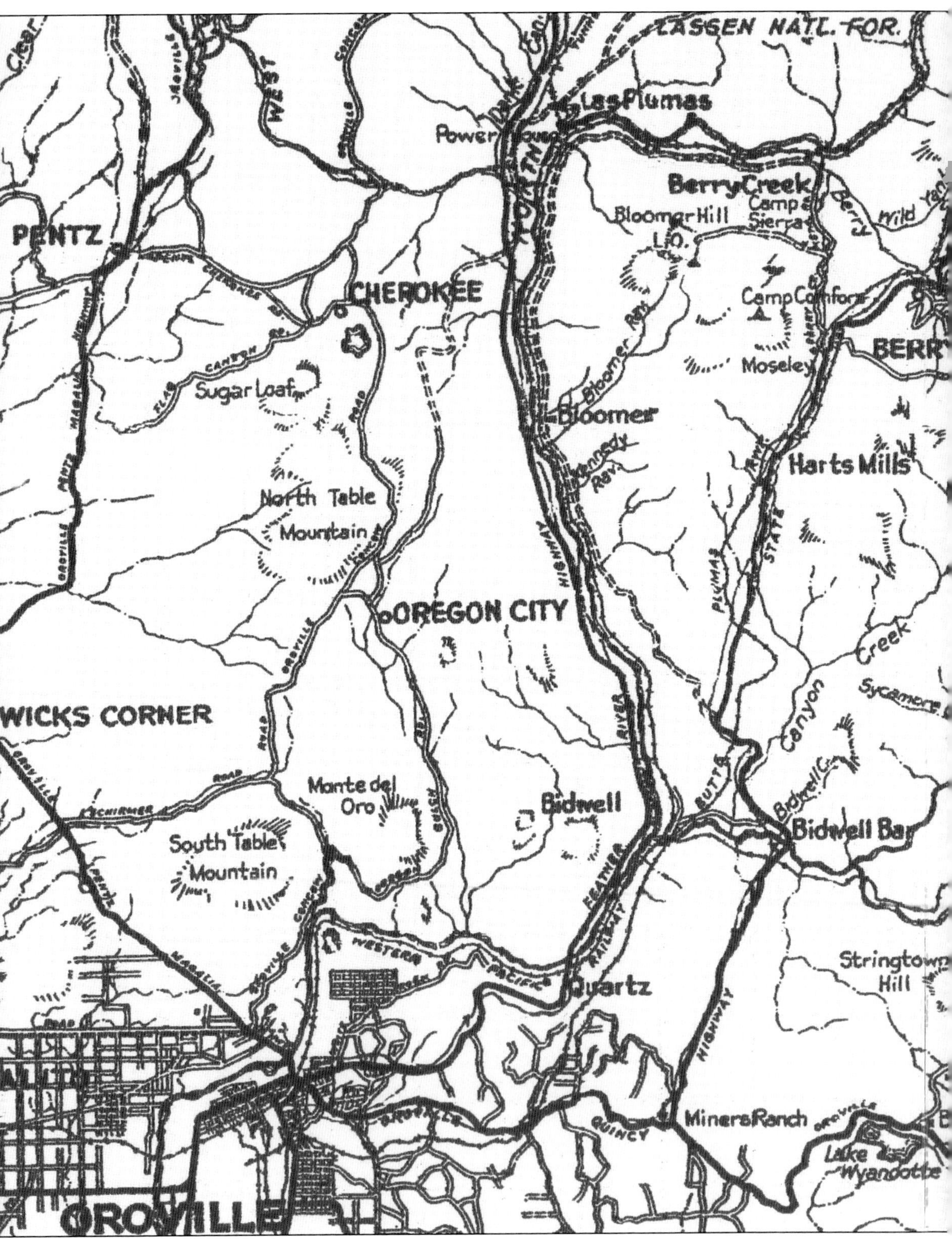
LASSEN NATL. FOR.
Las Plumas
Power House
Berry Creek
Camp Sierra
Bloomer Hill
L.O.
Camp Comfort
Moseley
PENTZ
CHEROKEE
Sugar Loaf
Bloomer
Kennedy Rav.
Harts Mills
North Table Mountain
OREGON CITY
WICKS CORNER
Canyon Creek
Sycamore
Monte del Oro
Bidwell
Bidwell Bar
South Table Mountain
Stringtown Hill
Quartz
Miners Ranch
Lake Wyandotte
OROVILLE

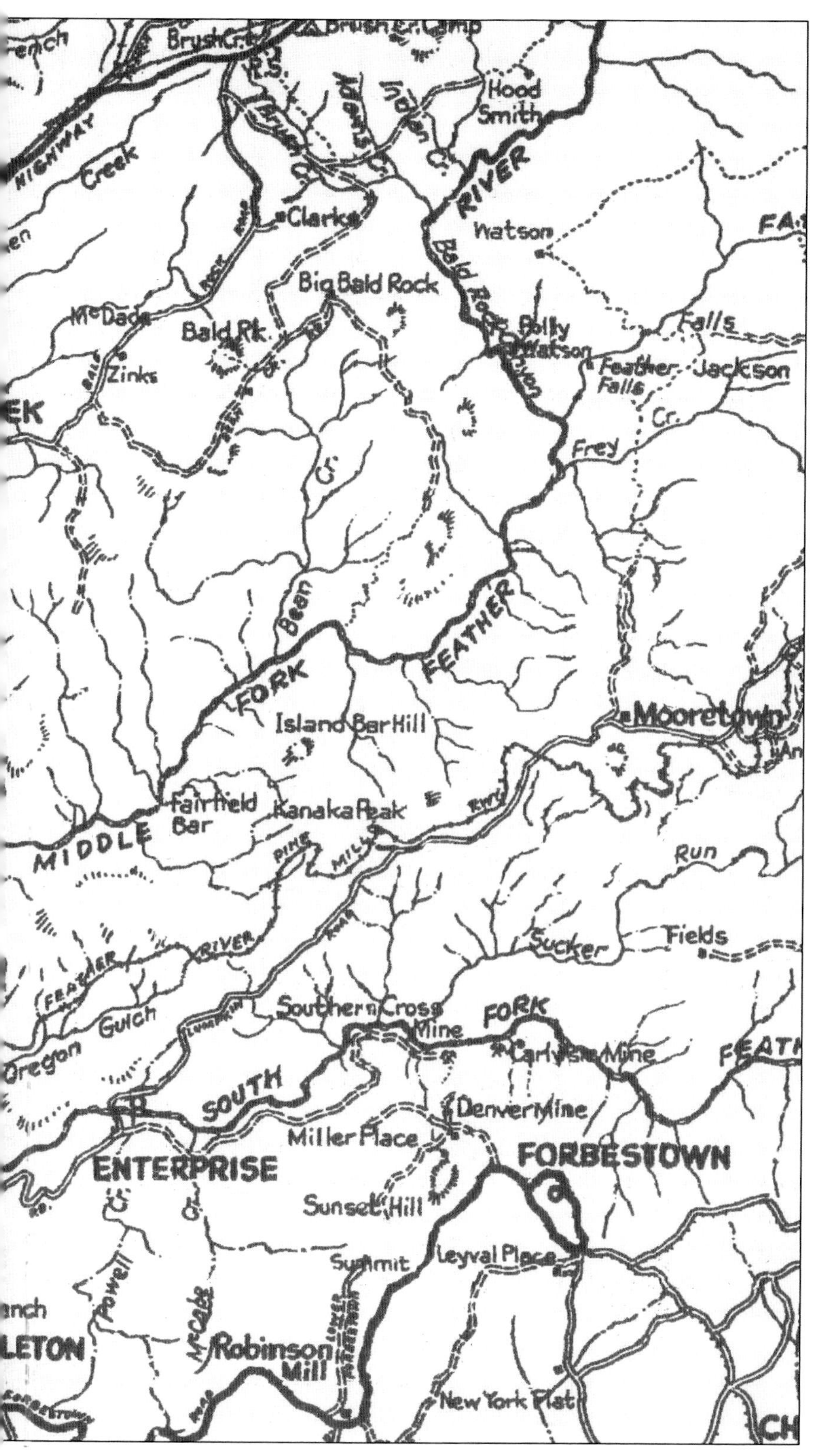

This map from around 1930 shows the locations of the various communities prior to their inundation by Lake Oroville. In this book, the city of Oroville on the lower left has been used as the point from which to describe distances and the locations of the various communities. In the upper middle of the map are the community of Las Plumas and the Big Bend Powerhouse. Just to the east is the rail junction of Berry Creek station. At the middle of the far right of the map is Mooretown, which eventually changed its name to Feather Falls Village. In the middle of the map is Bidwell Bar. Just to the east and a bit south from Bidwell Bar is the community of Enterprise. The Oroville Dam is located just above where the word "Quartz" appears on the map. (Courtesy of BCHS.)

Consistent with our mission to preserve history on a local level, this book was printed in South Carolina on American-made paper and manufactured entirely in the United States. Products carrying the accredited Forest Stewardship Council (FSC) label are printed on 100 percent FSC-certified paper.

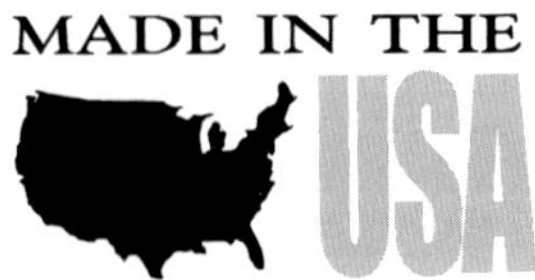